CHANTERELLE

DAVID WALTUCK *& Andrew Friedman*

CHANTERELLE

THE STORY AND RECIPES OF A RESTAURANT CLASSIC

FOREWORD BY ADAM GOPNIK

PHOTOGRAPHY BY MARIA ROBLEDO

The Taunton Press

The Taunton Press, Inc., 63 South Main Street, PO Box 5506, Newtown, CT 06470-5506

e-mail: tp@taunton.com

EDITOR: PAM HOENIG

COPY EDITOR: VALERIE CIMINO

INDEXER: HEIDI BLOUGH

JACKET & INTERIOR DESIGN: ERICA HEITMAN-FORD FOR MUCCA DESIGN

PHOTOGRAPHER: MARIA ROBLEDO

Library of Congress Cataloging-in-Publication Data

Waltuck, David.

Chanterelle : the story and recipes of a restaurant classic / author, David Waltuck.

p. cm.

Includes bibliographical references and index.

ISBN 978-1-56158-961-6 (alk. paper)

1. Cookery, French. 2. Chanterelle (Restaurant : New York, N.Y.) I. Title.

TX719.W3385 2008

641.5944--dc22

2008009754

Printed in Singapore

10 9 8 7 6 5 4 3 2 1

BuT 11/26/08

To my family.

To Karen, my wife and partner in all things.

To my wonderful children, Sara and Jacob.

And to the memory of my parents, Jeanette and Murray,

who nourished my soul and who took me out to dinner.

Contents

Foreword
Adam Gopnik

I loved the restaurant Chanterelle long before I managed to eat there. In the late '70s and very early '80s, a small ground-floor room in a storefront on a then-obscure street on the southern fringe of SoHo was transformed, apparently overnight, into something new and beckoning, as if by tasteful pixies. Before, there had just been another dark, industrial corner, at the intersection of Greene and Grand. Now the place glowed on its corner like a flickering gaslight. There were pale apricot walls (which you could just see as you walked by) below the old high, stamped tin ceiling, and three brass chandeliers above the old cast-iron columns. The exterior window was decorated every day with a menu written in a beautiful, swirling italic hand; the food the hand described, which was apparently available inside, was intriguing in its combination of obvious French materials with something new and more American: seafood sausage and roast squab with garlic, and soft-shell crabs with lime.

It didn't just look wonderful; it felt, somehow, new. Certain places, restaurants among them, don't just resonate with the style of their period, but announce a new style coming, and this little corner storefront did: It represented the SoHo art world in its approaching, second, higher period, when new signs of luxury would inflect minimalist austerity. At the time, I was living with my wife just around the corner in a fourth-floor loft, our first real home, and walking by the new place on the corner of Grand and Greene every night, we sensed that this little storefront represented not the old glamorous New York, to which one aspired, but a new New York style just coming into being, a nascent style in which a certain established idea of high-tech simplicity was being inflected with a witty old-world idea of high-minded pleasure, a style held in quotes but offered sincerely. (You see the same thing in, say, David Salle's paintings of the period, poetic darkness touched by a certain amount of pure black velvet.) We would borrow a friend's dog,

and late at night, contemplate the menu with aplomb, looking, as demurely as we could, inside.

Over time, we came to eat there, and to know the couple, David and Karen Waltuck, whose vision the restaurant represented (and the designer Bill Katz, who had helped them realize it). Not only was the food even better than its embroidery—subtle without being silly and simple without being plain—but we also soon realized that the Waltucks' lives mirrored our own, as they did those of a generation of young New Yorkers. They were struggling to combine a family and professional life while still remaining possessed of a vision, to which, for all the difficulties and sheer exhaustion of running a daily restaurant in a difficult city, they wanted to be faithful.

That vision, which the following pages annotate and explain, is hard to define, but it involves many things kept in balance, or tension: an idea of luxury reconciled with a hope for familiarity; a distaste for fancy cooking combined with a respect for haute cuisine. Most of all, and more perhaps than any other dining place I know of, their vision is marked by a desire not to have all the vectors of attention pointing inward, at the plates and what's on them, but pointing upward, metaphorically, toward that ceiling and its chandeliers—toward the possibility of an elevated evening, something out of the ordinary, a three-hour engineered transcendence of the mundane. I've been lucky enough to have had unforgettable meals in many places; but I think I've shared more beautiful evenings under their particular stars than any other. Though designed as a stage set, their place feels like a hearth.

It still does. The amazing thing is that David and Karen have continued to produce that kind of experience night after night, in the premises on Harrison Street they went to in the '80s (following the art world as it moved a little south), without dropping a stitch of sober charm along the way. What was once a period piece has become a classic, and their classicism depends, as it always does, on a daily renewal of energy, to be held under the restraint of an established style. Several books could be written about the life and times of Chanterelle: one an anthropological study of art-world dining habits, another a story about the transformations of French cooking in American hands. But this book is about the central drama, about how the Waltucks and their team managed to make a new kind of place, and how they continue to make it new each night. Turning these pages, I felt the excitement again of those lost rainy nights on the corner of Greene and Grand, staring inside at a new world held in a room. The best kinds of enchantment are enlarged rather than diminished by explanation; we come away as dazzled as ever by the magic, and more eager than ever to go inside.

The Chanterelle Story

Most people who make a living doing something they love can point to the moment when they discovered it, lightning struck, and they exclaimed, if only to themselves, *"That's* what I'm going to do for the rest of my life!"

My revelation occurred in midtown Manhattan, on a Saturday night in the early 1960s. It was then, long before it had a name or a location, that the first stirrings of what would, in time, become Chanterelle restaurant took hold in my mind.

I grew up in the Bronx, that sprawling, overwhelmingly middle-class, northernmost borough of New York City. Food wasn't a priority in the Waltuck home, although my two aunts, Gertie and Fanny, who lived in the same apartment building as we did and didn't have families of their own to nourish, often cooked for my parents, my brother, and me, preparing a hodgepodge of American and Middle European staples: stuffed cabbage, chicken fricassée, roast leg of lamb, braised pot roast, and a repertoire of soups that included matzo ball, mushroom barley, and borscht. The food was satisfying but inelegant: Drab pale green and brown tones ruled the day, and many house favorites were ladled out of gigantic pots or carved on a huge wooden board from the head of the table. Meals were casual affairs, with little emphasis on the rituals of dining: You sat down, you ate, you cleared the table, you went on with your life.

My parents, both New York City social workers, took a serious interest in the arts and were devoted to exposing their young children to some of the city's legendary culture. And so, occasionally, on Saturday nights, they would usher my brother and me into the car and drive us down into Manhattan for an evening of theater, always preceded by dinner in a restaurant. I was like a tourist in

the blur of flashing lights and neon that defined Times Square in those days. As the family car snaked its way down the West Side Highway to 42nd Street, eventually docking in an outdoor lot, I felt a thrilling shiver at being in The City, and this excitement grew as we navigated the sidewalks of the Theater District, its sounds and smells filling my senses to overflowing.

I can't recall which of the largely interchangeable Hell's Kitchen French restaurants was the first one we visited, but I will never forget the immediate and lasting impression it made on me. As we passed through the restaurant doors—through the looking glass, it seemed—into a world of lace curtains, tuxedoed waiters, and hushed voices, I was wonder-struck. The restaurant, and the ones that followed on subsequent Saturdays, awakened in me a kind of romance. The reassuring grace of the maitre d', the timeless elegance of the dining room, the soft, flattering lighting—these things were transporting. By the time we ordered dinner, I had the sensation that I was no longer in New York City, but in some otherworldly place devoted entirely to the comfort and contentment of its guests.

More than anything, I was spellbound by the food. In stark contrast to home, where meals were presented unceremoniously, courses were announced like late-arriving guests as they were set down before us. Each dish had four or five components—a fish or meat, a sauce, a starch, and a vegetable or two—all of them coming together in perfect harmony. And it was all so *pretty*—potatoes were artfully piped, vegetable purees had been shaped into quenelles, and meat and fish were beautifully portioned and arranged on the plate. The components of these edible compositions seemed to have been *transformed,* bearing little or no resemblance to the raw ingredients that went into them. There was magic in every flourish, from tomatoes trimmed to look like roses to leftovers wrapped in aluminum foil molded into the shape of a duck.

For me, these dinners were the main event of our trip into the city. When it was time to push off for the theater, I found myself wondering, *"Theater? Who needs theater?"*

Young boys are prone to obsessions, so while my friends were busy collecting baseball cards, I began what would become my lifelong love affair with food, at first by endlessly replaying those restaurant meals in my mind. I was especially impressed by the sauces, and I found myself thinking about them in school or while riding the subway. Before long, my appetite for food knowledge was insatiable. I began reading whatever I could get my hands on. In particular, I was drawn to the legendary food writer and culinary Francophile Richard Olney's *Simple French Food* and the seasonally arranged *French Menu Cookbook*.

I felt an urge welling up in me until it became impossible to ignore: Reading wasn't enough—I had to *cook*. I began by baking, because the formula-like recipes seemed inviting and straightforward to me, and I knew that my family would be willing to sample whatever breads and pastries I produced. My first forays were successful, but loaf after loaf of warm bread on the kitchen counter left me curiously unsatisfied. I concluded that baking, at least for me, was more craft than art, and I swiftly shifted to the savory realm that had turned me on in the first place. I started simply, making stocks, to see if I could achieve the gelatinous quality described in books. Tasting my first one, I recognized the sauce it might become. On another Saturday, I put an egg yolk in a bowl, added some mustard and lemon juice, and whisked them together, slowly drizzling olive oil into the mixture, staring with anticipation, then amazement, as it all held together in a creamy emulsion: mayonnaise!

I was hooked. I felt I could cook *anything*. I was single-minded in my pursuit of this passion, purchasing knives, ring molds, and other tools and equipment to supplement our family's resources, or making do with what we had, like the time I whipped up a fish mousse in

our blender, or took the subway down to Esposito Pork Store on Ninth Avenue in Hell's Kitchen (it's still there) to buy some pork skin, bringing it home and using it to make cassoulet.

My parents thought I was a little nuts, and maybe I was. I lived for Saturdays, when I was allowed to scurry all over town in hot pursuit of hard-to-pronounce ingredients, take over the kitchen, and cook my heart out. Every week I'd try something more challenging—quenelles, aspics, terrines, confit—and it all came naturally to me. Cleaning the sinks and stove at the end of each too-short session, I'd be overcome with pride, grinning from ear to ear, and thinking, "I can do this."

And then, there was my culinary guardian angel, my mother's friend Sarah Sameth, whose career as a French teacher conferred upon her an air of sophistication in our circle, one which was furthered by the name she adopted to honor her love of all things French—Josephine. Every so often, Josephine would take me to lunch at Lutèce, one of the great four-star restaurants of the day, where I was treated not only to sublime renditions of the food I was reading about and attempting to make, but also to my first vision of a famous chef. During each visit, André Soltner would emerge from the kitchen in his impeccably starched whites, his toque perfectly centered on his head, and make the rounds of the dining room. Regulars in business suits received a private audience with this papal figure; Josephine and I were happy to settle for a smile and a nod as he breezed by our table. When I nodded back, and we made eye contact, it was thrilling.

By the time I was in high school, I wasn't just reading recipe books; I had become equally intrigued by all aspects of a chef's world, such as ingredients and how they're sourced. I pored over Euell Gibbons's *Stalking the Wild Asparagus* and *Stalking the Blue-Eyed Scallop,* while, in the kitchen, my experiments grew ever more ambitious. I turned out complete meals on the order of those restaurant dinners that had first compelled me to cook. I was also consumed with the future, with thoughts of where my passion might take me when I could devote more and more time to it, perhaps even my entire life.

CHEF MEETS GIRL

For the past three decades, the realization of those food dreams has been Chanterelle, the restaurant that I own and operate with my wife, partner, front-of-the-house goddess, and mistress of details, Karen.

I can't tell the Chanterelle story without telling the David and Karen story: We are both creatures of the Bronx, who met back in high school but didn't begin dating until the summer of 1977. Despite having a home borough in common, we were a case study in opposites attracting: In sharp contrast to my near-painful shyness, Karen is fearlessly social and free-spirited. We also had vastly different experiences: To me, a teenage adventure was journeying down to the specialty shop Kalustyan's on Lexington Avenue in search of preserved lemons; to her it was spending a year in France in high school, and one in Rome in college.

Karen worked for a small women's boutique on the East Side and, before taking that job, had lived and traveled in South America and Europe. She loved her work, which took her on buying trips overseas.

Karen had never been all that interested in food—during her years abroad, she had survived on about fifty dollars per month, and had eaten whatever she could afford at local markets and could figure out how to cook. But, as we began a brief courtship carried out largely in the top New York City restaurants of the day, such as Café des Artistes, La Côte Basque, and the site of those midday excursions with Josephine, Lutèce, I was delighted that she quickly developed a fondness for fine dining.

At that time, I was enrolled at the Culinary Institute of America, about an hour and a half north of Manhattan, but I didn't care much for school. I had already been cooking for several years and found myself questioning the very things I was being taught. As much as I revered traditional French cuisine, my palate had developed to the point that I was tinkering with some of the basics. A big breakthrough came when I stopped cooking with celery, which I'd always felt had a very distinct, almost peculiar flavor. Many, if not most, stocks, sauces, soups,

Happier, and more tired, than ever: early days at Chanterelle.

and stews have carrot, onion, celery, and maybe garlic in their bases. Three of the four made sense to me, but I never understood the automatic inclusion of celery, and it was around that time that I ceased using it at home, despite what we did at school.

Adding to my dissatisfaction was the alternate universe in New York City that beckoned me: In addition to being a student, I was the brunch cook at the Empire Diner, at Tenth Avenue and 22nd Street in Manhattan, a place that looked like a truck stop but served surprisingly sophisticated food. The owner gave me free rein to create my own specials, which was an enormous break and confidence booster for a young toque. The freedom was exhilarating in contrast to the textbook cooking I was doing at school.

And, of course, there was Karen. Every Sunday, after driving into the city at the crack of dawn and working my shift, I'd spend the afternoon with the woman who was becoming the love of my life. I stayed later and later each week to be with her as much as possible, and began finding myself almost nodding off on the Taconic State Parkway on my drive back to campus, swerving all over the highway and occasionally explaining myself to a stone-faced state trooper.

Like a kid in a candy store: the original Chanterelle kitchen.

Bored with my studies, madly in love, and longing to work as much as possible in a real-world kitchen, I left school and went looking for a full-time gig in the city. I became sous chef to Charles Chevillot, the owner of La Petite Ferme, a beloved French restaurant with countryside undertones, which had moved from its original home on 10th Street to larger accommodations on the Upper East Side. Despite my highfalutin' title, I saw myself essentially as a glorified lunch cook, almost single-handedly turning out the bistro fare dictated by my employer. In an earlier time, this would have been gratifying work, but it was the dawn of a new era in western restaurant cuisine: There was a pioneering movement afoot in France as chef after chef broke the shackles of conformity and forged an individual style. Even in Manhattan, there was unprecedented interest in food, much of it goosed by writers such as *New York* magazine's Gael Greene, who was writing not just about the restaurants in Manhattan but also was traveling overseas and submitting dispatches on the gustatory scene in Paris. She and others were describing food with an enthusiasm and vocabulary previously reserved for the performing arts. The zeitgeist was irresistibly named *nouvelle cuisine,* and I was drawn to its emphasis on composition and presentation, with dishes emerging from the kitchen ready to be served rather than finished tableside by a waiter. Though it made room for lighter, almost spa-like approaches, including portions that many found scandalously small, it also held fast to certain elements of classic French cooking, retaining the focus on rigorous techniques, but breaking away from time-honored dishes in favor of new compositions that reinvented and redefined them. To New Yorkers, a dining public raised on the notion that there were two options for French dining—the "fancy" restaurant with Dover sole and duck *à l'orange* and the bistro with onion soup and *steak frites*—the novelty was enticing.

In many ways, I was taken with the idea of *nouvelle cuisine,* without having tasted much of it. But I could *imagine* what the food I was reading about tasted like, and I appreciated certain credos that were emerging: the devotion to seasonal, fresh ingredients, which is almost taken for granted today in restaurants of a certain caliber; the idea of making a personal statement, also now pretty much expected; and the emphasis on smaller portions and more courses, which was tailor-made to my Olney-inspired love of the meal as composition. Everything about it seemed to mirror my own evolution as a cook: I had started with the classics, had broken a few rules to suit my sensibility, and was beginning to have my own ideas.

I wasn't the only one in our apartment swept up with these seductive goings-on. Karen thought that she might want to join me in opening a restaurant one day. So, we made our first joint trip to France to see the revolution for ourselves, hitting as many two- and three-star Michelin restaurants as we could in the span of about two weeks. Somehow, against all odds, really, the food lived up to our almost ludicrously lofty expectations. I was more excited than ever to get back home and try my own dishes, bringing together the techniques I'd been honing with my ideas, which had by then been shaped by years of reading, tasting, cooking, and daydreaming.

Three restaurants also dazzled us with their brand of hospitality, each of them astonishingly accessible, eschewing in their own ways the precious, overformalized tone set by the vast majority of upscale establishments in France, and in New York City for that matter. One was Taillevent, Paris's exquisite gastronomic temple. We showed up as the very picture of American tourism, two young lovers of perhaps questionable means. But as we walked through the front door, none of that mattered; the owner, Jean-Claude Vrinat, was so gracious that he gave us the distinct impression he had been waiting for us all his life. At La Pyramide, in the shadow of ancient sycamore trees out in the countryside, we were enchanted by the image of Madame Point, widow of the late, great chef Fernand Point, sitting at a beautiful desk writing menus by hand, and by the sommelier, a man we placed in his eighties, who had an easy way with even the most precious wines, uncorking first-growth 1929 Bordeaux with astounding familiarity. And, at the original Le Bernardin, Karen was captivated by dining room empress Maguy Le Coze, a gazelle in her skintight Azzedine Alaïa,

who personified a word we hadn't associated with the restaurant business: *glamour.* It became a touchstone.

The flight home was a magic carpet ride. In the dim light of the airplane, with fellow passengers asleep all around us, we cuddled together and whispered our conclusions about everything we'd just taken in, applying our impressions of Taillevent, La Pyramide, and Le Bernardin to the restaurant we were thinking of opening ourselves. It didn't matter that we were unknown quantities in the restaurant world of New York City; we were so galvanized by our shared experience that there was no stopping us now.

"YOU GUYS SHOULD OPEN A RESTAURANT."

Back in the United States, I was more driven to cook than I had been since those early days in the Bronx. I had always experimented a bit, but the idea of drawing directly from French classics in a new way really lit me up. I was formulating concepts for dishes that merged old and new, such as a lobster ragoût with a bisque-inspired sauce flavored with Sauternes, lime, and curry (see page 131) and Squab Mousse with Juniper & Green Peppercorns (page 115). This, along with a love of un-shy flavors—less restrained than those found in many French kitchens—reflected the American, or the New Yorker, in me.

Inspiration came from a variety of sources, but mostly from reading about food. I'd see a recipe in a book, or a passing reference to a dish in a magazine, and write it down, filling notebooks with list after list of things I wanted to try. Sometimes I'd learn about what another chef was cooking, perhaps in *Gault Millau* magazine, which I couldn't wait to get my hands on each month, and treat it like a creative challenge, devising a recipe based on the name. There's no better example of this than the quintessential Chanterelle signature dish from day one through today, our seafood sausage. In the mid-1970s Gael Greene mentioned that Taillevent in Paris was serving a *boudin des fruits de mer*. Intrigued, I made a seafood filling, piped it into a sausage casing, grilled it, and sauced it with a *beurre blanc*. (Years later, on a trip to France, we dined at Taillevent again, and ordered their sausage. It was much larger and plumper than the one we serve, poached rather than grilled, and less robust, with strained out-shallots in their rendition of a *beurre blanc*. One of our regular customers was at Taillevent that night and told owner Jean-Claude Vrinat that our sausage was better. Vrinat took it in good humor and for years sent us a Christmas card every December.)

I began road-testing new dishes at home. Charles Chevillot was very generous about letting me special-order rare ingredients, and I'd also visit those same shops on Ninth Avenue that I had trekked to as a little kid, bringing my personal arc full circle. On one of these excursions it occurred to me that I'd been on a steady learning curve, from dinners in French restaurants with my parents, through my solo cooking lessons in the family kitchen, then to cooking school and early jobs, and now an exciting new phase of possibility and innovation.

As I experimented in earnest, I honed my personal style even further. Just as they are today, most of my compositions were based on harmonizing no more than two or three primary flavors with a sauce that pulled them all together. To achieve this, I chiseled away at ingredient lists until arriving at what I thought of as the essence of each dish. I also streamlined many of the building blocks of the kitchen in my ongoing quest to bring as much clarity as possible to every element. It turns out that ditching the celery was just the first of many liberties I would take with traditional recipes before I was through. For example, many chefs use tomato in their veal stock, but I chose not to, wanting to taste only the veal itself. If tomato was called for in a particular dish, I'd add it during the preparation. By the same token, I stopped putting herbs or peppercorns in my chicken stock, because the flavor of individual herbs or the heat of the peppercorns wouldn't be welcome in every recipe that called for the stock. I questioned *everything* and operated on sheer instinct, obsessively editing until each dish was a study in ruthless efficiency.

We needed an audience, of course, so, in 1977, in our studio apartment on East 77th Street, Karen and I began throwing monthly dinner parties for six or eight people. The result of all my imaginings, such as Lobster with Cider and Apples (page 132), and Rack of Lamb with Cumin-Salt Crust (page 213) all made their debut there.

For us the planning was a feast in itself: We'd talk about the menu for days, visualizing the meal as it would unfold for our guests, making sure not to repeat flavors or textures, and keeping the palate fresh enough to enjoy the next course. Then we'd get to work: I'd shop for ingredients and do as much advance preparation as possible, making stocks, sauces, and anything else that could be, or had to be, readied ahead of time. Karen, who had never planned on a life in the hospitality biz, was getting a crash course and really enjoying it. Just as I had my own favorite markets and resources, she made a tour of her own beloved purveyors, visiting the florist and trekking crosstown to 67 Wines and Spirits on Columbus Avenue, returning hours later, kicking the front door open with a mixed case underarm.

On the day of the dinner, I'd chain myself to the stove, while Karen would decorate our home with little flower arrangements and, after the style of La Pyramide's Madame Point, handwrite a menu in what has since become her signature flowing pen strokes.

On the appointed evening, always a Sunday, we'd hurriedly clean up the apartment and set the table. Around sunset, give or take an hour, our good friends and occasional family members would arrive. The dinners were intoxicating, in every sense of the word. Hour after hour ticked by as we ate, drank, laughed, argued, and occasionally sang the night away until we were in a state of communal bliss. At some point, our apartment no longer felt like an Upper East Side studio; I had that same sense I'd had as a child, that I was in an otherworldly place devoted entirely to the comfort and contentment of its guests, achieved through the dispensing of food and hospitality. Only it was *my* food and Karen's hospitality. In those moments I saw myself through the eyes of the kid I used to be, and he was, once again, grinning ear to ear and thinking, "I can do this."

The passion lives on: in the Chanterelle kitchen in our current home on Harrison Street.

A weekly ritual: Karen designs the flower arrangements.

My feelings were reflected by our guests, all of whom told us the same thing: "You guys should open a restaurant." They believed we were on to something, not just with my food, which seemed to find a definable style rather quickly, but also with Karen's unique, heartfelt, and unassuming charms as a hostess. While I always knew that I would open my own place, I had never imagined doing it so quickly. I thought that I would cook under the tutelage of others for years, but it was dawning on me that all those Saturday sessions in my family's kitchen had laid a better foundation than I realized. I was becoming comfortable and confident, starting to believe I could please a dining room full of hungry and demanding New Yorkers. And, of course, there was Karen, the embodiment of everything I wanted our restaurant to be: cultured, earthy, and with an unpretentious manner and innate sense of style.

Opening a restaurant in the 1970s was a much less weighty proposition than it is now. We believed we could get our doors open for as little as $35,000, though when all was said and done, we ended up spending just over $100,000, still a far cry from the multimillion-dollar investments people make today.

We were also emboldened by the fact that two American couples had already cleared a path into the world of fine dining in New York City: Barry Wine, who owned the Quilted Giraffe with his wife, Susan, hadn't cooked anywhere other than their restaurant, nor had Karen Hubert and Len Allison of Hubert's. Not only were there Americans in the kitchen, but there was English on the awning: it was significant that these establishments served French, or French-leaning, food under a non-French moniker. That's why, when Bill Katz, our good friend, mentor, and personal Diaghilev, who would go on to design the restaurant, suggested the name Chanterelle, we decided to let it stand alone, without affixing a "Le" or "La" to it. This wouldn't be noteworthy today, but at the time it was audacious.

GRAND STREET, HERE WE COME

We went looking for a space, and were very close to settling on one that would seat about sixty guests. But when we ducked into a nearby Brazilian joint for lunch one day, I was taken with its small size. Having never actually been a chef, I realized that it would be a better idea to hedge my bets with a restaurant I knew I'd be able to manage, so we found another spot—a shuttered bodega that had been a corset factory's showroom once upon a time—on Grand Street in SoHo. Everybody in New York knows SoHo now, with its famous boutiques and restaurants, but at the time it was the next frontier of Manhattan, the world of curvy, named streets that existed below the neatly ordered and numbered grid system. We weren't trying to make a statement. The fact of the matter was that we couldn't afford to be uptown, or even on a major thoroughfare like West Broadway, but our starting rent of $850 per month on Grand Street seemed manageable.

In hindsight, though, Chanterelle was a restaurant that was meant to be downtown, in the wide-open, skyscraperless land of artists' lofts. Existing off the grid gave us permission, if only from ourselves, to do things our way, and there was a raw, creative freedom in the air down on Grand Street that was invigorating. In many ways, the act of transforming that old bodega into Chanterelle felt like the work of an artist, especially because the overall vision for the space was created by our guardian angel, Bill Katz, himself an artist. Part of Bill's vision was to celebrate the 19th-century architecture that enveloped us. To do this, he left unobstructed the views through the expansive windows to give diners the feeling of being at one with the neighborhood, with its desolate nocturnal streets and cast-iron storefronts, while at the same time giving passersby a glimpse of the festivities within.

The more we discovered about the space, the more we loved it: As we chipped away the Pepsodent®-green paint, we encountered mahogany wainscoting buried beneath the walls and a sumptuous tin ceiling. There was no antechamber; as soon as you stepped through the front door, you were in our dining room.

The realization of our shared dream was so close we could taste it, but while we were full of enthusiasm, we were out of money. One night, we found ourselves sitting in our lovely dining room at one in the morning, wondering what in the world we were going to do. Just then, a young couple on roller skates wheeled up to our door and stuck their heads in. It turned out they were Susan and Louis Meisel, owners of a gallery on Prince Street, on their way home from a late night skating at the Roxy. We were at such a low point that we let it all spill out, telling these two strangers our entire story, right up to our current moment of professional destitution. Louis smiled at us and said, "Don't worry about it," and the two of them glided off into the night.

They contacted us a few days later, and we arranged a dinner in the nearly finished restaurant for the two of them and a number of potential investors they had lined up. The dinner was a smashing success, and by the end of the night we had raised the remaining monies we needed to get our doors open. We were once again on our way.

Down the home stretch, as many decisions as possible were made to ensure our vision of the restaurant as a surrogate home: Instead of overhead lights, we had chandeliers. Instead of a podium at the door, we moved in an antique wooden desk that once belonged to Karen's grandmother Clara. Instead of a coat closet, we placed an antique American armoire purchased from a nearby antiques shop next to the desk. We were unmistakably a restaurant—there were, after all, ten tables—but these touches set a personal tone. To heighten the effect, we also decided to forgo any signs of commerce: there would be no register, no bar, no bottles on display, and no window into the kitchen.

Bill's design was as spare as it was elegant. In time, one perceptive critic would observe that just as his sets for ballets made brilliant use of space, providing a compelling stage for the dancers, the dining room he created for us didn't call undue attention to itself. It was a home for the food and the service—an apt reflection of the paring down I had been doing in the kitchen. In keeping with our desire to not distract our guests from each other or the food, we decided not to hang any art on the walls. But one of our new investors, a legendary New York City gallery owner, kept trying to convince us that he had just the right painting for our dining room. The ongoing dialogue inspired Bill to suggest that we feature art on our menu cover, an inspired suggestion that led to one of our most treasured traditions (see page 16).

Since our dinner-party days, we had given a lot of thought to what we wanted a meal at Chanterelle to be, and as the opening approached, we came to the conclusion that we would serve formal food in an informal setting—no, not informal; what we sought was not a lack of formality, but a *toned-down* formality. We wanted people to feel like they were coming to a dinner party in a fantastic, idealized dining room, unself-conscious but well thought out—a place that seemed like it had always been there, but was fresh. There would be no captain in a tuxedo, but service on the same level as the places that stood on such ceremony. Karen wanted the experience to be nothing less than perfect, but without the condescension and obsequiousness that often came with it.

As for the food, I wanted diners to have the feeling that I'd had as a kid in those French restaurants. I wanted them to find everything beautiful to look at and intense and unforgettable to eat. I focused on sauces, on proudly old-fashioned terrines, quenelles, aspics, and consommés, and on ingredients that were beyond the reach of the average person in those days, such as wild mushrooms, oysters, truffles, and sea urchins. We were a small, intimate restaurant, but we wanted the effect to be *big*—indelible flavors and warm service—our idiosyncratic take on a three-star French restaurant, such as could only exist below Houston Street in 1970s New York.

Serving such meals was more challenging than it might sound: For all of the growing excitement about food, purveyors of fine ingredients were hard to come by. We found our sources as we went along, like the young New Jersey couple who noticed our mushroom-themed name and pulled up in their car to introduce themselves and sell us a variety of wild mushrooms they had foraged, or

the Oregon farmer from whom we purchased others. On another day, a voluble and enthusiastic guy named George Faison pulled up in his station wagon, introduced himself, and told me about the new business he and his partner were starting, to sell foie gras in America: D'Artagnan.

Despite our proudly American name, and the decision we had made (also nearly scandalous at the time) to write our menu in English, we were always going to adhere to certain European traditions—we offered a rich and varied cheese board from the day we opened, and we always waited until after dessert to offer coffee, accompanied by *petits fours,* unless the customer asked for it earlier.

Karen also made a bold decision about the dining room staff, forgoing the usual hierarchy of captains, waiters, and busboys. Breaking the hiring mold in "fancy" restaurants of the day, she was open to all looks and types and didn't exclude women or people without prior restaurant experience. "You can teach technique," she likes to say, "but you can't teach smart." Her number-one priority was finding people who were engaging, focused, natural, and sincere. The result was that guests would have the feeling that they had stumbled upon a co-ed troupe of conspicuously young, unconventionally groomed butlers.

The atmosphere at Chanterelle has always been creative. Not unlike our clientele, many of our staff members were, and are, in the arts themselves, like the four dancers who once worked at the restaurant and shared a loft around the corner.

We also made a decision *not* to enforce a dress code, something that is all but extinct in Manhattan today, but back then, if you arrived in shirtsleeves at an upscale restaurant, you'd be loaned a jacket and tie. Not only did we want our guests to be comfortable, but the idea that uptown people in tuxedoes would be seated side by side with artists in blue jeans and woolly sweaters was also, to our way of thinking, quintessentially New York. Karen was fast developing the philosophy that each couple or group who entered the restaurant would have its own idea of what a meal at Chanterelle should be, and that we should tailor the experience accordingly. Ten tables, ten worlds.

The corner where it began: at the intersection of Grand and Greene streets in SoHo.

THE ART OF CHANTERELLE

❦

The honor roll: Bill Katz (pictured with us above) painted the artistic representation (on the facing page) of the artists whose work has graced our menus.

When Bill Katz first suggested that we feature art on Chanterelle's menu covers, we loved the idea, in part because it reminded us of the legend of La Colombe d'Or, the restaurant in the south of France where such artists as Picasso, Matisse, Klee, and Calder had exchanged paintings for food. Before we knew it, he had arranged for us to use a print by Marisol, the image of a hand holding a delicate flower, on our inaugural menu.

Marisol was the first in an extraordinary group of artists whose work has graced our menus over the years. Bill, our dear friend cum curator, established that our covers would change every six months, and they've featured a phenomenal range of artists, photographers, composers, and writers, including Merce Cunningham and John Cage, Cindy Sherman, Francesco Clemente, Cy Twombly, Allen Ginsberg, and Roy Lichtenstein, to name just a few. Sometimes the artwork is there to mark a special event, like the benefits that we host for our friend Bill T. Jones. On occasion, somebody will ask us if he or she can do one; for example, one day Bill Cosby was having dinner at the restaurant and inquired, "What's the deal with the menus?" When it was explained to him, he said, "I want to do one." We agreed, then, with Bill Katz, he improvised an original monologue that was ultimately accompanied on the menu cover by a beautiful Edward Henderson drawing.

Karen and I, as well as the entire staff, always eagerly await the day Bill arrives with the latest addition to our collection; after all these years, it remains an honor and a thrill. One of our greatest pleasures at the restaurant is telling visitors the story of past menu covers, which line the walls of our sitting room. For us, each of them recalls a specific time in the history of Chanterelle, captured forever by talents we revere, the perfect fusion of food and art.

Lorna Simpson

Cletus Johnson

John Cage

Richard Prince

Susan

Gregory Hull

Lynn Davis

Philippe Petit

Donald Baechler Adam Fuss

Rothenberg

Daniel Oates

Maurice

Eric Fischl

Ellsworth Kelly

Annie Leibovitz

Tom Levine

April Gornik

Robert Allen Ginsberg

Howard Hodgkin

Bill Cosby

Robert Mapplethorpe

Maurice Grosser

Cindy Sherman

Jasper Johns

Joe Brainard

Robert Indiana

Kara Walker

Lenny Kalzer

Robert Wilson

Juan Hamilton

Jennifer Bartlett

Glenn Ligon

Louise Nevelson

Roy Lichtenstein

Philip Taaffe

Gretchen Bender

Mike Starn

Sanders

Bill Katz

Vija Celmins

Gert Laas

Timothy Greenfield-Sanders

Smith

Michael Auder

Jack Shear

Merce Cunningham

Kiki

Elizabeth Murray

Robert Longo

Alex Katz

Marisol

Edward Henderson

David Seidner

Lord

Ross Bleckner

Jo Baer

Emma Gold

Keith Haring

Cy Twombly

Andrew

Francois Morellet

Francesco Clemente

Nan Golden

Doug Starn Donald

John Dugdale

Terry

James Brown

Terry Winters

Robert Rauschenberg

Malcolm Morley

Kunié Sugiura

John Duff

Mathew Barney

Virgil Thomson

A part of history: the stunning view from the dining room on Grand Street.

A DECADE TO REMEMBER

Without a wine or beer license, we opened in November 1979. For the first week, we served friends and family only, inviting them for dinner so we could get our act together before we began charging customers. Early on, it was quite a scene: In our first months, a time when we would have been happy to serve *any* customers, we were both humbled and thrilled to welcome a steady procession of icons. It's never been our style to trumpet the boldface names who have frequented Chanterelle—in fact, one of the charms of the restaurant is that many of them have dined as anonymously as anyone else, and were treated just the same by Karen and the rest of the staff. Nonetheless, I want to share a few names here because I think they give a sense of what it was like on Grand Street when Chanterelle was born: Bill Katz and his partner Willy Eisenhart often dined at the restaurant with artists and writers, many of whom we got to know, and some of whose artwork was eventually featured on our menu covers, including Virgil Thompson, Edward Albee, Bill T. Jones and Arnie Zane, and Tom and James Levine. Other neighbors included Agnes de Mille, Louise Nevelson, Leo Castelli, Richard Avedon, Robert Mapplethorpe, Keith Haring, Adam Gopnik, and magazine magnate Malcolm Forbes, who would *vroom* up on his motorcycle. (When he passed away, years later, he left both Karen and me, along with other restaurateurs he was fond of, a final, posthumous gratuity.)

We were young and idealistic and we did everything ourselves: Karen would answer phones all day, then disappear at some point to run around the corner and buy cheese from the recently opened emporium Dean & DeLuca, then come flying in the door, picking up the phone to take a reservation on her way to the refrigerator, then change for dinner. In the days before we began serving lunch, we had only eight people on hand for our nightly "family" (restaurant-speak for "staff") meal. At the end of each night, I'd meticulously clean the kitchen and Karen would clean the dining room until a waiter, more seasoned than she, suggested she let the dishwasher do it for her. We were closed on Monday, but that was

the day I came in to do a lot of my deep prep for the coming week, and it was often the day that Karen would visit her favorite flower purveyor and create that week's arrangements in the dining room, just the way she had for those dinner parties in our apartment. She'd also use the dining room as her office, doing the books at one of the tables. Gradually, we added people to the team, but for us the work simply never stopped. The restaurant was our life: It felt as if we were always getting ready to open or breaking the place down for the night, with the adrenaline burst of cooking and serving dinner propelling us into the next morning.

At the outset, I hired a prep cook to help me during the day, but during service I was alone in the kitchen, and it was madness, one of the many surefire signs that while Karen knew how to make people feel at home and I knew how to cook, we really had little idea of how to run a restaurant. We learned as we went, making some embarrassing rookie decisions. Karen, in keeping with her reverent desire to please our guests, booked the tables with extreme conservatism to make sure nobody would ever have to wait for their agreed-upon seating time. (She also believed that always having one table open maintained a welcoming, anticipatory air in the dining room, and so strove to have one table enticingly vacant, if only for a few minutes.) We had no air conditioner when we first opened, and in the winter an old heat-generating gas blower kept our diners warm. The same was true in the kitchen: I can't remember what we thought was more important than the walk-in refrigerator we declined to install, but it was a pound-foolish decision to be sure: After dinner each Saturday night, with nearly forty-eight hours to go before our next service and no way to keep perishables from perishing, we'd often have to give away about a thousand dollars' worth of food to our staff.

We served a $35 prix-fixe menu. I changed the menu weekly, and Karen, still operating according to Madame Point's example, handwrote our menus.

After the European fashion, we planned to close for the month of August and for the week after New Year's Eve, and that's just what we did for the first few years.

If all of this sounds a bit idiosyncratic, that's because it is, and our little secret behind the scenes is that for all of our ambition, Chanterelle was, and is, at the end of the day, a mom-and-pop restaurant. We were spending our lives there, so the staff became family, and were treated as such: I began throwing my now-traditional Chinese New Year's feast for the staff and a Thanksgiving dinner that included family, friends, and whatever staff members might be stranded far from home.

In the days before we opened, curious neighbors saw us attacking the cast-iron columns outside the space, chipping away at the old paint with ball peen hammers. One of them told Gael Greene about us, and she came in within two weeks after we served our first meal. Two weeks after that, we were on the cover of *New York* magazine, and her rave review ran with the headline "The Daring Young Man on Grand Street."

On the heels of this attention, uptowners began to find their way down to Grand Street and, before we knew it, we were booked beyond our wildest dreams. We had no place for customers to wait. They'd stream out the door and onto the sidewalk. Karen or one of her surrogates would escort them down the street to La Gamelle, a cozy restaurant and bar, then return to retrieve them when their table was ready. The neighborhood was so desolate after dark that most of our customers, unaccustomed to downtown, dared not make the walk themselves, and the same was true after their meal, when one of our team would venture over to West Broadway to find them a taxi.

For years, it felt like we were hosting a never-ending party. There are things about it that seem as vivid today as they did all those years ago, like the way powdery white winds would blow past the window on winter nights, turning the dining room into a snow globe. Or how cabs would pull up, the passengers would realize how remote our location was, and keep going. Or the curious street characters who wandered in from the Bowery almost nightly in our first few months to see what all the fuss was about, drawn to this little beacon of light in what used to be a ghost town after dark.

As time went on, I grew more confident in my own instincts and began to make my food even more personal, weaving in dishes informed by my own history—an hors d'oeuvre based on blintzes, a soup inspired by borscht, duck spring rolls born of my love for Chinese food, and so on.

Reviewers were almost unanimously kind, although some were kinder than others. "If you don't like the review," went a house joke, "just wait a week. There'll be another." Then, in 1987, Bryan Miller gave us four stars in the *New York Times*. We were ecstatic, and poured Champagne for the entire dining room. It was the biggest sea change in our lives since Gael Greene's write-up, and it came with a new set of challenges. Instantly, our reservation lines were overwhelmed; the phone company told Karen that we'd need ten rollover numbers to avoid a busy signal, and, from then on, training reservationists ostensibly meant teaching them how to say "I'm sorry" in the most gracious way possible. Sometimes the kitchen was barely organized chaos, but for us, each night was a new adventure: The restaurant had a genuine buzz about it and we never knew who might show up or how late the evening would go. One night film director Milos Forman was at one table with Phillip Petit, and Mikhail Baryshnikov was at another. We were way behind in the kitchen, and I remember a waiter frantically pacing back and forth on the other side of the line, pleading with me, "Where's Baryshnikov's meat? Where's Baryshnikov's meat?"

A ROOM OF OUR OWN

When our ten-year lease expired in 1988, we decided to move to more luxurious quarters and began looking for a new space, eventually finding our current home, the Mercantile Exchange Building, a beautiful landmark location in Tribeca that we were able to secure only with the help, generosity, and support (both moral and financial) of three extraordinary regulars who suddenly became what the theater people call "angels," making a special investment in our future. And so, on the last night of our lease, Halloween, we threw a staff costume party in the dining room. We had already moved everything into storage, including the chandeliers, while we built out the space. With bare lightbulbs illuminating our evening, we polished off the wine that we had strategically left behind, stopping the party at the stroke of midnight, because that's when we had to be out. We didn't soap up the windows like so many restaurateurs do, because we weren't closing; we were just moving. But we couldn't resist one final gesture, inspired as much by the holiday as anything else, scraping off all but four letters of our name, leaving a new one—Hell—stenciled on the glass.

After a period of a few months during which we made some essential structural changes to the space, we reopened Chanterelle in its new home. (Things were also new at our personal home: Our daughter, Sara, was born during this time, followed two years later by our son, Jacob, adding untold joy and richness to our lives.) Having operated out of a bare-bones facility for ten years, we felt, and still feel, spoiled by some of the amenities, like the fact that we have an office and spacious wine cellar downstairs (or that we even have a useable downstairs at all) and an anteroom where people can wait for their table and that doubles as an informal gallery of past menu covers. We have a service entrance, so deliveries are no longer wheeled through the front door, and guests no longer pass by the kitchen on their way to the restroom.

But even in these more luxurious quarters, we strived to remain true to all the things that made Chanterelle special, and we have continued to do our best to maintain them to this day: The menus still feature Karen's unmistakable script, the unadorned space still includes her soaring flower arrangements, she and I still collaborate on a daily basis, and I'm happy to report that we're still married. We still hang coats in an armoire near the front door, although it's a larger one than we had in our old quarters; we still have a diverse, talented staff that functions in harmony, with no busboys in sight; we're still honored to have a different artist's work grace our menu covers twice a year; and we still serve dishes

The human touch: Karen writing a new menu in her unmistakable script.

that are inspired, as much as anything, by those evenings out with my parents. I've learned a lot since then, but I don't think I'll ever stop trying to conjure the feeling that Chanterelle is a dream of a restaurant, first imagined by a little, food-loving kid, that somehow, magically, came true.

How to Use this Book

I've tried to organize this book to make it as user-friendly as possible. Readers who want to prepare a full, five- or six-course tasting menu at home to rival the ones we serve at Chanterelle can mix and match dishes to their heart's desire to do just that. For guidance in selecting and planning a menu, see the essay on the facing page.

By the same token, each recipe is meant to be a free-standing offering, inviting you to cook and enjoy it on its own or as part of a meal comprising your own recipes or those from other chefs and books.

The chapters are ordered according to the progression of a meal: hors d'oeuvres followed by salads and starters, followed by main courses and then desserts. The one major adjustment I've made to the structure of a Chanterelle meal is that we do not offer side dishes on our menu, but I've presented some here: They can be served with the suggested main courses or with others, and I've provided some guidance for which sides go best with which type of dish, though my suggestions are by no means exhaustive.

In the back of the book you'll find recipes for certain basics, such as stocks and pasta dough, as well as a useful list of sources from which you can order hard-to-find foods and cooking equipment.

Finally, I encourage you to bring your own palate to these recipes; most of them indicate to season to taste with salt and pepper, and many leave the exact amount of lemon juice, soy sauce, or some other flavoring agent up to your sensibility. I mean this sincerely: Some cooks prefer more acidity or salinity in their cooking than others, and you should make these dishes your own to some extent by letting your own preferences be your guide.

Notes on Composing
and Planning a Menu at Home

&

I've cooked all of the dishes in this book at Chanterelle and prepared many of them at home as well. So, I thought it would be a good idea to share some notes about how to select and plan a menu of Chanterelle dishes for entertaining from a home kitchen.

The first decision home cooks need to make about dinner parties is how much they want to be in the kitchen and how much they want to be at the table. I mention this because I've noticed that more and more home cooks are, in some ways, functioning like restaurant chefs when they host dinner parties, spending most of the time in the kitchen, emerging just long enough to eat each course, then disappearing again to cook or finish the next course. I don't see anything wrong with this, but I do think it's important for each cook to make a decision about where he or she wants to spend the majority of an afternoon or evening.

If you enjoy passing time the way I used to at our pre-Chanterelle dinner parties, sitting down just long enough to eat—or operating out of one of the increasingly popular open home kitchens that allow you to cook and socialize simultaneously—then the sky's pretty much the limit as far as what you can cook and serve. Even so, there are some factors that should be taken into consideration, such as how much space is available for prep and plating and how many burners and ovens are in your kitchen.

If you want to socialize at your own dinner parties, then you need to find a middle ground between taste and practicality, planning a menu of dishes that complement one another, with one eye on minimizing the amount of cooking that must be done just before serving. If this describes your situation, I recommend that you select dishes that can be made in advance and kept warm, or reheated, as well as a few dishes that can be served at room temperature. For example, avoid hors d'oeuvres that call for deep-frying, serve at least one course that's presented cold or at room temperature, and make sure that the components of your main course do not all need to be cooked *à la minute.* One ideal main-course equation is a braised meat plus a puree that can be kept warm in a double boiler and a vegetable that's quickly sautéed just before serving. If the components can be served family style, either from a buffet or passing them at the table, that'll make life that much easier.

To some extent, this book was written with the idea of freeing you up to be at the table: Many of the recipes have make-ahead notes, and if a dish features more than two components, I've indicated when one or two can be optional, such as the spring rolls that accompany the duck dish on page 193.

Seasonality should also be a consideration in menu planning. You should try to employ not just a range of in-season ingredients, but also a variety of techniques that people associate with the season, such as braising in the fall and winter and grilling in the summer. Also, take advantage of the conveniences

continued

Fall and Winter Menu

- Squab Mousse with Juniper & Green Peppercorns (page 115)

- TRIO OF HOT SOUPS

  Celery Soup with White Truffles (page 66)

  Lentil & Black Truffle Soup (page 68)

  Onion Consommé with Onion & Fontina Ravioli (page 64; omit the pastry)

- Sautéed Bay Scallops with Duck Fat, Tomato & Basil (page 122)

- Brined Roast Pork Loin with Fennel Jus & Fennel Flan (page 219)

- Bartlett Pears Served Two Ways (page 275)

offered by a season: There's just no reason for a cook, even one who likes playing the role of chef, to cook every course in the summer, when cold food—either made in advance and chilled, or something that's never touched by fire—will be welcome, even *expected,* by your guests and easier on your schedule, a win-win proposition if ever there was one.

Other dishes are just naturals for entertaining, or for multicourse meals. For example, the seafood sausage, one of our signature dishes, looks impressive on the plate, but in reality, the sausage must be made in advance, so this impress-your-friends recipe is actually a perfect year-round choice.

To illustrate all of this, let's look at a few possible menus.

FALL AND WINTER

At the restaurant, I might serve the five courses on page 23 in the fall and winter.

The squab mousse is simply a perfect entertaining dish for any occasion: It *has* to be made ahead and is an elegant, sophisticated way to begin any meal. You could even eliminate the plating step, packing the mousse into a terrine or crock, serving it with toast points, and inviting everybody to help themselves from the center of the table.

Serving three hot soups might seem a bit "restaurant" for home cooking, but all three of them are relatively straightforward to make and can be prepared in advance. That said, you could, of course, serve just one soup: The celery root and white truffle would be the most impressive.

The bay scallops with duck fat is the *à la minute* dish in this lineup, but if it seems like too much to pull off midmeal, a scaled-down version of Osso Buco of Monkfish with Preserved Lemon (page 153), which can be made ahead and reheated at the last second, may be substituted. Or you could serve full portions of the monkfish dish and eliminate the pork, making the fish the main course.

Or, you can still serve the brined roast pork, but make it less demanding by replacing the fennel flan, which must be unmolded and presented restaurant style on the plate, with Braised Fennel (page 242), which is more forgiving in the oven and can be served family style, even from the same platter as the sliced pork. You'll hit all the same flavor points as you would with the original dish but save yourself a lot of time and mental energy.

SUMMER

To simplify this menu, you could eliminate one or two courses starting with either the tartares or the blossoms and finishing with the snapper or the lamb.

As far as uncomplicating the dishes themselves: You could make one of the beet tartares, and one fish tartare, streamlining the preparation and presentation. As with the squab mousse, you could also make just one fish or beet tartare and serve it on crackers or toast points as an *amuse-bouche.* As for the lamb, you could prepare a larger roast in place of chops (i.e., a roast rack or leg). The finishing of the sauce with goat cheese needs to be last minute, but the thyme-lamb jus is just fine on its own and can be made ahead and kept warm. (I haven't mentioned the blossoms or the snapper because both are already quite user-friendly and lend themselves to advance cooking.)

SPRING

As always, one or more courses can be cut: For two savory courses, the lobster or the asparagus followed by the turbot or the rabbit would be a fine meal; for three, the lobster, turbot, and rabbit. If making an aspic is intimidating, you could instead make a simpler lobster salad with some greens and/or fennel, dressed with one or both of the sauces (red pepper coulis or saffron aïoli). Alternatively, you could replace the dish with Vegetables and Shellfish à la Grecque (page 91), which not only can be made ahead, but also does not require clarifying or gelling a broth. (It can also be made with fewer components, such as just mussels and artichokes, for example.)

The asparagus dish requires expensive ingredients (truffles) and some delicate last-minute cooking (poached eggs), but just asparagus with truffle sauce and Parmesan would be delicious as well. Or, you can eliminate this as a course and use the asparagus as a vegetable with the rabbit to keep a very springtime theme. I also want to put in a word for the turbot, which might seem difficult, but in fact is not. Everything up to cooking the fish and finishing the sauce is done ahead. The fish can be sautéed instead of grilled, or a somewhat thicker and less delicate fish such as halibut or wild striped bass may be substituted. You could also skip the sauce altogether and go for a homier version, serving turbot or sole sautéed with brown butter and peas with or without the pancetta and pearl onions.

Another suggestion for a second course, which would not require much delicate or last-minute work, is Spring Greens Soup with Pike Quenelles (page 73), which could even be served without the pike quenelles if desired. The rabbit dish could be replaced with our other rabbit dish, Stuffed Saddle of Rabbit with Coarse Mustard & Tarragon (page 198), which is similar in flavor and feeling but requires less last-minute work and is more forgiving in terms of doneness.

I haven't mentioned dessert alternatives for these individual menus, because my plan B for all of them is the same: Purchase some premium store-bought ice cream and serve it with one or more of the *petits fours* on pages 279–281. I promise you, everybody will go home very, very happy.

Spring Menu

- Lobster with Bouillabaisse Aspic (page 92)

- Grilled Asparagus with Black Truffles, Shaved Parmesan & a Poached Egg (page 119)

- Grilled Turbot with Peas, Pearl Onions & Pancetta (page 148)

- Rabbit Chops with Fines Herbes & Cream (page 197)

- Fig & Goat Cheese Tart with Huckleberry Ice Cream (page 267)

HORS D'OEUVRES

At Chanterelle, there's no older or more inside joke than using the word *nuts* as a stand-in for *amuse-bouches,* the bite-size treats offered as a welcome from the chef. When we began serving them in the early 1980s, the idea of sending out free food confounded our waiters. "It's the Chanterelle version of when you go to a bar and get nuts," I explained. The waitstaff began coming into the kitchen requesting "nuts for two" or "nuts for three," and the tradition has endured for more than twenty years. Just what constitutes an *amuse* (as the phrase is often abbreviated) is open to interpretation, but we adhere to the classic ideal of something that can be popped into the mouth, or served in a thimble-like vessel and knocked back like a shot. Of course, in a home setting, where they're called *hors d'oeuvres, amuses* are nothing new and the recipes in this chapter have been selected with the realities of home cooking and entertaining in mind: Most can be prepared entirely, or substantially, in advance and warmed, fried, assembled, or plated just before serving. A note on yields: Almost all of the recipes in this book serve four people, but because it's difficult, if not impossible, to produce small enough quantities of some of their elements, many of the recipes in this chapter make enough hors d'oeuvres for more than four. Where possible, I've provided instructions for refrigerating or freezing extra servings, as well as serving suggestions for extra sauces, dips, and other components.

Herbed Crêpes with Black Caviar & Crème Fraîche

2 large eggs

½ cup all-purpose flour

2 tablespoons olive oil

¾ teaspoon minced fresh dill

¾ teaspoon minced fresh flat-leaf parsley

½ teaspoon minced fresh chives

Pinch of kosher salt

Black pepper from a mill

⅔ cup water

Canola oil or nonstick cooking spray, for greasing pan

6 chive spears for large pouches or 24 for small pouches

3 or 4 tablespoons crème fraîche

1 to 2 tablespoons black caviar (see headnote)

MAKES 6 LARGE OR 24 TO 28 COCKTAIL-SIZE HORS D'OEUVRES, ENOUGH TO SERVE 6 TO 8

Inspired by an appetizer served at the Quilted Giraffe, one of the American-owned French restaurants that preceded Chanterelle in New York City, these little beggar's purses are all about accentuating and complementing the caviar, a lively variation on the Russian tradition of blini as an accompaniment. These are especially appropriate for black-tie and other formal events because the crème fraîche and caviar echo the black-and-white motif.

For recipes like this, where the caviar isn't the star of the dish, I use American paddlefish caviar. (This is a bit of a misnomer because only eggs from sturgeon are officially considered caviar, but I use the name freely.) It's much less expensive than sevruga, osetra, or other Caspian Sea varieties. American caviar is closest to sevruga, with small eggs and an inky color. It varies in quality, but should provide the desired salinity here.

When making these crêpes, the first one may not be perfect because it takes time for the heat of the pan to become regulated and for the cook (this means you) to get into a crêpe-making rhythm. But never fear: This recipe makes enough batter so you can discard one crêpe and still have enough for the yield indicated.

You can vary the amounts of each herb so long as there are 2 teaspoons total.

To make the crêpes, whisk the eggs, flour, olive oil, dill, parsley, chives, salt, a grind or two of pepper, and the water together in a medium bowl until just combined. Set aside to rest at room temperature for at least 20 minutes, or cover with plastic wrap and refrigerate overnight.

When ready to proceed, dampen a paper towel with canola oil and brush a 9-inch nonstick sauté pan with just enough oil to grease it. Heat the pan over medium heat for 2 to 3 minutes (you want it to be hot, but not so hot that the crêpes will brown or burn; if you make it too hot, or not hot enough, you can adjust the heat after the first crêpe). Using a small ladle or a ¼-cup measure, filling it halfway, spoon in 2 tablespoons of the crêpe batter while tipping the pan to coat just the bottom with the batter, then pour any excess back into the bowl. (You will end up using about 1 tablespoon of batter per crêpe.) Cook the crêpe briefly, until it sets but does not brown, about 30 seconds, then use a rubber spatula to turn it over gently and cook the other side. Transfer the crêpe to a plate. Repeat with the remaining batter, transferring each to the plate as they are done cooking. (They will be served at room temperature, so don't worry about keeping them warm.) Re-grease the pan as necessary with another swipe of oil.

Bring a large pot of water to a boil. Fill a large bowl halfway with ice water. Drop the whole chives into the boiling water and blanch for 10 seconds. Use tongs to transfer them to the ice water to stop the cooking and set the color. Drain and set aside. (The blanching will make the chives easier to tie.)

For large purses, transfer one crêpe to a clean, dry surface. Spoon 1 teaspoon of the crème fraîche and ½ teaspoon of the caviar into the center. Gather the sides of the crêpe up to form a pouch and secure it by tying a chive strand around its neck.

For hors d'oeuvre–size purses, cut each crêpe into quarters. Spoon ¼ teaspoon of the crème fraîche and a few pearls of caviar into the center of each quarter. Fold the pointed end over the filling, then gently roll up the crêpe and secure it by tying a chive strand around its middle. Serve immediately.

From left to right: Deviled Quail Eggs with Black Caviar (page 43), Herbed Crepes with Black Caviar & Crème Fraîche (page 28), Curried Crab Cannoli with Coriander & Cucumbers (page 34)

Chinese Spoons with Fried Oysters, Sweet & Sour Pickles & Curry Mayonnaise

Fried oysters are something special in their own right, but in this hors d'oeuvre, the oysters are just the beginning. The mollusks are complemented by sweet-and-sour marinated cucumbers and a curry mayonnaise. There's no texture or flavor category that isn't at least grazed by these little spoons—from creamy to crunchy, from sweet to sour to fishy, they have it all. They offer as much action in a single mouthful as you'll find anywhere.

The best caviar for this is trout, which has a brilliant red color and is less bulbous than the more familiar salmon variety. You can also use black caviar, but I much prefer the way the red stands out against the other ingredients. You may replace the caviar by topping each spoon with a leaf or two of cilantro for an herbaceous effect that's different, but also delicious.

Note that you will need oyster shells or Asian soup spoons (which have a nice, deep bowl—a perfect mouthful) for serving these.

Make the pickles by combining the cucumber, vinegar, sugar, and salt in a medium bowl and gently tossing them together. Cover with plastic wrap, refrigerate, and let marinate for at least 1 hour or overnight. Drain the liquid before serving.

Put the flour in a wide, shallow bowl and dredge the oysters to lightly coat them.

To fry the oysters, pour the oil into a large skillet to a depth of 2 inches and heat to 350°F. Meanwhile, line a large plate or platter with paper towels. Carefully add the oysters to the hot oil, a few at a time, and pan-fry until golden and crispy, about 1½ minutes per side. Use a slotted spoon to transfer them to the paper towels, season with salt and pepper, and let them drain of excess oil.

Meanwhile, arrange 24 porcelain soup spoons or cleaned oyster shells on a clean, dry surface and place 1 teaspoon of the pickles in each. When the oysters are fried and drained, place an oyster in each spoon or shell, top with a ¼ teaspoon dollop of Curry Mayonnaise, and finish with a sprinkling of caviar, if using. Serve immediately.

½ cup English (hothouse) cucumber, cut into ⅛-inch dice

3 tablespoons rice vinegar

2 tablespoons sugar

1 teaspoon kosher salt

1 cup all-purpose flour

24 medium oysters, shucked and drained of their liquid (see page 32)

Canola oil, for frying

Kosher salt

Black pepper from a mill

2 tablespoons Curry Mayonnaise (recipe follows)

2 tablespoons red caviar (optional)

MAKES 24 HORS D'OEUVRES, ENOUGH TO SERVE 6 TO 8

½ cup canola oil

1 tablespoon curry powder

1 large egg yolk

1 teaspoon freshly squeezed lime juice

½ teaspoon Dijon mustard

1 tablespoon water

MAKES ABOUT ¾ CUP

Curry Mayonnaise

This mayonnaise is a fine accompaniment to shellfish and is especially delicious on a soft-shell crab sandwich.

I always use Sun Brand® Madras curry powder, a nicely balanced, if slightly salty, curry that is sold in an orange tin.

Pour the oil into a medium heavy-bottomed saucepan. Add the curry powder, stir to mix, and cook over medium-low heat until the mixture is fragrant, 4 to 5 minutes. Remove from the heat and let the mixture cool.

Put the egg yolk, lime juice, mustard, and water in a food processor fitted with a steel blade and process for 30 seconds. With the motor running, slowly add the cooled curry oil and blend into a thick emulsion. (You may also make the mayonnaise by hand, using a whisk and adding the oil very slowly.) The mayonnaise will keep in an airtight container in the refrigerator for up to 24 hours. Let it come just to room temperature before using.

OYSTERS

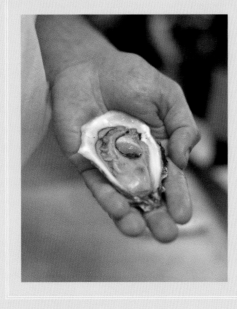

I prefer East Coast oysters to West Coast oysters for the simple reason that I think they have more flavor.

To shuck oysters, put a towel in one hand and grasp the oyster, cupped side down, using the towel to protect your hand. Insert a shucking knife in the gap between the halves of the shell and work the knife until the shell "pops" open, then use the knife to cut the muscle that attaches the oyster to the shell.

To clean oysters, make sure you open them over a container, gathering the oysters and juice inside. Agitate them in their liquid to clean them, then lift them out, strain the liquid into another container, save it (you can freeze it), and use it to add flavor to any mollusk-based soup.

Crispy Bacon-Wrapped Oysters with Rémoulade

A riff on the New Orleans–born hors d'oeuvre angels on horseback, these bacon-wrapped oysters made their first appearance at Chanterelle as a garnish to the collard green cannelloni on page 82. They were so addictive that I decided to serve them on their own, adding an herbed rémoulade to provide some cool, creamy relief. These are a guaranteed crowd pleaser.

This recipe produces about 1 cup of rémoulade. Depending on personal taste, you may only use about half of it. Serve the extra with sautéed or fried fish or slathered on sandwiches.

I often use Wondra® flour (a mixture of wheat and barley flour) as the breading for items that will be fried. If you read its package, you won't find this option mentioned there because Wondra is meant to be used as a thickening agent, but a lot of chefs use it for frying and sautéeing because it makes for a very light coating and gets crispier than all-purpose flour.

To make the rémoulade, put the mustard, egg yolk, and cornichon brine in a food processor fitted with a steel blade. Process for 30 seconds, then, with the motor running, slowly pour in the olive oil through the feed tube to form a thick, emulsified mayonnaise. If it seems too thick, add a few drops of hot water and pulse to incorporate. Transfer the mayonnaise to a medium bowl; don't rinse out the food processor bowl. Add the shallot, cornichons, and capers to the processor and pulse to coarsely chop. Gently fold the chopped mixture into the mayonnaise. You should have about 1 cup of rémoulade. Season to taste with salt and a few additional drops of cornichon brine if desired. (The rémoulade will keep in an airtight container in the refrigerator for 2 to 3 days; let come to room temperature before serving.) Fold in the parsley, chives, chervil, and tarragon just before serving.

To prepare the oysters, arrange the bacon pieces on a clean, dry surface. Place an oyster on each piece and fold over the ends of the bacon, overlapping them a bit, to encase the oysters. Secure the bacon wrap with a toothpick through the center of the oyster. (The bacon-wrapped oysters can be refrigerated for up to 2 hours at this point; let come to room temperature before flouring and frying. Do *not* flour before refrigerating.)

Preheat the oven to 250°F.

Put the flour in a shallow bowl and carefully dredge each bacon-wrapped oyster, being careful to not let the oysters fall out. Tap off any excess flour.

Pour canola oil into a deep, heavy-bottomed skillet to a depth of 2 inches. Set over medium-high heat and heat the oil to 350°F. Meanwhile, line a large plate or platter with paper towels. Carefully add the oysters to the hot oil, a few at a time, and pan-fry until golden and crispy, about 1½ minutes per side. Use a slotted spoon to transfer them to the paper towels, season with salt and pepper, and let them drain of excess oil.

Remove the toothpicks, if desired, then arrange the oysters on a warm platter and serve with the rémoulade in a bowl alongside.

2 teaspoons Dijon mustard

1 large egg yolk

1 tablespoon brine from a jar of cornichons, strained, plus 4 cornichons, stems removed

¾ cup olive oil

1 medium shallot, peeled

1 tablespoon plus 1 teaspoon capers, drained

Kosher salt

1 teaspoon minced fresh flat-leaf parsley

1 teaspoon minced fresh chives

1 teaspoon minced fresh chervil (optional)

1 teaspoon minced fresh tarragon

8 slices bacon, each cut crosswise into 3 equal pieces

24 medium to large oysters, such as Blue Point or Wellfleet, shucked (see sidebar on the facing page), drained of their juice, and patted dry

About 1 cup Wondra or all-purpose flour, for dredging

Canola or other neutral oil, for frying

MAKES 24 HORS D'OEUVRES, ENOUGH TO SERVE 6 TO 8

Curried Crab Cannoli
with Coriander & Cucumbers

9 thin, round wonton or dumpling wrappers, 4 inches in diameter (don't use Suey Gow or pot sticker wrappers, which are too thick), cut in half

Canola oil, for frying (see recipe), plus ½ cup

Nonstick cooking spray

8 ounces lump or jumbo lump blue or Maine Jonah crabmeat

1 cup diced (⅛-inch) English (hothouse) cucumber

½ cup coarsely chopped fresh cilantro

Curry Mayonnaise (page 32)

Kosher salt

Black pepper from a mill

MAKES 12 CANNOLI, ENOUGH TO SERVE 6 AS AN HORS D'OEUVRE

This hors d'oeuvres—essentially a pick-up-able way of serving a crab salad—packs a lot of flavor and texture into a neat little tube, with a fun, alliterative name to boot. To make up for the small serving size, the salad is dressed with a potent lime-curry emulsion.

I got the idea for making cannoli with wonton wrappers from a cook in my kitchen who wrapped the skins around a piece of shelving pipe, then dipped the pipe into a deep fryer. To this day, I use Metro shelf rods, cut into 8-inch lengths, but at home, a wooden dowel will work. If this all seems a bit industrial, you can fry the wrappers and use them as chips, piling the crab salad on top.

My first choice in crab is blue crab, which has a very clean, sweet, oceanic quality that is superior to other crab varieties. That said, in a recipe like this, where the crab is dressed with curry and lime, Maine crab can also be used. Its flavor isn't as delicate, it has smaller, less luxurious flakes, and it must be drained in cheesecloth, but it's a viable alternative.

To make the cannoli shells, remove the wonton wrappers from their package and drape over a damp paper towel to keep them from drying out.

Pour canola oil into an electric fryer or tall pot to a depth of 6 inches. Turn on the fryer or set the pot over medium-high heat, and heat the oil to 325°F. Line a large plate or platter with paper towels.

Spray a dowel with nonstick cooking spray. Drape the halved wontons on the rod (this may have to be done in several steps, depending on the length of the dowel), wrapping each skin around the dowel and sticking the edges together with a bit of water. Very carefully, lower the dowel into the hot oil, release it, and fry the cannoli shells until they are browned and crisp, 3 to 4 minutes, using tongs to turn the dowel and ensure even frying. (The shells will float, making the turning necessary.) Use tongs to remove the dowel from the oil and set it on the paper towels to let the shells drain and cool. Once cool to the touch, gently slide the cannoli shells off the rod. (Some of the shells inevitably break, even in the Chanterelle kitchen, so 3 of the 9 wrappers used here are provided for a security margin.) The cooled shells will keep in an airtight container at room temperature for up to 24 hours.

To make the filling, sort through the crabmeat to remove any shell or cartilage fragments. If the crabmeat is watery, squeeze it in a piece of cheesecloth or put it in a fine-mesh strainer and press down with a rubber spatula or the bottom of a ladle to remove any excess liquid. Combine the crabmeat, cucumber, and cilantro in a large bowl and stir gently to incorporate while taking care to not break up the crab pieces. Add the mayonnaise and use a wooden spoon to combine. Season to taste with salt and pepper, being careful not to overseason, as the curry powder may be salty.

Use a teaspoon or demitasse spoon to divide the crab mixture evenly among the cannoli, carefully filling the shells. Serve within 15 to 20 minutes; otherwise the shells will begin to soften.

Brandade Fritters
with Lemon-Saffron Aïoli

I didn't discover brandade as a child because it wasn't on the menu in those restaurants that my parents took me to on our theater nights. But this Provençal staple, a creamy puree of salt cod, potatoes, garlic, and olive oil, triggers the same emotions for me, an example of the transformative and magical qualities of cooking. Here, brandade—which is usually served with a salad and a slice of bread—is turned into a fish cake or fritter, perfect for hors d'oeuvres duty.

Put the salt cod in a large bowl and gently pour in enough cold water to completely submerge it. Soak for 1 hour, then drain and refresh with enough cold water to completely submerge the fish again. Repeat the process, changing the water every hour, until the water is no longer salty to taste, which should require a total of 4 or 5 changes. Drain the salt cod. (It can be refrigerated overnight at this point, if desired.)

Put the soaked cod, milk, and water into a large saucepan over medium heat, bring to a low simmer, and cook until the fish is flaky and falling apart, about 45 minutes. Use tongs or a slotted spoon to transfer the cod to a plate to cool. Add the potatoes to the cooking liquid and simmer until tender to a knife tip, about 20 minutes. Drain in a strainer set over a bowl; reserve the cooking liquid.

Meanwhile, heat the olive oil and garlic in a small heavy-bottomed sauté pan over the lowest possible heat. Simmer until the garlic is very soft (enough that it can be pureed but is not browned), about 15 minutes. Remove from the heat and let the garlic cool in the oil.

Flake the cod by hand into the food processor, discarding any bones. Add the potatoes and the garlic with its oil, and process until smooth. If the mixture looks dry, add up to 1 cup of the reserved potato cooking liquid to moisten it, processing to incorporate.

Transfer the puree to a large bowl. Fold in the breadcrumbs to thicken it, then season to taste with pepper. (It will not need salt.)

Put the flour in a wide, shallow bowl. Form the puree by the ½-teaspoon-full into small marble-size balls and roll them in the flour to lightly coat.

Preheat the oven to 250°F. Line a plate with paper towels.

Pour canola oil into a deep, heavy-bottomed skillet to a depth of about 1 inch and heat to 350°F. Working in batches, add a few of the fritters to the hot oil and pan-fry until golden brown, 3 to 4 minutes, turning them with a slotted spoon after about 2 minutes. Use the slotted spoon to transfer the fritters to the paper towels to drain of excess oil. Season with salt, transfer to an ovenproof platter, and place in the oven to keep warm. Repeat with the remaining puree.

To serve, neatly rearrange the fritters on the platter and top each one with a drop of the aïoli before serving immediately.

1 pound salt cod

4 cups whole milk

4 cups cold water

1½ pounds russet potatoes (about 3 medium potatoes), peeled and cut into large chunks

1 cup olive oil

20 garlic cloves, peeled

¼ cup plain dry breadcrumbs

Black pepper from a mill

1 cup all-purpose flour

Canola oil, for frying

Lemon-Saffron Aïoli (page 295)

MAKES 50 TO 60 FRITTERS, ENOUGH TO SERVE 10 TO 12

Sesame-Scallion Shrimp Toasts

8 ounces shrimp (any size), peeled and deveined

1 large egg white

½ teaspoon kosher salt

½ teaspoon sugar

¼ teaspoon Tabasco® sauce

1 teaspoon Asian fish sauce

¾ cup heavy cream

2 tablespoons finely chopped scallion greens

¼ teaspoon toasted sesame oil

6 slices white bread, crusts removed

2 tablespoons white sesame seeds

1 tablespoon black sesame seeds, or an additional tablespoon of white sesame seeds

Canola oil, for frying

1 cup Tamarind Dipping Sauce (page 53) and 1 cup Ginger-Soy Dip (recipe follows) (if only using one sauce, use 2 cups)

MAKES 24 TRIANGLES, ENOUGH TO SERVE 6 TO 8

This is straight-up, old-school Chinese American stuff, the kind of thing I ate as a kid in Chinese restaurants in the Bronx. The classic would have chopped pork fat in the filling, but that's too decadent even for me.

Put the shrimp, egg white, salt, sugar, Tabasco, and fish sauce in a food processor fitted with a steel blade. Pulse the mixture, slowly adding the cream through the feed tube to make a smooth puree. Transfer to a medium bowl and stir in the scallion greens and sesame oil. Taste and adjust the seasoning with salt, sugar, and/or Tabasco as needed.

Spread the mixture over one side of the bread, using all of it to generously coat the slices. Put the white and black sesame seeds in a small bowl and toss them together, then sprinkle over the coated slices. Use a sharp knife to cut each slice of bread twice on the diagonal, creating 4 triangles from each slice.

Preheat the oven to 250°F.

Pour canola oil into a wide, deep nonstick pan to a depth of about ⅛ inch and heat well over medium-high heat. Meanwhile, line a plate with paper towels. Add a few shrimp toast triangles to the pan without crowding and cook until crispy and golden, about 4 minutes, then use a metal spatula to turn them over and cook until crispy and golden on the other side, another 4 minutes. As the triangles are done, transfer them to the paper towels to drain, then transfer to an ovenproof plate and keep warm in the oven. Repeat with the remaining shrimp toast triangles.

Transfer the shrimp toasts to a platter. Serve immediately with either or both dipping sauces alongside.

Ginger-Soy Dip

¼ cup plus 2 tablespoons soy sauce

1 tablespoon toasted sesame oil

2 tablespoons balsamic vinegar

½ cup plus 2 tablespoons mirin

¼ teaspoon red chile flakes

3 tablespoons peeled and finely grated fresh ginger

2 tablespoons finely chopped scallion greens

MAKES ABOUT 1 CUP

You can also use this dip for the duck spring rolls on page 48, or as a dressing for raw fish preparations.

Whisk all the ingredients together in a medium bowl. Let steep for at least 30 minutes at room temperature before serving. (The dip will keep in an airtight container in the refrigerator for up to 3 days; let come to room temperature before using.)

Clockwise from top left: Vegetable Spring Rolls with Tamarind Dipping Sauce (page 52),
Sesame-Scallion Shrimp Toasts (page 36), Duck & Foie Gras Dumplings (page 46)

"Blintzes" of Fresh & Smoked Salmon with Caviar Cream

½ cup heavy cream, plus more for serving

3 tablespoons crème fraîche or sour cream

1 teaspoon sherry vinegar

1 cup diced (¼-inch) sushi-grade salmon with skin removed (from about an 8-ounce fillet)

¼ cup diced (¼-inch) smoked salmon (about 4 ounces)

½ teaspoon freshly squeezed lemon juice, plus more to taste

Pinch of kosher salt

1 large egg

2 tablespoons cold water

Six 12-inch *feuille de brik* sheets or large spring roll wrappers

Canola or other neutral oil, for frying

2 tablespoons American black caviar, such as paddlefish

MAKES 24 PIECES, ENOUGH TO SERVE 6

Years ago, while dining at one of New York's finest restaurants—an upscale, American-owned establishment with French-leaning food—I was served a miniature bagel topped with a drizzle of truffle sauce. I was startled to see a Jewish American staple in that setting. I was also instantly liberated. It had never occurred to me to bring foods from my own ethnic heritage into Chanterelle, but as I sat there eating this gussied-up bagel, I thought, "Why not?"

It wasn't long before little nods to knishes, blintzes, and other Middle European favorites began to find their way onto my menu. This is one such dish, which combines the form of a blintz with another cornerstone of my culinary heritage, smoked salmon. To balance the flavor and make the dish suitable to the elegant surroundings of Chanterelle, I add fresh salmon and finish the blintzes with a simple caviar cream. Try to find a nice, smoky salmon, such as a Norwegian-style one.

Rather than make blintz dough, I use *feuille de brik,* the crêpe-like wrappers found in North African cooking. They can be purchased from specialty suppliers and are usually sold frozen. *Feuille de brik,* also sometimes spelled *feuille de brick* or *bric,* are very much my first choice for this dish, as they are much thinner and more delicate than spring roll wrappers. That said, you may use spring roll wrappers as an alternative.

To make the caviar cream, put the cream, crème fraîche, and vinegar in a medium bowl and stir together. Cover with plastic wrap and set aside to thicken at room temperature for 20 to 30 minutes, then transfer to the refrigerator to chill for at least 1 hour and up to 2 hours. If it becomes too thick, stir in a teaspoon or two more cream to make it pourable.

Put the fresh and smoked salmon in a medium bowl. Add the lemon juice and salt, toss gently, and set aside.

Prepare an egg wash by whisking the egg and water together in a small bowl.

Arrange the *feuille de brik* sheets on a clean, dry surface, with one corner pointed at you. Using a pastry brush, brush each one with a thin coat of egg wash. Place 3 tablespoons of the salmon filling in the center of each wrapper. Then, if you think of each corner as a compass point, fold the south corner upward and hold it down with a thumb as your pointer fingers fold in the east and west corners, encasing the filling. Roll the *feuille de brik* carefully and tightly away from you, sealing the blintz with a bit more egg wash if necessary.

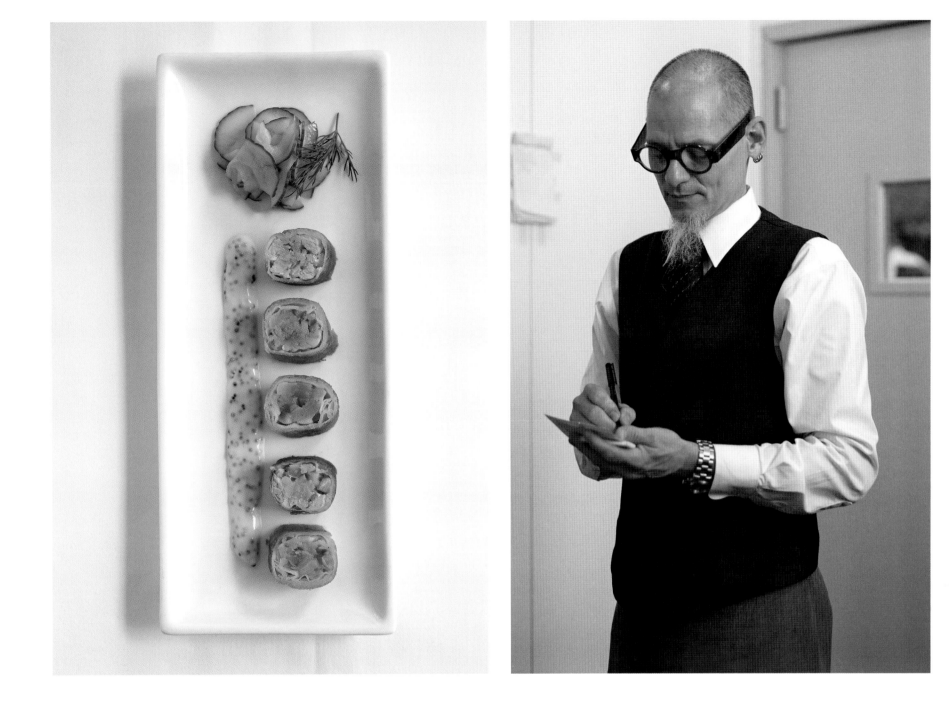

Line a plate with paper towels. Heat a wide, heavy-bottomed sauté pan over medium heat for 3 to 4 minutes. Pour in the oil and heat until a scant drop of water sizzles when flicked into the pan, about 2 minutes. Carefully place the blintzes in the hot oil and fry until crispy (the filling will be slightly undercooked in the center), 2 to 3 minutes per side. Use tongs to remove them from the oil to drain on the paper towels.

Use a serrated knife to cut each blintz into quarters. Stir the caviar into the cream. Arrange the blintz pieces on a platter. Serve hot, with the caviar cream alongside as a dip.

Nori Rolls of Hamachi Tartare

5 ounces sushi-grade hamachi (yellowtail) fillet, cut into ⅛-inch cubes

3 tablespoons minced scallion greens

1 tablespoon drained and finely chopped pickled ginger

Pinch of kosher salt, plus more to taste if necessary

¼ teaspoon toasted sesame oil

½ teaspoon freshly squeezed lemon juice, plus more to taste

1 tablespoon wasabi tobiko

2 sheets sushi nori

¼ cup julienned (2-inch-long) English (hothouse) cucumber

MAKES 16 PIECES, ENOUGH TO SERVE 4 TO 6

Thanks to the nori (seaweed) wrappers, this hors d'oeuvre looks like a cut sushi roll, with vibrant bursts of color provided by the wasabi tobiko, fish roe that's been colored green and flavored with wasabi. In reality, it's a tartare served in a sushi-like package. It's also part of a plated assortment of raw and cured fish that we serve at Chanterelle that changes from time to time based on what fish is available, and—to be honest—what I feel like cooking that day. I don't find a mat is necessary to roll these; just use a steady hand and keep the wrappers taut. The hamachi may be replaced by other fatty fish such as tuna, salmon, or Spanish mackerel.

Put the hamachi, scallion greens, and pickled ginger in a large bowl. Add the salt, sesame oil, lemon juice, and wasabi tobiko and use a wooden spoon to mix well but gently, taking care to not crush the fragile fish dice. Taste and adjust the seasoning with salt or more lemon juice, if necessary. (The tartare can be refrigerated in an airtight container for up to 2 hours. Do not make the rolls in advance, however, as they can become soggy.)

Lay the nori sheets, shiny side down, on a clean, dry surface. Spoon half of the hamachi mixture along one edge of one sheet of nori, from side to side, and press it down gently to flatten it. Top with half the julienned cucumber and roll the nori tightly, moistening the final edge of the sheet with a little cold water so that the sheet is sealed closed. (The cucumber should show in the center of the roll.) Repeat with the remaining nori, hamachi, and cucumber.

Using a very sharp knife, slice each roll into 8 pieces by first halving them, then aligning the halves alongside each other and cutting them again, to make 8 pieces. Finally, cut each piece in half again at an angle, for a total of 16 decorative pieces. Serve immediately.

Dry-Cured Tuna
with Spicy Mustard Vinaigrette

I'm not quite sure when I first decided to experiment with dry-curing fish, but I've become very fond of the technique and the result it produces, which I describe as "fish jerky." Fish, in this case tuna, is marinated for one to two days, then refrigerated on a rack for several days. As air circulates freely around it, the fish dries out and the texture becomes meaty, almost leathery. It's still recognizable as tuna, but it transforms into something new and exciting. The mustard vinaigrette is the perfect accompaniment.

Cured tuna is a fun ingredient to play with—I use it in our ever-changing assortment of fresh and cured fish, and you can toss pieces of it into salads. This preparation also works very well with salmon.

Note: You can also serve this as an appetizer by omitting the toast and arranging five slices of tuna on each of four plates. Drizzle decoratively with the dressing.

Whisk together the soy sauce, mirin, and ginger in a medium bowl. Put the tuna in a small shallow pan or baking dish, and pour over the marinade to submerge it completely. Cover with plastic wrap and refrigerate for 24 to 48 hours.

Remove the tuna from the marinade, shake off the excess, and pat dry with paper towels. Sprinkle on all sides with the sea salt and black pepper, then place it on a rack or trivet set over a pan or plate, so that air can circulate around it on all sides. Refrigerate the tuna for at least 3 days, or up to 4 days, so that it dries. During this time, it will darken on the outside and become firm to the touch.

(Don't worry, it will not stink up your refrigerator.) The longer it cures, the more leathery and chewy it will become.

To make the dressing, whisk together the Dijon and dry mustards, vinegar, and water in a medium bowl. Gradually whisk in the oil to form a thick emulsion. Add the kosher salt and cayenne.

Using a very sharp knife, slice the fish thinly crosswise into at least 20 slices. Arrange the toast bites on a clean, dry surface, and top each with a slice of tuna. Spoon ½ teaspoon of the dressing on each piece before arranging on a platter and serving.

1 cup dark soy sauce, such as Kim Lan®, an aged soy sauce from Taiwan

1½ cups mirin

One 3-inch piece fresh ginger, peeled and coarsely chopped

12 ounces (after trimming) sushi-quality tuna, preferably in an even rectangular shape about 2 inches wide, 2 inches thick, and 6 inches long

2 teaspoons fine sea salt

1 teaspoon freshly ground black pepper

2 tablespoons Dijon mustard

2 teaspoons dry mustard

2 tablespoons rice vinegar

1 tablespoon cold water

1 cup canola or other neutral oil

Pinch of kosher salt

Pinch of cayenne

5 slices white bread, toasted, crusts removed, and cut diagonally into quarters

SERVES 20 AS
AN HORS D'OEUVRE,
OR 4 AS AN APPETIZER

Deviled Quail Eggs with Black Caviar

Kosher salt

2 large chicken eggs

12 quail eggs

2 tablespoons mayonnaise

½ teaspoon Dijon mustard

⅛ teaspoon finely grated lemon zest

1 tablespoon American black caviar, such as paddlefish or hackleback

SERVES 4 TO 6 AS
AN HORS D'OEUVRE

This is our elegant take on an American classic. Don't worry: You don't have to peel enough quail eggs to make the filling, which uses chicken eggs. You can find quail eggs at some gourmet markets, or order them from D'Artagnan (see Sources, page 298).

Bring a medium heavy-bottomed saucepan of generously salted water to a boil. Fill a large bowl halfway with ice water.

Carefully add the chicken eggs to the boiling water and cook until hard-cooked, about 11 minutes. Use a slotted spoon to transfer them to the ice bath to cool. Carefully add the quail eggs to the boiling water and cook for 1½ minutes. Remove to the ice bath to chill.

Once cooled, carefully peel the eggs and cut each in half lengthwise. Remove the yolks from the egg halves and transfer them to a food processor fitted with a steel blade, reserving the whites of the quail eggs and discarding the whites of the chicken eggs, or saving them for another use. Add the mayonnaise, mustard, and lemon zest, and process the mixture to a fine paste. Season carefully to taste with salt, bearing in mind that the quail eggs will be topped with caviar. Transfer the deviled yolks to a pastry bag fitted with a small star tip and pipe the filling into the quail egg white halves. Top each with a scant amount of caviar and transfer to a platter before serving. (The eggs can be made up to 1 hour ahead of time, covered loosely with plastic wrap, and refrigerated. Serve cold.)

Roulade of Prosciutto, Foie Gras & Figs

5 ounces duck foie gras, preferably French or Canadian

Kosher salt

Pinch of sugar

2 tablespoons unsalted butter

1 tablespoon rendered duck fat, or 1 additional tablespoon unsalted butter

5 ounces dried figs (about 1 cup), stems removed and cut in half lengthwise

½ cup red wine

½ cup plus 1½ teaspoons ruby port

Black pepper from a mill

8 ounces very thinly sliced prosciutto

30 thin slices baguette, toasted in a 300°F oven until crisp but not browned, about 7 minutes

MAKES 30 PIECES, ENOUGH TO SERVE 6 TO 8

Rich, sweet, and chewy, these gourmet "roll-ups" add foie gras to the time-honored combination of prosciutto and figs. To be honest, I developed the recipe as a way to use the foie gras odds and ends that gather in the restaurant freezer. I've only made one change to the recipe over the years: Originally I used fresh figs, but I have found that dried have a more pleasing sweetness and are far more consistent in quality. I've presented the recipe here the way we make it at Chanterelle, but you can purchase a prepared foie gras mousse instead of making your own and you will lose absolutely nothing in flavor.

Preheat the oven to 200°F.

Season the foie gras generously with salt and the sugar and press it into a small terrine (the exact dimensions are not important; nor is whether the foie gras fills the terrine, because you will be processing the cooked foie gras into a mousse). Top the terrine with parchment cut to fit the terrine, then with aluminum foil, molding it around the edges of the terrine. Set the terrine in a roasting pan and fill the pan with enough warm water to reach halfway up the sides of the terrine. Carefully transfer the pan to the oven and bake the foie gras until an instant-read thermometer inserted into the center registers 95°F (just barely warm to the touch) and its fat has rendered and is floating on top, about 25 minutes. Carefully remove the pan from the oven and the terrine from the pan. Let cool completely.

Meanwhile, melt the butter and duck fat together in a small saucepan over medium-low heat. Remove from the heat and let the fats cool to room temperature.

Put the fig halves in another small saucepan. Pour in the wine and ½ cup of the port and bring to a boil over medium heat. Lower the heat to a simmer and cook until the liquid has reduced to a syrupy consistency and been absorbed by the figs, about 20 minutes. Remove

from the heat and let the figs cool. Transfer the figs and any remaining liquid to a food processor fitted with a steel blade and process until smooth. Transfer the puree to a bowl, cover with plastic wrap, and set aside. (The fig chutney will keep in an airtight container in the refrigerator for up to 3 days; you can use it right out of the refrigerator, but process it again for a few seconds to make it spreadable.)

Put the foie gras, duck fat, butter, and remaining 1½ teaspoons port in the food processor and puree the mixture. Season to taste with salt and pepper, then transfer to a bowl. (The puree will keep in an airtight container in the refrigerator for up to 3 days; bring to room temperature and whisk to a creamy consistency before using it in the roulade.)

Prepare a 12 x 17-inch baking sheet by lining it horizontally with a single piece of plastic wrap about 28 inches long and allowing 5 inches of wrap to hang over each end of the tray. Layer the prosciutto slices end to end horizontally along the 17-inch side. Continue row by row, slightly overlapping each slice, to cover the bottom of the tray with a "sheet" of prosciutto. Use an offset spatula to carefully spread a thin layer of the foie gras over the prosciutto. Finally, put the fig chutney in a pastry bag fitted with a medium plain tip and pipe out a tube-like length of chutney about ½ inch thick about ½ inch from one edge of the 17-inch side.

To roll, pull up on the plastic wrap and lift up the edge of the prosciutto nearest the fig chutney, then guide it up and over the chutney so it falls over the chutney, encasing it. Continue to use the plastic to roll the prosciutto over and over, around the fig center. Pull at the 5-inch surplus plastic at either end to tighten the roulade, and twist the ends to form a sausage-like tube. Transfer to the refrigerator and chill until serving or for up to 3 days. The roulade can also be quickly chilled for 30 minutes in the freezer.

To serve, use a very sharp knife to slice the roulade into ½-inch-thick rounds. Top each crouton with a piece of roulade and serve.

Braised Duck Leg Spring Rolls

3 duck legs, preferably Moulard (about 2½ pounds total)

Kosher salt

Black pepper from a mill

3 ounces dried shiitake mushrooms (about 10)

8 cups Red-Cooking Broth (page 293), strained

1 cup mung bean sprouts, coarsely chopped (Napa cabbage may be substituted)

¼ cup finely sliced scallion greens (from about 2 scallions)

2 teaspoons toasted sesame oil

1 teaspoon high-quality five-spice powder

1 tablespoon oyster sauce

2 large eggs, at room temperature

3 tablespoons cold water

Twenty 8-inch-square spring roll wrappers

½ cup hoisin sauce

1 tablespoon soy sauce

1 tablespoon honey

1 tablespoon rice vinegar

Canola oil, for frying

MAKES 20 SPRING ROLLS, OR 80 "BITES," ENOUGH TO SERVE 8 TO 10

I'm always on the lookout for ways to use duck legs, which are delicious but not quite elegant enough for the Chanterelle dining room. Years ago, I began braising the legs in my red cooking liquid and the result became a very popular "family" (staff) meal at the restaurant. As a Chinese food aficionado, I then started chopping the legs for use as a spring roll filling, adding bean sprouts and mushrooms. The result was put to use as a garnish on various duck dishes before we began cutting up the rolls and serving them as an *amuse*.

Preheat the oven to 375°F.

Arrange the duck legs, skin side up, on a sturdy rack set in a roasting pan. Season generously with salt and pepper. Roast the legs, without turning them, until they are browned and have rendered some of their fat, 15 to 20 minutes, periodically draining and discarding the fat as it accumulates in the pan.

Transfer the legs to a medium heavy-bottomed saucepan, add the mushrooms and Red-Cooking Broth, and set over high heat. Bring to a boil. Partially cover the pot, reduce the heat to a simmer, and cook until the duck meat is very tender and falling off the bones, about 1 hour. Drain and transfer the duck legs and mushrooms to a bowl to cool. (Once drained and cooled, the cooking liquid can be reserved for other uses; see page 294.)

When cool to the touch, pull the duck meat and skin off the legs and coarsely chop. Discard the bones, and transfer the meat and skin to a bowl. Remove and discard the stems from the mushrooms and coarsely chop the caps, adding them to the duck meat. Add the sprouts, scallions, 1 teaspoon of the sesame oil, the five-spice powder, and oyster sauce, and stir together until well incorporated. Season with salt and pepper to taste and a few more drops of the oyster sauce, if desired. (The filling can be refrigerated in an airtight container for up to 24 hours or frozen for up to 1 month.)

Whisk together the eggs and water in a small bowl. Arrange the spring roll wrappers on a clean, dry surface with one corner facing you and, using a pastry brush, brush each one with a thin coat of egg wash. Place 2 tablespoons of the filling on each wrapper, toward the lower corner. Then, if you think of each corner as a compass point, fold the south corner upward and hold it down with a thumb as your pointer fingers fold in the east and west corners, encasing the filling. Roll the wrapper and filling upward carefully and tightly, sealing it with a hint more egg wash if necessary. (The prepared spring rolls can be individually wrapped in plastic wrap, then in aluminum foil, and frozen for up to 1 month; defrost before frying.)

To make the hoisin dip, whisk together the hoisin sauce, soy sauce, honey, vinegar, and the remaining 1 teaspoon sesame oil in a small bowl. (The dip will keep in an airtight container in the refrigerator for up to 1 week; let it come to room temperature before serving.)

White Truffle Butter

Compound, or flavored, butters are one of the great culinary convenience[s]
refrigerated or frozen for extended periods of time, and tossed with or me[lted]
foods. When they soften and their flavor is unlocked, they have the effect
My favorite uses for truffle butter are spreading it on toast, tossing it with
it over grilled steak. You can also dress French fries with it to turn a casual
unexpectedly sophisticated.

Put the butter, truffle, porcini, and salt in a food processor
fitted with a steel blade. Pulse until the truffle and porcini
break down slightly, then process until you obtain fine
specks of truffle, stopping the motor and scraping down
the sides of the bowl with a rubber spatula as needed.

Pass the butter through
bowl, pressing down on it
spoon to extract as much t
or gently press into a small
refrigerate for up to 3 days

Creamy Tomato Soup

Flavored with brandy and thickened with heavy cream, this rich tomato so[up]
in small doses. This will make more than you need to accompany the sandw[ich]
extra for up to two days.

Melt the butter in a large heavy-bottomed soup pot over
medium-low heat. Add the onion and garlic and gently
cook, stirring occasionally, until the onion is soft and
translucent but not at all browned, about 15 minutes,
adding a splash of wine or water if it appears to be
drying out.

Add the brandy and raise the heat to high. Cook,
stirring, until almost completely evaporated, 2 to
3 minutes. Add the stock, tomatoes, tomato paste,
and basil and bring to a boil. Reduce the heat to medium
and simmer, uncovered, for 30 minutes.

Strain the soup throug[h]
saucepan, pressing down o[n]
flavorful soup as possible. [Cook on]
high heat for 5 minutes to
the flavor. Stir in the crea[m]
to a boil, then lower the he[at]
nicely thickened and richly
Season to taste with salt, pe
tomatoes aren't sweet.

Serve from sake cups, de[mitasse, or other]
attractive vessels.

To fry the spring rolls, pour the canola oil into an
electric fryer or tall pot to a depth of 6 inches. Turn on
the fryer or set the pot over medium-high heat and heat
to 350°F. Line a large plate or platter with paper towels.

Carefully add the spring rolls to the hot oil, a few at a
time, and deep-fry until golden and crispy, 3 to 4 minutes.

Use tongs to transfer them to the paper towels, season
with salt and pepper, and let drain of excess oil.

To serve, use a serrated knife to cut each spring roll
crosswise into 4 equal pieces before transferring to a
platter. Serve the dip alongside.

Eight ½-inch-thick slices good-quality white bread or brioche

6 tablespoons homemade (recipe follows) or store-bought white truffle butter, softened at room temperature

¾ cup grated Italian fontina cheese (about 6 ounces)

¼ cup (½ stick) unsalted butter, plus more if necessary

2 to 2½ cups Creamy Tomato Soup (recipe follows)

MAKES 32 TRIANGLES, ENOUGH TO SERVE 8 TO 10

Truffled Grille[ ]
with Creamy T[ ]

This play on the all-American pairi[ ]
cans of Campbell's®, Kraft® Singles[ ]
you smell the essence of truffle, tast[ ]
homemade tomato soup. Guests at[ ]
I recommend it to you as an hors d'[ ]

I use *pain de mie,* a brioche bake[ ]
sandwiches, but any high-quality w[ ]

The sandwiches can be served w[ ]
and one cup of soup for each of fou[ ]

4 cups packed Napa cabbage cored, quartered through the stem, and cut into 3-inch-long, ¼-inch-wide strips (from about ½ head)

3 cups julienned (3-inch-long) leeks (white and pale green parts from about 2 leeks), washed well (see Prep Talk, facing page)

2 cups julienned (3-inch-long) carrots (from 1 large carrot)

1 cup fresh mung bean sprouts (about 2 ounces)

⅔ cup thinly sliced rehydrated dried shiitake mushroom caps (from about 12 dried mushrooms, soaked in water overnight and squeezed of excess moisture)

One 10-ounce can bamboo shoot strips, drained

3 tablespoons canola or other neutral oil, such as grapeseed, plus several cups more for frying

1½ cups thinly sliced scallion greens (from about 2 bunches)

¼ cup Chinese oyster sauce

2 teaspoons toasted sesame oil

Kosher salt

Black pepper from a mill

1 large egg

2 tablespoons water

Twenty-four 8-inch square spring roll wrappers

1 cup Tamarind Dipping Sauce (recipe follows)

MAKES 96 COCKTAIL BITES, ENOUGH TO SERVE 20 TO 25 PEOPLE

Vegetable Spring Rolls
with Tamarind Dipping Sauce

My vegetarian take on a popular Chinese and Vietnamese appetizer, Chanterelle's spring rolls don't contain shrimp or pork, but they do get a huge flavor boost from the oyster sauce in which the vegetables are tossed before being rolled in the spring roll wrappers, and an almost beefy quality from the dried mushrooms, a mainstay of Chinese cooking. (Do *not* use fresh shiitakes; dried are essential for giving this an authentic character.) They also benefit from one of the irrefutable truths of cooking: *Everything* tastes better fried.

Chinese food wasn't part of our menu when we first opened, but I grew up eating and loving it, and began weaving Chinese and other Asian influences into our repertoire after Karen and I made an extended trip to the Far East in the early 1980s.

When making these rolls, be careful not to overcook the vegetables; you want each one to retain its individual flavor and crunch, with all their colors showing when the rolls are cut into bite-size pieces. The rolls can also be served whole, as part of a buffet or meal.

Note that the mushrooms must be soaked overnight before preparing this hors d'oeuvre.

Put the cabbage, leeks, carrots, sprouts, mushrooms, and bamboo shoots in a large bowl and gently toss.

Heat a large heavy-bottomed sauté pan over high heat. Add the 3 tablespoons canola oil. When it is shimmering but not yet smoking, add the mixed vegetables and cook, tossing or stirring continuously, until they are just wilted but still *al dente* (you want cooked but slightly crunchy vegetables, like those in many Chinese dishes), 3 to 4 minutes. Transfer them to a fine-mesh strainer or colander and shake gently over the sink to drain.

Wipe out the bowl that held the vegetables and transfer the cooked vegetables to the bowl. Add the scallions, oyster sauce, and sesame oil, and toss well or stir together gently with a wooden spoon. Season with salt and pepper to taste. Let the mixture cool before proceeding. (The spring roll filling can be refrigerated in an airtight

container for up to 2 days or frozen for up to 1 month; defrost before proceeding.)

Crack the egg into a small bowl. Add the water and whisk together to make an egg wash.

Set the spring roll wrappers on a clean, dry surface and cover with a damp paper towel to keep them from drying out. Remove one wrapper and set it on the work surface with one corner pointing at you. Using a pastry brush, brush its surface with a thin coat of egg wash. Place 2 tablespoons of the filling in the center of the wrapper. Then, if you think of each corner as a compass point, fold the south corner upward and, holding it down with a thumb, fold in the east and west corners, encasing the vegetable filling. Roll the wrapper and filling away from you, carefully and tautly, sealing the wrapper with a little more egg wash if necessary. Repeat with the remaining wrappers, egg wash, and filling. (The spring rolls can be tightly wrapped, individually, in plastic wrap and refrigerated overnight, or frozen for up to 1 month; frozen rolls don't require defrosting before frying.)

To fry the spring rolls, pour canola oil into an electric fryer or tall pot to a depth of 6 inches. Turn on the fryer or set the pot over medium-high heat and heat the oil to 350°F. Meanwhile, line a large plate or platter with paper towels. Carefully add the spring rolls to the hot oil, a few at a time, and deep-fry until golden and crispy, about 5 minutes. Use a slotted spoon to transfer the rolls to the paper towels to drain of excess oil.

After all the rolls have been fried and drained, use a serrated knife to cut each one into four equal pieces. Arrange them on a serving platter and serve with the dipping sauce alongside.

Tamarind Dipping Sauce

This dip is also excellent with Sesame-Scallion Shrimp Toasts (page 36) and as a dip for crudités.

Heat a medium heavy-bottomed saucepan over medium-high heat for about 2 minutes. Pour in the oil and heat until it is shimmering but not smoking. Add the garlic and ginger and sauté until lightly browned and fragrant, 2 to 3 minutes. Stir in the vinegar, sugar, tamarind, ketchup, sambal, fish sauce, 2 cups of the water, and the lime juice. Bring to a boil, then reduce the heat to a rapid simmer and cook, stirring occasionally, for 10 minutes.

Meanwhile, in a small bowl, whisk together the cornstarch and the remaining 2 tablespoons water. Stir this into the simmering sauce and cook until the sauce begins to thicken. Strain through a fine-mesh strainer set over a bowl, pressing down on the solids to extract as much flavorful liquid as possible. Discard the solids.

Serve the dip at room temperature. It will keep in an airtight container in the refrigerator for up to 2 weeks. Let it come back to room temperature before using it.

2 tablespoons canola or other neutral oil, such as grapeseed

2 tablespoons coarsely chopped garlic (from about 4 cloves)

½ cup peeled and coarsely chopped fresh ginger (from a 4-inch-long piece)

3 tablespoons sherry vinegar

2 tablespoons sugar

3 tablespoons tamarind concentrate

3 tablespoons ketchup

½ teaspoon sambal (ground chile sauce; red chile flakes may be substituted)

2 tablespoons Asian fish sauce

2 cups plus 2 tablespoons cold water

½ teaspoon freshly squeezed lime juice

1 tablespoon cornstarch

MAKES ABOUT 2 CUPS

SOUPS

At Chanterelle, as in many restaurants, soups almost always are selected in harmony with the seasons but in contrast to the weather: The defining ingredient is a seasonal touchstone, such as asparagus in the spring, tomatoes in the summer, and celery root in the fall, but we serve cold soup on hot days and warm soup on chilly days. More than almost any other food, soup goes right to the soul, so even a simple one can make a big impression. I also value the purity of soups: Most of them, whether broth-based or pureed, celebrate one or two primary ingredients, focusing almost exclusively on them, with all other elements there to offer emphasis or contrast. Whether for everyday or special-occasion cooking, soup also offers convenience. Most of these recipes can be made in advance, promising a quick lunch or dinner or a course that can be readied ahead of time for a dinner party. At Chanterelle, we use soups in two distinctly "restaurant" ways that I find extra-special at home. The first is by offering a "shot" of soup as an *amuse,* or palate-teaser, presented just after guests are seated at the table. The other is by occasionally offering a tasting of three complementary soups (see Soup Trios, page 56). Both traditions make a big splash at the table, and I encourage you to adapt them at home.

Chilled White Asparagus Soup with Smoked Salmon

2 tablespoons canola or other neutral oil

1 large yellow or white onion, coarsely chopped

About 2 tablespoons dry white wine

2 quarts Chicken Stock (page 292) or water

2 pounds white asparagus, bottoms trimmed and cut into 1-inch pieces

2 cups heavy cream

Kosher salt

White pepper from a mill

½ lemon

4 ounces smoked salmon, cut into small dice

1 tablespoon olive oil

1 tablespoon chopped fresh dill

1 tablespoon chopped fresh chives

Four ¼-inch-thick slices baguette, toasted in a 300°F oven until crisp but not browned, about 7 minutes

SERVES 4

This soup is made with little more than white asparagus, stock, and cream, with a little lemon to punch up the flavor of the asparagus and help preserve its whiteness. It's augmented by fresh herbs and a baguette crouton topped with a quick "tartare" of salmon.

Because this soup is served cold, season it aggressively so that the flavors shine through the chill—something you should keep in mind whenever seasoning preparations that will be served cold.

I've presented this soup in a number of ways at Chanterelle: as a dish unto itself; as part of a trio of cold soups; and as a cold *amuse-bouche*. If you'd like to serve the soup as an *amuse,* omit the baguette and salmon and pour the soup into chilled demitasse cups. It will serve up to 20 people this way; to serve fewer, halve or quarter the recipe accordingly.

SOUP TRIOS

Periodically at Chanterelle we offer a trio of either hot or cold soups as a first course. It's a unique and scene-stealing offering at home. Serve each guest about ½ cup of each soup presented in matching bowls, or in an eclectic combination of vessels to reflect the differences among the soups themselves.

Trio of Cold Soups

Cold Roasted Red Pepper Soup (page 58)

Green Gazpacho with Crabmeat (page 63) or Chilled Beet Soup with Crème Fraîche & Caviar (page 59)

Chilled White Asparagus Soup with Smoked Salmon (this page)

Trio of Hot Soups

Celery Soup with White Truffles (page 66)

Lentil & Black Truffle Soup (page 68)

Onion Consommé (page 64; omit the pastry)

Heat the canola oil in a large heavy-bottomed saucepan over medium-high heat. Add the onion and sauté until softened but not browned, about 4 minutes. (If the onion seems to be browning at all, sprinkle with a little of the wine.) Raise the heat to high, add the wine, and cook until almost completely evaporated. Pour in the stock and add the asparagus. Bring to a boil, then reduce the heat to a low simmer and cook until the asparagus is soft to a knife tip, about 20 minutes.

Working in batches, puree the contents of the pot in a blender, then strain through a fine-mesh strainer set over another heavy-bottomed saucepan, pressing down on the solids with a rubber spatula or wooden spoon to extract as much of the flavorful liquid as possible. Stir in the cream and gently reheat over medium-low heat. Season with salt, pepper, and a few drops of lemon juice. Let the soup cool to room temperature, then cover with plastic wrap and refrigerate for at least 4 hours or overnight if possible.

When ready to serve, remove the soup from the refrigerator and let warm slightly at room temperature. Taste and adjust the seasoning if necessary. If the soup seems excessively thick, thin it with a few drops of cold water.

In a small bowl, toss the salmon with the olive oil and a few drops of lemon juice, and season with salt and pepper.

Divide the soup among 4 wide, shallow bowls and garnish with the dill and chives. Put a heaping spoonful of salmon mixture on each crouton and float one crouton on the soup in each bowl. Serve immediately.

Cold Roasted Red Pepper Soup

6 large red bell peppers

½ cup plus 2 tablespoons olive oil

1 teaspoon kosher salt

2 tablespoons sherry vinegar

½ teaspoon minced garlic

1½ cups canned or bottled tomato juice

¼ cup finely diced country bread or baguette with the crust removed (see Prep Talk, this page)

2 tablespoons chopped fresh flat-leaf parsley

SERVES 4

Readers who devour cookbooks from cover to cover might feel a twinge of déja vu when they get to the seafood chapter, because this soup is a thinned-out version of the sauce on the yellowtail with saffron orzo (page 162). Garnished with tiny croutons, this is a very satisfying, complete soup. If it's available to you, a very fine dice of Spanish ham sprinkled over the surface is a wonderful finishing touch.

Preheat the oven to 400°F.

Coat the peppers generously with 2 tablespoons of the oil, place on a baking sheet, and roast until they are charred and their skins are wrinkled and separating from the flesh, about 45 minutes. Remove from the oven and transfer to a heatproof bowl. Quickly cover the bowl with plastic wrap or a damp cloth, and let the peppers steam in their own heat for about 10 minutes. Carefully remove and discard the skins, seeds, and stems, reserving the flesh and juice.

In a blender, combine the roasted peppers and their juice, the salt, vinegar, garlic, tomato juice, and the remaining ½ cup olive oil. Process until very smooth. Strain the soup through a fine-mesh strainer set over a bowl. Cover with plastic wrap and refrigerate for at least 1 hour or overnight.

When ready to serve, spread the diced bread on a baking sheet and bake until crisp and lightly browned.

To serve, divide the soup among 4 wide, shallow bowls and garnish with the parsley and croutons.

PREP TALK

Dicing Bread

It's very difficult to dice bread finely for croutons, but freezing the bread ahead of time helps, and the fine dice will thaw quickly.

Chilled Beet Soup
with Crème Fraîche & Caviar

Another dish with roots in my Jewish American upbringing, this is essentially a strained borscht that's flavored with vinegar and sugar and dolled up with crème fraîche and caviar. At Chanterelle we often serve this as an *amuse,* presented in a sake glass, though we have also offered it as a soup on the menu from time to time. Canned chicken broth is actually preferable to homemade here, because homemade tends to gel when cold, which you don't want. If you'd prefer to use homemade, dilute it with half water.

Put the beets, broth, onion, and vinegar in a large heavy-bottomed saucepan over medium-high heat. Bring to a boil, then reduce the heat to a simmer and cook until the beets are quite tender to a knife tip, about 40 minutes. Strain through a fine-mesh strainer set over a bowl, reserving the beets and onion.

Transfer the beets and onion to a food processor fitted with a steel blade and pulse until fairly smooth, though some texture will remain. Transfer to a fine-mesh strainer set over the bowl holding the broth, pressing down on the solids to extract any remaining liquid. Measure 1 cup of the remaining puree and add it to the broth, discarding the surplus puree. Stir the soup well and season with the salt and sugar. Chill and season to taste once again before serving. (The soup will keep in an airtight container in the refrigerator for up to 3 days.)

To serve, divide the soup evenly among 4 wide, shallow bowls and top with a dollop of crème fraîche and a sprinkling of chives, dill, and caviar.

1½ pounds beets (about 3 medium-large beets), peeled and quartered

5 cups high-quality low-sodium store-bought chicken broth or water

1 medium Spanish onion, coarsely chopped

1 tablespoon red wine vinegar

1 teaspoon kosher salt

1 tablespoon plus 2 teaspoons sugar

¼ cup crème fraîche or sour cream

1 tablespoon chopped fresh dill

1 tablespoon chopped fresh chives

4 teaspoons American black caviar, such as paddlefish

SERVES 4, OR 16 AS HORS D'OEUVRES IN SMALL GLASSES

Chilled, Jelled Tomato Consommé with Shrimp, Chervil & Caviar

If there is such a thing as a composed soup, then this is it: a jellied tomato soup decorated with a spot of tomato, a blob of black caviar, and a Jackson Pollack–like drizzle of chervil mayonnaise. It's a soup that seduces with textures as much as with flavors: the voluptuous mouth-feel of the gelatin-infused consommé, the crunch of the shrimp, the creamy mayonnaise, and the pearls of caviar.

This soup requires a lot of effort, from clarifying the stock to making a concassée, but I think it's worth it, not just for the range of tastes and textures but also because this is one of the dishes in the book guaranteed to elicit gasps of delight based on its appearance alone. (The stock is more difficult than most to clarify because the egg whites don't coalesce into a solid raft, so it must be carefully strained.)

Don't be shy when seasoning the individual components; because they are served cold, all the flavors, including salt, will be somewhat dulled.

Put the garlic, 2 of the carrots, 2 of the onions, the tarragon, bay leaves, and canned tomatoes in a large heavy-bottomed pot. Pour in the tomato juice and stock, set over medium-high heat, and bring to boil. Reduce the heat to a simmer and cook for 30 minutes.

Strain the broth through a fine-mesh strainer set over a bowl, pressing down on the solids to extract as much of the flavorful liquid as possible. Cover the bowl with plastic wrap and refrigerate to chill completely. (To speed the process, you can set the bowl in an ice bath.)

When you're ready to pull the stock out of the refrigerator, whisk the egg whites together in a medium bowl just until frothy.

Pour the chilled stock into a large pot over low heat. Add the egg whites, along with the remaining chopped carrot and onion, and cook, stirring occasionally, until the egg whites form a "raft," a unified, floating mass on the surface of the broth, about 1 hour of total cooking time.

Pour the stock into a cheesecloth-lined colander set over a large heavy-bottomed saucepan. You should have 4 cups of broth; if you have more, bring the stock to a boil and reduce to 4 cups. Remove from the heat and sprinkle in the gelatin, allowing it to dissolve. Place the pan over medium heat and whisk to fully incorporate the dissolved gelatin. Season generously to taste with salt.

Transfer the consommé to a bowl, cover with plastic wrap, and refrigerate overnight or for up to 2 days.

To cook the shrimp, combine the wine, lemon juice, 2 tablespoons of salt, and the water in a medium saucepan and bring to a boil. Let boil for 10 minutes, then add the shrimp and cook until firm and pink, about 1 minute. Use a slotted spoon to transfer them to a plate, and cool them quickly in the refrigerator.

---

2 medium garlic heads, in their skins, coarsely chopped

3 large carrots, unpeeled, coarsely chopped

3 large Spanish onions, peeled and coarsely chopped

1 cup coarsely chopped fresh tarragon

2 bay leaves, preferably fresh

2 cups canned plum tomatoes, with their juice (about 18 ounces)

4 cups canned or bottled tomato juice

8 cups Chicken Stock (page 292) or water

8 large egg whites

1½ teaspoons powdered gelatin

Kosher salt

1 cup dry white wine

Juice of ½ lemon

6 cups water

8 medium shrimp (about 8 ounces), peeled and deveined

2 ounces fresh chervil leaves and stems (about 2½ cups lightly packed)

1 large egg

½ teaspoon Dijon mustard

1 teaspoon tarragon vinegar or white wine vinegar

½ cup mild olive oil, or ¼ cup plus 2 tablespoons olive oil mixed with ¼ cup canola oil

3 very ripe medium plum tomatoes, peeled and cut into concassée (see Prep Talk, page 62)

2 tablespoons American black caviar, such as paddlefish

SERVES 4

To make the chervil mayonnaise, bring a large pot of water to a boil and fill a large bowl halfway with ice water. Carefully place the chervil in the boiling water, blanch for 10 seconds, then quickly transfer it to the ice bath to shock it. Squeeze the water from the chervil and chop coarsely. Put the chervil, the whole egg, mustard, and vinegar in a food processor fitted with a steel blade and process until well incorporated. With the motor running, slowly pour in the oil through the feed tube to form a smooth mayonnaise pale green in color. Season with a pinch of salt. (Do not refrigerate for longer than an hour or two or the mayonnaise will take on an unappealing khaki color.)

To serve, evenly divide the consommé among 4 wide, shallow bowls. Put 2 shrimp in the center of each bowl. Sprinkle the tomato concassée around the shrimp, then drizzle the chervil mayonnaise decoratively over the soup. Top each serving with 1½ teaspoons of caviar. Serve immediately.

Peeling Tomatoes & Making Concassée

To peel tomatoes, bring a pot of water to a boil. Fill a medium bowl halfway with ice water. Use a paring knife to cut a shallow "X" in the bottom of each tomato, then carefully cut out the stem. Carefully lower the tomatoes into the boiling water and blanch for 30 seconds. Use tongs or a slotted spoon to remove them from the water and plunge them in the ice water. Drain, then peel the tomatoes, using the knife if necessary to help the skin come off.

To make tomato concassée, cut the tomatoes in half, gently squeeze out the seeds, and cut the flesh into ¼-inch dice.

Green Gazpacho with Crabmeat

One of the great culinary resources of New York City is the Union Square Greenmarket. I was walking the market one morning when the summer harvest was at its great, green peak: Everywhere I looked there were lush bunches of herbs, piles of cucumbers, and baskets piled high with green peppers. I wanted to gather up all that green goodness and go back to my kitchen and make something. I remembered hearing of a green gazpacho—to this day, I don't know where—and decided to try that. Back at Chanterelle, I processed vegetables along with some serrano pepper for heat and a variety of herbs to give it a potent garden aroma. I finished the soup with olive oil and lemon juice, and rounded it out with crabmeat. Then I decided to make the crab the co-star of the dish, with the gazpacho acting almost like a sauce.

Put the crabmeat in a medium bowl and squeeze out any excess water. Gently pick through it to remove any bits of shell or cartilage, taking care to not break up the pieces any more than necessary. Add 1 tablespoon of the oil, ½ tablespoon of the lemon juice, ½ teaspoon of the salt, and 1 grind of black pepper and toss gently to combine. Taste and adjust the seasoning with more salt, pepper, and lemon juice, if necessary. Cover with plastic wrap and refrigerate for up to 2 hours.

Bring a large pot of water to a boil. Fill a large bowl halfway with ice water. Blanch the chives, dill, sorrel, parsley, and watercress for 10 seconds, then quickly transfer them to the ice bath to stop the cooking and set the color. Drain and squeeze out any excess water, then coarsely chop the herbs.

Put the chopped herbs, chile, cucumber, grapes, water, and the remaining ½ cup oil and 2 tablespoons lemon juice in a blender and process until smooth. Transfer the soup to a bowl, cover with plastic wrap, and refrigerate for up to 2 hours.

To serve, set a 2- or 3-inch ring mold in the center of a wide, shallow bowl and fill it with one-quarter of the crabmeat salad, pressing down firmly. Gently lift the ring away from the salad and repeat with the remaining 3 bowls. (Alternatively, you can simply mound one-quarter of the salad in the center of each bowl.) Ladle equal amounts of the chilled gazpacho around the crabmeat in each bowl. Garnish with the caviar, if desired, and serve.

PREP TALK

Blanching Leafy Herbs

Blanching fresh herbs brightens and sets their green color and softens their flavor. The easiest way I know to blanch parsley and other leafy herbs such as tarragon and cilantro is to tie them in cheesecloth before submerging them in the boiling water. This facilitates removing the herb from both the hot water and the ice water in which it's shocked.

8 ounces fresh lump crabmeat

½ cup plus 1 tablespoon olive oil

2½ tablespoons freshly squeezed lemon juice, plus more to taste

2 teaspoons kosher salt

Black pepper from a mill

2 cups loosely packed fresh chives cut into 2-inch segments

1 cup loosely packed fresh dill fronds

2 cups loosely packed fresh sorrel leaves, with the center ribs removed

2 cups loosely packed flat-leaf fresh parsley leaves

2 cups loosely packed watercress, with stems

1 tablespoon coarsely chopped fresh serrano chile

1 large English (hothouse) cucumber

¾ cup seedless green grapes

½ cup cold water

1 to 2 teaspoons American black caviar, such as paddlefish (optional)

SERVES 4

Onion Consommé
with Onion & Fontina Ravioli

6 large Spanish onions, unpeeled, thickly sliced

¾ cup canola or other neutral oil

1 teaspoon sugar

⅓ cup brandy

⅔ cup ruby port, plus more to taste

1 cup dry white wine

10 cups Veal Stock (page 294)

2 bay leaves, preferably fresh

5 large egg whites

1 tablespoon red wine vinegar

1 medium carrot, cut into ½-inch dice

1 medium Spanish onion, cut into ¼-inch dice

Kosher salt

Onion & Fontina Ravioli (recipe follows)

SERVES 4

This recipe reflects my lifelong desire to take classic French flavors to a new level; it is a variation on the idea of French onion soup that intensifies the flavor so much that I think you'll find it unforgettable. At Chanterelle, we serve the soup with Gruyère pastries, my nod to the convention of topping French onion soup with toast and cheese. Instead of floating toasted bread in the consommé, we present it as a miniature turnover. Here, I've replaced the pastries with onion and fontina ravioli that can be made as far ahead as you like, and reheated in just a few minutes.

The consommé on its own is wonderful, so don't hesitate to serve it without the ravioli, if you prefer.

Put the sliced onions and oil in a large heavy-bottomed pot over medium-low heat and cook slowly, stirring occasionally, until the onions give off their liquid, then begin to brown and shrivel, about 40 minutes. Sprinkle with the sugar, raise the heat to medium, and cook, stirring often, until the onions are deeply caramelized, about 10 minutes. Add the brandy, port, and wine, bring to a boil over high heat, and reduce the liquid, scraping up any browned bits stuck to the bottom of the pot, until nearly dry, about 10 minutes. Add the stock and bay leaves and bring to a boil. Lower the heat to a simmer and cook until the broth has reduced somewhat and is richly flavored, about 40 minutes. Strain through a fine-mesh strainer set over a bowl. Let cool, then cover and refrigerate overnight until completely cold, at least 2 hours or overnight.

Skim any fat from the top of the soup, then pour into a medium heavy-bottomed saucepan. Add the egg whites, vinegar, carrot, and diced onion and whisk together well. Bring to a gentle simmer very slowly over medium-low heat, stirring every few minutes until the egg whites and vegetables come to the top and form a solid mass, or "raft." Stop stirring and allow the broth (and raft) to cook over very low heat for about 20 minutes. Use a slotted spoon to skim off and discard the raft. Strain the consommé through a cheesecloth-lined colander set over a bowl, then season it to taste with salt and a splash of port, if desired. (The consommé can be refrigerated in an airtight container for up to 3 days or frozen for up to 2 months; reheat gently before proceeding.)

Bring a large pot of generously salted water to a boil, then carefully drop in the ravioli and boil until they rise to the surface, 2 to 3 minutes.

Ladle the consommé into 4 wide, shallow bowls. When the ravioli are done, use a slotted spoon to divide them among the bowls. Serve immediately.

Onion & Fontina Ravioli

These are also delicious as an appetizer or pasta course, sauced with a simple herbed cream or warmed cream infused with bay leaf.

In a wide, deep sauté pan set over medium-low heat, slowly cook the onions, butter, and wine, stirring occasionally, until the onions are golden brown and very soft, about 1 hour. Sprinkle with the sugar and raise the heat to medium, cooking for another 5 minutes to brown the onions a little more. Drain the onions in a colander set in the sink and let cool.

Transfer the cooled onions to a bowl, fold in the cheeses and nutmeg, and season with salt and pepper to taste. Mix well.

Roll the pasta dough out using a hand-crank machine or a stand mixer fitted with the pasta attachment, set to the thinnest setting. Using a ravioli mold or ravioli cutters, make at least 24 ravioli containing 1½ to 2 teaspoons filling each, taking care not to overfill the ravioli. Dust each one with a scant amount of flour to keep them from sticking. (They can be refrigerated for up to 3 days; see page 257 for instructions for freezing ravioli.)

1½ large Vidalia onions, cut into ¼-inch dice

2 tablespoons unsalted butter

¼ cup dry white wine

½ teaspoon sugar

2 tablespoons freshly grated Parmigiano-Reggiano cheese

1 cup grated Italian fontina cheese

Pinch of freshly grated nutmeg

Kosher salt

Black pepper from a mill

1 recipe Pasta Dough (page 297)

All-purpose flour as needed

MAKES ABOUT 24 RAVIOLI

Lentil & Black Truffle Soup

2 tablespoons unsalted butter

2 medium leeks (white and pale green parts), cut into ⅛-inch dice and washed well (see Prep Talk, page 53)

1 cup diced (⅛-inch) carrot

1 medium garlic clove, finely minced

4 cups Hock Stock (page 294) or Chicken Stock (page 292)

One 13-ounce can black truffle juice

½ cup French green lentils (lentilles du Puy), rinsed and picked over

1½ ounces fresh, flash-frozen, or canned black truffles, minced

3 tablespoons Madeira

½ teaspoon freshly squeezed lemon juice, plus more to taste

Kosher salt

SERVES 4

Soups are one of the great foods that can celebrate a winning combination of ingredients, because their elemental nature doesn't require much more than a well-matched pair to succeed. Case in point: the classic duo of lentils and black truffles, which creates a supremely earthy effect that I emphasize by putting some truffle juice (the liquid by-product of canned truffles, also made and sold on its own) in the broth. I also include a little Madeira and a stock made with ham hocks for a subtle, smoky undercurrent and added richness.

Warm a large heavy-bottomed pot over medium-low heat for about 1 minute. Add the butter and let it melt, then add the leeks, carrot, and garlic and cook, stirring frequently, until soft but not browned, about 20 minutes. Pour in the stock and truffle juice, raise the heat to medium, and bring to a simmer. Add the lentils and truffles, reduce the heat to low, and cook until the lentils are soft but still hold their shape, another 40 minutes. Stir in the Madeira and lemon juice.

Use an immersion blender to blend the soup in the pot, pulsing for just a few moments to thicken it while maintaining the texture. The soup should appear more opaque, but not entirely pureed. (Alternatively, you can puree one-quarter of the soup in a regular blender, then return it to the pot.) Season to taste with salt if necessary. (The soup can be refrigerated in an airtight container for up to 2 days and reheated gently.)

Ladle the soup into 4 wide, shallow bowls and serve.

Lobster Minestrone

Kosher salt

2 live lobsters (1¼ pounds each)

½ cup olive oil

2 large carrots, unpeeled,
cut into chunks

2 large onions, unpeeled,
cut into chunks

1 tablespoon minced garlic

½ cup brandy

1 cup dry white wine

10 cups Chicken Stock (page 292),
high-quality low-sodium store-bought
chicken stock, or water

2 cups canned tomatoes,
with their juice (about 18 ounces)

½ cup diced (¼-inch) leeks (white
and light green parts), washed well
(see Prep Talk, page 53)

½ cup diced (¼-inch) zucchini skin

½ cup diced (¼-inch) yellow
squash skin

½ cup diced (¼-inch) carrot

½ cup canned navy beans

Black pepper from a mill

2 tablespoons fresh basil
cut into chiffonade (optional;
see Prep Talk, this page)

SERVES 4

This is another of my childhood favorites, elevated to Chanterelle levels with a foundation of lobster stock and lobster meat in the soup itself. The servings here are generous, with half a lobster per person.

You can vary the vegetables, substituting turnips, celery root, or butternut squash for any of the vegetables. (The guideline is a total of 2 cups of diced vegetables.) You can also add ½ cup cooked small pasta such as elbows, orzo, tubetti, or small bowties or use the pasta to replace the beans.

Bring a large pot of salted water to a boil. Kill the lobsters quickly by holding each one to face you, then driving a knife between the eyes and pulling it down through the head, like a lever. Separate the claws and tail from the bodies by twisting them off. Cut the heads into 6 pieces each and set aside. Put the claws in the boiling water for 1 minute, then add the tails and boil for 2 more minutes. Use tongs to remove the claws and tails from the water and set the pieces aside to let cool to room temperature. When cool to the touch, remove the meat from the shells; it will be slightly undercooked. Remove the digestive tract and cut the meat into ¼-inch dice. Transfer the lobster meat to a bowl, cover with plastic wrap, and refrigerate for up to 24 hours.

Heat the oil in a large heavy-bottomed saucepan over high heat. When it is shimmering and just starting to smoke, add the lobster heads and coarsely cut carrots, onions, and garlic. Cook, stirring from time to time, until the lobster shells are red and very fragrant and the vegetables have browned, about 10 minutes. Pour in the brandy and wine and reduce the liquids until almost evaporated, about 5 minutes. Add the stock and tomatoes and bring to a boil. Reduce the heat to a simmer and cook until about 4 cups remain, about 30 minutes.

Strain the reduced stock through a fine-mesh strainer set over a large heavy-bottomed saucepan, then return it to the stovetop and bring to a simmer over medium-high heat. Add the diced vegetables and cook for another 10 minutes. Add the beans and cook for another 10 minutes. The vegetables should be very tender.

Season the soup to taste with salt and pepper. Just before serving, add the lobster meat, stirring just long enough to heat it through. Divide the soup evenly among 4 wide, shallow bowls. Sprinkle with the basil, if desired. Serve immediately.

PREP TALK

Cutting Chiffonade

Chiffonade literally means "ribbons." To cut leafy herbs such as basil or greens such as spinach into ribbons, stack a few leaves and roll them up tautly, like a cigar. Cut the roll crosswise and the pieces will unravel in ribbons.

Duck Soup with White Beans & Greens

½ cup rendered duck fat

1 cup diced (¼-inch) leeks (white and light green parts), washed well (see Prep Talk, page 53)

4 garlic cloves, coarsely chopped

1 large onion, coarsely chopped

8 cups Duck Stock (page 296)

¾ cup (about 8 ounces) dried navy beans, soaked overnight in enough cold water to cover and drained

2 bay leaves, preferably fresh

1 teaspoon fresh thyme leaves

1 duck leg and thigh confit, store-bought or homemade (page 194)

Kosher salt

Black pepper from a mill

Dash of red wine vinegar

1 cup coarsely chopped Swiss chard leaves, escarole, or beet greens

1 tablespoon coarsely chopped fresh flat-leaf parsley

SERVES 4

My French-leaning version of an Italian soup featuring white beans, escarole, and pork sausage, this soup replaces the traditional pork with duck confit. It's a full-flavored, hearty soup that is in regular rotation on our lunch menu. This recipe calls for ½ cup of duck fat; if possible, use fat that has been used to make confit, which will add an intense, garlicky, herbaceous undercurrent to the base. Otherwise, you can use purchased rendered duck fat.

Melt the duck fat in a large heavy-bottomed saucepan over medium heat. Add the leeks, garlic, and onion and cook over medium-low heat, stirring occasionally, until the vegetables are softened but not browned, about 10 minutes. Add the stock, beans, and bay leaves. Raise the heat to high and bring to a boil, then reduce the heat so the liquid is simmering and cook for 1 hour.

Add the thyme, stir, and continue cooking for 30 minutes more. The beans should be quite tender. If they aren't, you may need to add more stock or water and continue cooking until they are tender.

While the soup is cooking, preheat the oven to 400°F.

Put the duck confit on a rack set in a roasting pan or on a baking sheet. Roast until the fat has rendered and the skin turns crispy, about 10 minutes. Remove from the oven and, once the duck is cool enough to handle, pull the meat off the bones and chop coarsely or shred by hand. Set aside.

When the beans are done, use tongs to fish out and discard the bay leaves. Taste the soup and adjust the seasoning with salt, pepper, and a dash of vinegar. Add the Swiss chard and cook until wilted, just a minute or two. Taste again and adjust the seasoning, bearing in mind that the confit is salty.

Divide the confit among 4 wide, shallow soup bowls. Ladle some soup over the confit and garnish with the parsley. Serve immediately.

Come as You Are: Hospitality

⚘

When you call Chanterelle, a person—rather than an automated operator—will *always* answer the phone. That's because, to me, Chanterelle is all about people: about our guests and our staff, and a sincere human connection between the two.

I don't think that any reviewer has ever written about Chanterelle without examining, or at least commenting on, the style and sensibility of our service—the stripped-down architectural elegance; the absence of artwork on our walls, music in the air, or flowers on the tables; and the refreshing, unpretentious quality of our dining room team.

I am flattered to have been credited with forging a unique style, but the accolades should really go to my family members, who raised me to appreciate what a person does, not what he or she looks like. I am thankful for having been brought up in New York City, where both individuality and art have always flourished. When we first opened Chanterelle in SoHo, and artists and locals arrived, it never occurred to us to slap a jacket and tie on them, as many restaurants would have done at the time; we were simply honored to have them there and to serve them. And the same goes for all of our customers: We are there to serve them, not to have them impress us or to dictate how they might do that.

We don't put on airs ourselves, and we don't want the people who work with us to do so, either. For all of our ambition, at heart, David and I are still two kids from the Bronx. Being Americans, we called our restaurant simply Chanterelle, without adding "Le" or "La," and we wrote the menu in English. We also hired women for our team in 1979, when only one other high-end restaurant could say the same.

This attitude has served us all well, helping to maintain our genuine pleasure in our profession after thirty years. Restaurant hours, especially if you're the owner or chef, almost demand that your workplace be your home, so our staff has become like family, and we shudder to think of how it might have been otherwise. David has a line about restaurants that make their employees stifle their true selves: "The bitterness gets in the soup."

We've also tried to make every guest feel special, both in our original home and in our Tribeca digs. There's no bad table in the house, no psychological Siberia to which we relegate the last party to be seated. One of our hallmarks is that we relate to each table uniquely: I'm fond of saying that every party is its own world. At the same time, there is a constant in the dining room: our staff, all of whom are captain-caliber professionals, intelligent and skilled enough to maintain a high level of service while meeting clients' needs on their own terms. To put it another way, seventeen worlds collide on a nightly basis at Chanterelle and the result, every time I hope, is something you won't find anywhere else.

—KAREN WALTUCK

FIRST COURSES

¶ Once upon a time, meals began almost exclusively with a salad, some kind of cold, dressed vegetable, or a soup. All of that has changed in the three decades since Chanterelle served its first dinner. Today a first course, especially in a sophisticated urban restaurant, is less likely to be a salad than something else. In fact, it's quite possible that it will bear no resemblance to a salad whatsoever, meaning it will have no greens or vinaigrette and might very well be hot rather than cold. ¶ There is literally no limit, beyond size, to what might be an offer to begin a meal today. A starter might be vegetarian, or feature fish or meat; it might have one component or several; and it might be old-fashioned or revolutionary. You might think that this would be unappealing to a classicist such as myself, but as somebody who came of age during the era of nouvelle cuisine, I find it perfectly natural and creatively stimulating. ¶ To my mind, the best starters and salads are a bit whimsical, whet the appetite for the rest of the meal, and are versatile enough to precede a wide variety of other dishes. To put it another way, these are *fun* dishes, enjoyable to think about and amusing to the palate: They set the tone for what is to follow and, one hopes, get people excited about what will follow, giving them a sense of what might come next, but—almost paradoxically—leaving the options tantalizingly wide open.

Asparagus Flan with Morel Mushroom & Oyster Sauce

Asparagus and morels are both ingredients of spring, and they have become an all-but-mandatory pairing for this season on American restaurant menus from coast to coast. When a combination becomes this ubiquitous, it falls to each chef to create his or her own signature treatment(s), and this is one of the many ways I've called on it over the years. The asparagus is pureed and gently baked into savory flans; the morels are sautéed and folded into a light cream sauce that's perked up with lemon juice and Madeira.

If you're wondering why there's spinach in this recipe, it's not for its flavor. In order to get maximum flavor from the asparagus, it's cooked longer than usual, which leaches out its green color. The spinach is purely cosmetic, to return some of the green to the flan.

Bring a large pot of generously salted water to a boil. Meanwhile, fill a large bowl halfway with ice water.

Carefully put the asparagus stalks in the boiling water and cook until thoroughly limp (this makes them easier to process), about 10 minutes, adding the spinach after 8 minutes. Drain the asparagus and spinach and quickly transfer to the ice water to stop the cooking, then drain and dry them on a clean kitchen towel.

Place the asparagus and spinach in a food processor fitted with a steel blade and process until very smooth. Transfer the puree to a cheesecloth-lined colander set over a bowl. Gather the sides of the cloth over the puree to form a bundle, set a few plates on top of the cheesecloth to weigh it down, and set the bowl with the colander in the refrigerator overnight to extract as much liquid from the puree as possible.

Preheat the oven to 250°F. Grease four 4-ounce ramekins with canola oil.

In a large bowl, whisk together ½ cup of the cream, the whole egg, egg yolk, and nutmeg, season with salt to taste, then incorporate the drained puree. Fill the ramekins

evenly with the flan mixture (they should be about seven-eighths full) and place in a roasting pan. Carefully add warm water to the pan so that it comes halfway up the sides of the ramekins. Cover the pan loosely with aluminum foil and bake until the flans are set (a knife inserted into the center should come out clean), about 1 hour. Remove them from the water bath and keep them covered and warm. (The flans can be made up to 2 hours in advance and kept covered with plastic wrap at room temperature; reheat them in the water bath, covered with foil, in a preheated 250°F oven for 10 minutes.)

Meanwhile, strain the oysters in a cheesecloth-lined strainer set over a bowl, reserving the liquor. Heat a large heavy-bottomed sauté pan over medium heat. Add the butter and let it melt. Add the morels and sauté until they begin to give off their juice, about 3 minutes, then drain the morels and reserve their liquid. Return the morels to the pan and cook, still over medium heat, until browned and dry, about 5 minutes. Pour the reserved morel juice, mushroom stock, and ⅓ cup of the strained oyster liquor

continued

Kosher salt

2 pounds pencil-thin asparagus, bottoms trimmed, 12 tips cut off, wrapped in plastic, and refrigerated

2 cups loosely packed spinach leaves, tough stems trimmed and washed well

Canola oil, for greasing ramekins

1½ cups heavy cream

1 large egg

1 large egg yolk

⅛ teaspoon freshly grated nutmeg

12 oysters, shucked (see page 32), with their juice

2 tablespoons unsalted butter

1 pound morels, cut in half and washed (see Prep Talk, page 80)

⅓ cup Mushroom Stock (page 290) or homemade or high-quality low-sodium store-bought chicken stock

1 tablespoon Madeira

1½ teaspoons minced fresh chervil

1½ teaspoons minced fresh tarragon

1½ teaspoons minced fresh flat-leaf parsley

1½ teaspoons minced fresh chives

½ teaspoon freshly squeezed lemon juice

SERVES 4

into the pan and simmer until reduced by half, about 5 minutes. Add the Madeira and remaining 1 cup cream and reduce until lightly thickened, 3 to 4 minutes. (It's all right to let the sauce get a little dry because no matter how well the oysters have been drained, they will release some liquid into the sauce.) Toss in the oysters and cook until just warmed through. Swirl in the chervil, tarragon, parsley, chives, and lemon juice.

While the sauce is cooking, bring a small pot of salted water to a boil. Add the reserved asparagus tips and cook for 2 minutes. Drain and refresh under gently running cold water. Drain again.

To serve, unmold the flans by running a knife around the inside of each ramekin and inverting it onto a plate. Ladle some morel sauce around the flan. Garnish each plate with 3 asparagus tips and serve.

Crab Ravioli with Almond Oil & Avocado

A light, refreshing play on ravioli, with paper-thin slices of golden beets in place of the pasta, these little knife-and-fork crab sandwiches are paired with a salad built on the combination of avocado and almond oil. Additional crunch and a jícama-like sweetness are provided by fresh water chestnuts; if you can not get fresh, do *not* substitute canned, which are flavorless.

Put the beet in a small saucepan with a tight-fitting lid (or cover tightly with aluminum foil). Pour in enough water to come one-third up the sides of the beet. Set over medium-high heat and bring the water to a simmer. Cover, reduce the heat to a simmer, and cook until the beet is tender to a knife tip, 2 to 2½ hours, checking occasionally to make sure the water has not evaporated and adding more if necessary. Transfer the beet to a plate to cool, then peel it and set aside.

To make the vinaigrette, whisk together the almond oil, lemon juice, salt, and 2 grinds of pepper from the mill in a small bowl. Dress the crabmeat with half of the dressing. Add the water chestnuts, toss, taste, and adjust the seasoning if necessary.

Cut the beet lengthwise into paper-thin slices, using a mandoline if you have one. Cut each slice into a 2-inch round, preferably using a fluted cutter. You'll need 24 rounds.

To serve, lay out 3 rounds of beet on each of 4 salad plates. Divide the crab salad evenly among the slices, then top each with another beet round. These are the "ravioli." In the center of each plate, place a few leaves of the lettuce chiffonade and, over that, 2 slices of avocado. Drizzle the lettuce and avocado with most of the remaining dressing, then drizzle a little around the plate and over the beet ravioli as well. Sprinkle everything with sea salt, decorate the ravioli with sprigs of chervil, and serve.

1 very large, preferably round, golden beet (about 1¼ pounds)

½ cup roasted almond oil

2 teaspoons freshly squeezed lemon juice

½ teaspoon kosher salt

Black pepper from a mill

8 ounces jumbo lump crabmeat, picked over for shell or cartilage fragments

3 tablespoons peeled and diced fresh water chestnuts (from 2 or 3 water chestnuts)

1 head Boston lettuce, leaves separated, rolled, and sliced into 1-inch-wide chiffonade

1 medium ripe avocado, peeled, pitted, and cut into eighths lengthwise

Sea salt to taste (preferably fleur de sel)

12 sprigs fresh chervil

SERVES 4

Cannelloni with Collard Greens

1 pound collard greens, washed well in several changes of cold water, large stems removed and cut into large pieces

8 cups Hock Stock (page 294)

12 oysters (preferably Pemaquid or other large East Coast variety), shucked (see page 32) and drained well in layered paper towels, reserving ¼ cup oyster liquor

½ cup (1 stick) unsalted butter, cubed

3 tablespoons mascarpone cheese

1 tablespoon freshly grated Parmigiano-Reggiano cheese

Kosher salt

1 recipe Pasta Dough (page 297)

3 slices bacon

¼ cup Chicken Stock (page 292) or high-quality low-sodium store-bought chicken stock

Canola or other neutral oil, for frying

Wondra or all-purpose flour, for dusting oysters

2 tablespoons minced fresh chives

I don't know what kind of crazy mood I was in when I came up with this dish, which marries elements of American Southern cooking, such as collard greens cooked in a pork-infused liquid, with Italian tradition, namely cannelloni and mascarpone and Parmesan cheeses, the whole thing garnished with pan-fried bacon-wrapped oysters. Maybe I was just hungry for big flavors.

Note that you will need a pasta machine to properly roll out the dough for the cannelloni. If you don't have one, a rolling pin is an option, although I suggest buying sheets of fresh pasta instead to guarantee a consistent thickness.

Put the collard greens and hock stock in a large heavy-bottomed pot and bring to a simmer over medium-high heat. Cover, reduce the heat to maintain a simmer, and cook for 1 hour. Drain the greens in a strainer over a large bowl. Wipe out the pot, return the strained stock to the pot, and set over high heat. Stir in the reserved oyster liquor, bring to a boil, and reduce to about ⅔ cup, about 20 minutes. Still working over high heat, whisk in the butter, a few cubes at a time. Remove the sauce from the heat and keep it covered and warm.

When the greens are cool enough to handle, squeeze out any excess liquid and finely chop. Wipe out the bowl that held the stock and put the greens in the bowl. Add the mascarpone and Parmesan, stir to combine well, and set aside.

Bring a large pot of salted water to a boil.

Using one-quarter of the dough at a time, pass it through progressively thinner settings of a hand-crank pasta machine until the machine is on the finest setting. When several thin sheets are finished, cut the sheets into four 4-inch squares.

Preheat the oven to 400°F.

Cook the pasta in the boiling water until *al dente,* about 3 minutes. Shock it under cold water to get it cold enough to work with, then drain on paper towels.

Cut each slice of bacon crosswise into 4 pieces. Roll up an oyster in each piece and secure with a toothpick. Chill the 12 bacon rolls until ready to fry.

Spoon 3 tablespoons of collard green filling into each pasta square and roll into a tight cylinder, leaving the ends open. These are the cannelloni. Place in a shallow baking pan with the chicken stock and cover with aluminum foil. Warm in the oven for 7 to 8 minutes.

Heat about ½ inch of canola oil in a wide, deep sauté pan over medium-high heat. Dust the bacon rolls lightly with flour and pan-fry in the hot oil until crispy, about 3 minutes. Drain on paper towels.

To serve, cut a cannelloni in half crosswise and put one half in a large, shallow bowl. Rest the other half on top. Ladle some sauce around the cannelloni. Remove the toothpicks from 3 bacon-wrapped oysters and arrange the oysters around the cannelloni. Garnish with chives. Repeat with the remaining cannelloni, sauce, oysters, and chives and serve immediately.

Fennel-Marinated Oysters

1 cup olive oil

½ cup fennel seeds, coarsely ground in a spice mill or coffee grinder

20 oysters, preferably Pemaquid or other large East Coast variety

1 teaspoon pastis, such as Pernod® or Ricard®

2 teaspoons freshly squeezed lemon juice

½ teaspoon kosher salt

Seaweed or coarse salt as a bed for the oyster shells

1 small bulb fennel, outer layers removed, cored, and very finely diced (if done ahead, toss with some marinade to prevent the fennel from browning), fennel fronds reserved for garnish

1 lemon, peeled, sectioned, seeds removed, and sections cut into ¼-inch pieces

2 ripe plum tomatoes, cut into concassée (see Prep Talk, page 62)

2½ teaspoons American black caviar, such as paddlefish

SERVES 4

One of the most productive questions a chef can ask himself is, "I wonder what would happen if . . . " It's a natural question that arises when you spend enough time in the company of ingredients, and it can lead to some successful experimentation. In this case, I wondered what would happen if you marinated raw oysters like you would fish in a ceviche. I've always believed that the flavors of fennel and oysters are complementary, so I made a simple fennel oil for use in the marinade and was delighted with the results. These oysters are often included in the Quintet of Oysters we serve at Chanterelle—an assortment of five oyster preparations on one plate, meant as a sort of mini-tasting. But I'm so fond of this preparation that I wanted to include it on its own here. It's topped with a bit of caviar, really there just for the salty accent it provides and for a final opulent flourish. Take note that you need to prepare the fennel oil the day before and that the oysters need to marinate for at least 24 hours.

Pour the olive oil into a small heavy-bottomed saucepan. Add the ground fennel seed and heat over medium heat until the oil is warm and the fennel aromatic, about 10 minutes; don't allow the ground seed to brown. Remove from the heat and let cool. Cover and let sit at room temperature overnight or for up to 3 days. (Don't strain the oil.) When ready to proceed, pour the oil through a fine-mesh strainer into a medium bowl.

Shuck the oysters (see page 32). Drain them, saving the liquor for another use or discarding it. Reserve the bottom (rounded) shells.

Add the Pernod, lemon juice, and salt to the bowl with the fennel oil and whisk well. Add the oysters, cover with plastic wrap, and refrigerate for at least 24 or up to 48 hours.

To serve, drain the oysters. (They will retain enough liquid to help make the dressing in the finished dish.) Make a bed of seaweed or coarse salt on each of 4 plates and arrange 5 oyster shells on top. Place 1 oyster in each shell. Top each oyster with ½ teaspoon diced fennel bulb, 2 or 3 pieces of lemon, ¼ teaspoon of the tomato concassée, and ⅛ teaspoon caviar, and decorate with a small piece of fennel frond. If the oysters seem to need it, add a drop or two of the remaining marinade. Serve immediately.

Warm Oysters with Sauerkraut & Caviar

I first began serving oysters with wilted Savoy cabbage years ago, when seemingly every chef in France was turning out irreverent takes on classic dishes, such as pairing fish with choucroute—a previously unheard-of duo. It occurred to me that sauerkraut, which, of course, is made with cabbage, would bring more flavor to this dish, with its own distinct brininess complementing that of the oyster.

As elegant and delicious as this is, it's also very easy to make: A quick sauce is fashioned from the oysters' poaching liquid, cream, butter, and lemon; the oysters and sauce are spooned into half-shells; and a pinch of caviar on top reinforces the oysters' salinity.

You can present the filled shells atop coarse salt or seaweed to keep them from tipping over. If using seaweed, blanch it, then shock it in ice water to brighten its green color.

20 oysters, preferably Pemaquid or other large East Coast variety

Juice of ½ lemon

¾ cup heavy cream

½ cup sauerkraut, drained but not rinsed and coarsely chopped

Black pepper from a mill

2 tablespoons chopped fresh chives

2 tablespoons chopped fresh dill

1 to 2 tablespoons American paddlefish or other black caviar

SERVES 4

Preheat the oven to 300°F.

Shuck the oysters (see page 32), save the rounded bottom shells, and reserve the liquor. Rinse the shells, pat dry, put them on a baking sheet, and keep warm in the oven.

Pour the oyster liquor, lemon juice, and cream into a heavy-bottomed, nonreactive saucepan, bring to a boil, and reduce by half. Stir in the sauerkraut, add a couple of grinds from the pepper mill, lower the heat to medium, and cook out any excess moisture, about 5 minutes. (You want to reduce the sauce until it is extremely thick before adding the oysters; no matter how well drained they are, they will give off some liquid and thin the sauce.) Add the oysters and cook until the edges just begin to curl, about 2 minutes. Remove from the heat and stir in the chives and dill.

Make a bed of seaweed or coarse salt on each of 4 plates and arrange 5 oyster shells on top. Spoon an oyster with some sauerkraut and sauce into each shell, then top with some caviar. Serve immediately.

Vegetables & Shellfish à la Grecque

À la grecque is French for "in the Greek style" and refers to vegetables, most famously artichokes, cooked in olive oil and lemon juice. My version is a shellfish dish that takes the *à la grecque* preparation as its starting point, adding coriander, shallots, white wine, tomato, saffron, and oregano for a lovely, aromatic, arrestingly rust-tinted broth that is then emulsified with olive oil—if you know a good, smooth one (as opposed to a harsh or aggressive one), use it. The result is a creamy sauce that coats the shellfish and vegetables. This is a perfect example of a starter that can double as a light lunch. It's very satisfying and complete.

You can add vegetables, or substitute some. Possibilities include pearl onions, button mushrooms, and yellow squash.

Put the shallots, garlic, coriander, water, wine, tomato paste, saffron, bay leaves, peppercorns, and oregano in a very large heavy-bottomed pot over medium-high heat and bring to a boil. Reduce the heat to medium-low and simmer for 20 minutes. Strain through a fine-mesh strainer set over a bowl. (At this point, you can let it cool completely, then cover and refrigerate for up to 3 days or freeze for 2 weeks.)

When ready to proceed, pour the broth into a large heavy-bottomed saucepan and bring to a boil.

Meanwhile, use a sharp paring knife to "turn" the artichokes, cutting them down to their bottoms, but leaving some of the peeled stem. Carefully place the artichokes in the boiling broth and cook until tender but not too soft, about 25 minutes. Use a slotted spoon to transfer them to a plate and let cool.

Carefully drop the shrimp into the hot liquid and cook for 1 minute. Use the slotted spoon to transfer them to a bowl to cool. Put the mussels in the pot, transferring them as they open to a separate bowl. Discard any that don't open after 5 minutes. Add the scallops to the boiling broth, removing them to a separate bowl after 2 minutes. Follow with the zucchini for 1½ to 2 minutes, then the carrot for 3 minutes. The vegetables should be tender but still slightly *al dente*.

Reduce the cooking liquid over high heat to about ⅔ cup, cooking for about 10 minutes. Transfer the reduction to a small bowl and let cool completely. Using an immersion blender, gradually add the olive oil to the reduction to form an emulsion. Stir in the lemon juice and season with salt to taste.

Scoop the chokes out of the artichokes and cut the hearts into quarters. Remove the top shell from each mussel and cut the scallops in half horizontally. Divide the vegetables and shellfish between 4 shallow soup bowls. Evenly divide the sauce among the bowls and garnish with the basil. Serve immediately.

1½ cups coarsely chopped shallots (about 3 large shallots)

¼ cup coarsely chopped garlic (about 6 cloves)

2 tablespoons coriander seeds

8 cups water

6 cups dry white wine

1 tablespoon tomato paste

½ teaspoon saffron threads

4 bay leaves, preferably fresh

1 teaspoon black peppercorns

1 tablespoon dried oregano

2 large artichokes, trimmed, outer leaves removed, and stems peeled

8 ounces medium shrimp, peeled and deveined

8 ounces mussels (preferably Prince Edward Island), rinsed and debearded

4 medium dry sea scallops (about 4 ounces)

1 small zucchini, cut into ⅛-inch-thick rounds

1 medium carrot, cut into ⅛-inch-thick rounds

1 cup good-quality extra-virgin olive oil

1 teaspoon freshly squeezed lemon juice

Kosher salt

2 tablespoons fresh basil cut into chiffonade (see Prep Talk, page 70)

SERVES 4

Two 1¼-pound lobsters

1 medium bulb fennel,
cored and cut into ½-inch chunks

2 large Spanish onions,
cut into ½-inch chunks

3 garlic heads, unpeeled,
cut in half horizontally

2 cups canned whole tomatoes,
with their juice (about 18 ounces)

½ cup plus 1 teaspoon pastis,
such as Pernod or Ricard

½ teaspoon crumbled saffron threads

3 small pieces dried orange peel

3 bay leaves, preferably fresh

10 cups Fish Stock (page 290)

1 small Spanish onion,
coarsely chopped

1 medium carrot, coarsely chopped

5 large egg whites

1 teaspoon powdered gelatin

Kosher salt

1 medium red bell pepper

¼ cup plus 1 teaspoon olive oil

½ teaspoon sherry vinegar

¼ teaspoon Dijon mustard

1 medium bulb fennel, trimmed
and shaved on a mandoline or
very thinly sliced by hand

1 tablespoon freshly squeezed
lemon juice

Black pepper from a mill

¼ cup Lemon-Saffron Aïoli
(page 295)

SERVES 4

Lobster with Bouillabaisse Aspic

I'll admit it: I first imagined this dish as a seafood terrine, but quickly realized that the amount of gelatin it would have taken to hold it together would have made the end result too solid. I decided to try a different tack, infusing a stock with the flavors of a bouillabaisse (pastis, tomatoes, saffron), then making a gelled soup from it and topping it with lobster—it worked beautifully. In many respects this is a deconstructed bouillabaisse with certain essential elements present: saffron in an aïoli, and the rouille, a red pepper–based condiment traditionally served with bouillabaisse, reimagined as a red pepper coulis. If you want to skip one component, leave out the aïoli.

Bring a large pot of salted water to a boil.

Kill the lobsters quickly by holding each one to face you, then driving a large knife between the eyes and pulling it down through the head, like a lever. Cut the heads into 6 pieces each and set aside. Separate the claws and tail from the bodies. Put the claws in the boiling water for 1 minute, then add the tails and boil for 2 more minutes. Use tongs to remove them from the water and set aside to cool to room temperature. Remove the meat from the shells; it will be slightly undercooked. Remove the digestive tract, transfer the lobster meat to a bowl, cover with plastic wrap, and refrigerate until ready to use, for up to 2 days.

Put the reserved lobster heads, fennel chunks, onion chunks, garlic, tomatoes, ½ cup of the pastis, the saffron, orange peel, bay leaves, and stock in a large heavy-bottomed pot. Bring to a boil, then reduce the heat to medium-low, and simmer until 6 to 7 cups remain, about 1 hour. Strain the broth through a fine-mesh strainer set over a large bowl, cover with plastic wrap, and refrigerate until completely cold, for up to 3 days.

Pour the cold broth into a medium heavy-bottomed saucepan over low heat. Add the chopped onion, carrot,

and egg whites, whisking them into the broth. Slowly bring to a simmer, stirring occasionally. When the egg whites and vegetables form a "raft" on top of the broth, stop stirring, but continue to simmer until the raft firms up and becomes solid as the egg whites cook, 20 to 30 minutes. Use a slotted spoon to remove and discard the raft. Strain through a cheesecloth-lined colander set over a bowl. Wipe out the saucepan and return the strained broth to it. Set over low heat and sprinkle in the gelatin, stirring to dissolve it. Season generously to taste with salt. Transfer the aspic to a pan, cover with plastic wrap, and refrigerate to firm it up, for at least 2 hours and up to 2 days.

To make the red pepper coulis, preheat the oven to 400°F.

Rub the pepper with 1 teaspoon of the olive oil and set on a baking sheet. Roast in the oven, turning to ensure even cooking, until wrinkled and charred all over. Transfer to a heatproof bowl, cover with plastic wrap, and let steam in its own heat for about 10 minutes. Remove the plastic and, when the pepper is cool enough to handle, remove the skin and seeds, using a paring knife

to scrape them if necessary. Put the pepper's flesh and juice in a food processor fitted with a steel blade. Add the vinegar, mustard, and ¼ teaspoon salt. Blend and, with the motor running, slowly drizzle in the remaining ¼ cup oil in a thin stream to form a vibrant, red emulsion. (The coulis can be refrigerated in an airtight container for up to 4 hours.)

To make the fennel salad, put the sliced fennel in a medium bowl. Add the lemon juice, the remaining

1 teaspoon pastis, 1 teaspoon salt, and a few grinds of pepper. Toss and let stand at room temperature for at least 10 minutes or refrigerate for up to 4 hours.

To serve, ladle one-quarter of the aspic into each of 4 chilled soup plates and place 2 tablespoons of the fennel salad in the center. Lay 1 lobster claw and half a lobster tail on top of each. Drizzle each serving with 1 tablespoon of the aïoli and 1 tablespoon of the coulis and serve immediately.

Steamed Zucchini Blossoms with Lobster & Shrimp Mousseline & Lemongrass Butter

½ cup coarsely chopped shallots

4 Thai lime leaves, thinly sliced

2 stalks lemongrass, outer layers removed, tender inner layers sliced and bruised to release their juice

1 cup dry white wine

2 tablespoons freshly squeezed lime juice

2 cups heavy cream

½ pound (2 sticks) unsalted butter, cubed and chilled

Kosher salt

8 ounces shrimp, peeled, deveined, and coarsely chopped

6 ounces precooked lobster meat (from one 1¼-pound lobster)

2 large egg whites

¼ teaspoon Tabasco sauce

½ teaspoon sugar

1½ teaspoons Asian fish sauce

8 large or 12 medium zucchini blossoms, fuzzy orange pistils removed

8 or 12 baby zucchini, tips trimmed with a diagonal cut (use the same number as you do zucchini blossoms)

15 fresh Thai or regular basil leaves, thinly sliced

SERVES 4

This dish sounds Italian—zucchini blossoms are one of the quintessential summer foods in Italy—but the truth is that this is a nifty way of serving a quenelle, essentially gift-wrapping it in a sweet, steamed, golden package, sauced with a Asian-inspired lemongrass butter. It's an elegant presentation that's easily achieved, a rare thing. The size of zucchini blossoms, and zucchini, varies dramatically, so I've indicated a range of eight to twelve for each here; the larger they are, the fewer you will need.

Many fish stores sell precooked lobster meat, which would be a good time-saving choice in this recipe.

Put the shallots, lime leaves, lemongrass, wine, and lime juice in a large heavy-bottomed saucepan over medium-low heat, bring to a simmer, and cook until the pan is nearly dry, about 10 minutes. Add ½ cup of the cream, raise the heat to medium, and bring to a boil. Reduce the heat to medium-low and whisk in the cold butter cubes a few at a time until they're completely emulsified and the sauce is smooth and thickened. Season to taste with salt and strain it through a fine-mesh strainer set over a bowl. (The lemongrass butter can be made up to 1 hour in advance of serving and kept warm in a double boiler; don't let it solidify or it will separate when reheated.)

Bring a small pot of water to a boil.

Put the shrimp, lobster, egg whites, Tabasco, sugar, fish sauce, and 1 teaspoon salt in a food processor fitted with a steel blade and process until smooth. With the machine running, add the remaining 1½ cups cream through the feed tube in a slow stream and process until evenly combined. Drop a small spoonful of the filling into the boiling water to poach for a minute or two. Remove from the water, let cool enough to taste, then correct the seasoning of the remaining filling with additional salt, Tabasco, and/or fish sauce if necessary.

Fill a pastry bag fitted with a medium plain tip with the seafood filling. Prepare a 12-inch steaming basket or stacked baskets set over a pan of simmering water. Pipe the mousse evenly into the zucchini blossoms, leaving just enough room to fold the tops of the blossoms over and under to securely encase the filling.

Leaving the base intact, slice each baby zucchini lengthwise, 4 slices for small zucchini, 5 for larger ones, so that the vegetable can be fanned yet remain whole when cooked. Transfer the blossoms and the baby zucchini to the steamer to cook until the blossoms feel firm when gently pressed, 5 to 6 minutes.

Ladle the lemongrass butter evenly among 4 salad plates. Place 2 or 3 blossoms and 2 or 3 zucchini fans on top of the butter and garnish with the basil. Serve immediately.

Grilled Seafood Sausage with Beurre Blanc Sauce

This dish, served in exactly this way, was one of the first things I cooked for one of those dinner parties Karen and I used to throw in our apartment nearly thirty years ago, and it's been a favorite at Chanterelle since we opened our doors in 1979. It's a study in contrasts: the salinity of the fish against the smoky flavor imparted by the grill; the vinegar and butter in the sauce; and the sauce and sausage themselves.

The idea of a seafood sausage might sound intimidating, but it's surprisingly approachable. First, although it features a variety of fish and shellfish, the only one that needs to be cooked before being put into the sausage is the lobster (if you like, you can purchase already cooked diced lobster meat from many fishmongers; you may also substitute half a pound of crabmeat). Second, the sauce is a very straightforward affair that asks little of you other than patient reducing.

The one daunting task, of course, is stuffing the sausages, but there are actually two ways to pull this off at home. One is to use a sausage-stuffing attachment for an electric mixer. The other is to put the stuffing in a pastry bag and pipe it into the casings; but beware—don't rush this step or you risk tearing the casing.

Attention to a few details is key to getting these to come out right: Be sure to start with cold fish and shellfish, to preserve its freshness and make it easier to handle; add the cream very, very slowly so that the mousse holds together well; and poach the sausage at a gentle simmer.

To make the sausage, bring a large pot of salted water to a boil.

Kill the lobster quickly by holding it to face you, then driving a knife between its eyes and pulling it down toward you, like a lever. Separate the claws and tail from the body. Put the claws in the boiling water for 1 minute, then add the tail and boil for another 2 minutes. Use tongs to remove them from the water, and let cool to room temperature. Remove the meat from the shells (it will be slightly undercooked) and remove the digestive tract. Coarsely chop the meat.

Put 2 tablespoons each of the chopped shrimp and scallops, and all of the sea bass, in a food processor fitted with a steel blade. Add 1 teaspoon of the salt and the egg white. Process to a mousse texture, then, with the machine still running, very slowly add 1 cup plus 2 tablespoons of the cream through the feed tube in a steady, thin stream. Transfer the mousse to a large bowl and fold in the remaining seafood, as well as the brandy, port, cayenne, and pine nuts. Stir in the remaining ½ teaspoon salt. The filling should be fluffy, light pink, and firm.

continued

FOR THE SAUSAGE:

One 1¼-pound lobster or 6 ounces precooked lobster meat

6 ounces shrimp (any size), peeled, deveined, coarsely chopped, and chilled

6 ounces dry sea scallops, coarsely chopped and chilled

8 ounces striped sea bass, skinned, any pin bones removed, cut into 1-inch chunks, and chilled

1½ teaspoons kosher salt

1 large egg white

1¼ cups plus 2 tablespoons heavy cream

1 teaspoon brandy

2 teaspoons ruby port

⅛ teaspoon cayenne

¼ cup pine nuts, toasted in a 300°F oven until lightly colored, about 10 minutes

2 feet pork casings, washed under cold running water, letting the water run through them to rinse out the salt

FOR THE BEURRE BLANC SAUCE:

½ cup finely diced shallots

1 cup dry white wine

¼ cup red wine vinegar

¼ cup heavy cream

½ pound (2 sticks) unsalted butter, cut into large cubes and chilled

Kosher salt

Black pepper from a mill

TO COOK THE SAUSAGE:

¼ cup (½ stick) unsalted butter, melted

SERVES 4

Prepare a pastry bag with a ½-inch plain tip and fill it with the mousse. Pipe the mixture into the pork casings by scrunching the casing onto the pastry tip and gently but tightly filling the casing. Use a pin to puncture the casing if an air pocket develops. Use cotton butcher's twine to tie the sausage at 5-inch lengths, securing the links at both ends.

Bring a large pot of water to a boil, then reduce the heat to a gentle simmer. Add all the sausage to the water and poach until firm and opaque, about 30 minutes. Turn off the heat and hold the sausage in the pot for 5 minutes. Use tongs to remove it from the water, drain well, and chill until ready to broil, preferably overnight. (The sausage can be wrapped in plastic wrap and refrigerated for up to 3 days.)

Meanwhile, to make the beurre blanc, put the shallots, wine, and vinegar in a nonreactive saucepan set over medium-high heat. Bring to a boil and reduce, stirring frequently, until the pan is almost dry, about 15 minutes. Whisk in the remaining ¼ cup cream and simmer the sauce to reduce and thicken it, about 3 more minutes. Lower the heat to medium and whisk in a few cubes of the cold butter at a time until they are all incorporated into a thick, emulsified butter sauce. Season with salt and pepper to taste. Keep warm in the top of a double boiler for up to 1 hour.

Preheat the broiler and arrange the chilled seafood sausages on a broiler pan. Score each sausage diagonally at ½-inch intervals and brush generously with the melted butter. Broil the sausages on one side only until browned, about 3 minutes. Move the pan down to a lower rack, turn the links over, and cook until warm all the way through, about another 2 minutes.

Arrange 1 sausage on each of 4 plates and spoon some beurre blanc sauce decoratively around the plate. Serve immediately.

Pike Quenelles
with Black Truffles & Lettuce

A touchstone that takes me back to those pre-theater dinners with my parents, quenelles—gently poached dumplings—are one of the proudly old-fashioned French preparations that we've always made room for on the Chanterelle menu, and probably always will. Not that my approach to making them is old-fashioned: The classic recipe features a panade, or breadcrumb mixture, that binds the fish, but I've found relying on egg white results in a lighter, fluffier, more luxurious quenelle. I also use Asian fish sauce to intensify the ocean flavor. Quenelles turn up all over the place on my menu, from soups to main courses.

This quenelle dish pays tribute to a trout mousse with a truffle sauce served by Fernand Point at La Pyramide restaurant, although my version is considerably different, except for, of course, the combination of truffles and fish.

In a food processor fitted with a steel blade, puree the pike, egg white, fish sauce, and 1 teaspoon of the salt. Slowly, with the motor running, add 2 cups of the cream through the feed tube until fully incorporated. Using the back of a wooden spoon or a rubber spatula, pass the mixture through a fine-mesh strainer set over a bowl, separating any remaining fish sinew from the puree. Gently fold in the cayenne and nutmeg. Cover with plastic wrap and refrigerate until very cold, about 20 minutes.

Line a plate with paper towels. Pour the wine, 2 cups of the fish stock, and the water into a large heavy-bottomed saucepan over high heat. Add the remaining 2 tablespoons salt and bring to a simmer. Drop a small spoonful of the pike puree into the boiling water to poach for a minute or two, allowing it to cool slightly before tasting. Based on the flavor, adjust the puree's seasoning with more salt

and/or fish sauce if necessary. Use a large tablespoon to form 8 quenelles with the puree (see Prep Talk, page 101) and carefully place them in the poaching liquid. Reduce the heat to low (or so there is no visible bubbling) and poach the quenelles until their color lightens, about 5 minutes. Use a slotted spoon to turn them over and continue poaching until they are firm, uniformly light, and slightly puffy, another 5 minutes or so. Use a slotted spoon to gently lift out and transfer them to the lined plate to drain and cool. (The quenelles can be refrigerated for up to 3 days; wrap the plate well with plastic and let come to room temperature before proceeding with the recipe.)

Spread the softened butter over the bottom of a large heavy-bottomed sauté pan or sauteuse (see page 145) and place the quenelles on top. Pour in the remaining 1 cup

continued

12 ounces pike fillet (other white fish such as halibut or hake may be substituted), skin removed, cut into 1-inch chunks, and chilled

1 large egg white, chilled

¾ teaspoon Asian fish sauce

1 teaspoon plus 2 tablespoons kosher salt

3½ cups chilled heavy cream

Pinch of cayenne

Pinch of freshly grated nutmeg

2 cups dry white wine

3 cups Fish Stock (page 290)

4 cups water

2 tablespoons unsalted butter, softened at room temperature

1 cup canned black truffle juice

2 tablespoons medium-dry Madeira, plus more to taste

2 tablespoons finely chopped fresh, flash-frozen, or canned black truffle

Black pepper from a mill

½ teaspoon freshly squeezed lemon juice, plus more to taste

3 cups Boston lettuce sliced into ½-inch-wide ribbons (from about 1 large head)

SERVES 4

stock, the truffle juice, and Madeira, and add the chopped truffles. Bring to a boil, reduce the heat to medium, cover, and cook for 5 minutes, turning the quenelles as they puff up slightly during the cooking process. Remove the pan's lid and reduce the liquid by half, another 2 to 3 minutes. Add the remaining 1½ cups cream and bring to a boil, then reduce the heat to medium-low, cover, and simmer for 4 to 5 minutes. Remove the lid, raise the heat to medium, and cook the sauce until it has thickened and the quenelles are noticeably puffed, another 2 to 3 minutes. Season the sauce to taste with salt and pepper, lemon juice, and a bit more Madeira, if desired. Add the lettuce to the pan, very gently mixing it in and allowing it just to wilt.

To serve, use a slotted spoon to place 2 quenelles on each of 4 plates. Spoon the sauce and lettuce alongside the fish and serve immediately.

PREP TALK

Making Quenelles

There are two ways to make quenelles. The simplest is to purchase an oval ice cream scoop with a bowl sweep that will release each quenelle with the press of the scoop's trigger. The traditional method is to scoop some of the item with a tablespoon, then work the food back and forth between two tablespoons until you end up with a football-shaped orb. Dip the spoons in warm water between quenelles to keep them from becoming sticky.

Terrine of Smoked Salmon with Cucumber-Vodka Granita

1 large English (hothouse) cucumber, coarsely chopped

¼ cup citrus-flavored vodka

1 tablespoon plus ½ teaspoon freshly squeezed lemon juice

½ teaspoon kosher salt

One 8-ounce piece smoked salmon, cut into 1-inch chunks

½ pound (2 sticks) unsalted butter, melted and slightly cooled

2 tablespoons heavy cream

10 ounces thinly sliced smoked salmon

¼ cup American black caviar, such as paddlefish (about 96 grams)

4 slices white bread, toasted, crusts removed, and quartered diagonally

SERVES 8

The foundation of this dish is the Russian tradition of pairing caviar and vodka, the clear, odorless spirit cleansing the palate between samples of the exquisitely fine, salty fish eggs. The terrine incorporates other elements you might find at a caviar tasting—smoked salmon, cream, and an accompaniment of toast points—and the vodka is present in a granita, or shaved ice, featuring cucumber and lemon. This is an almost absurdly luxurious starter, a fantasy of a caviar plate recast in the Chanterelle style. It's also visually stunning, with the black caviar popping against the pink salmon and the light green granita in its sidecar alongside.

You will need to purchase smoked salmon in two forms: one half-pound piece for dicing, plus a quantity of presliced salmon; it's the only way to get the two sizes and shapes called for here. As with the blintzes in the hors d'oeuvres chapter, I suggest you use a Norwegian-style salmon.

This recipe serves 8; there's just no way to make a smaller terrine.

To make the granita, put the cucumber, vodka, 1 tablespoon of the lemon juice, and the salt in a food processor fitted with a steel blade and process until smooth. Pour the mixture into a shallow metal pan, cover, and freeze until ice crystals form, about 1 hour. Stir the granita a bit, then freeze for another 2 hours, or overnight, scraping the crystals with a fork 3 or 4 times to create a fluffy, shaved ice.

Put the smoked salmon chunks in the food processor (after first wiping it clean). With the machine running, puree the salmon while adding the melted butter in a slow stream through the feed tube. As the mousse comes together, pour in the remaining ½ teaspoon lemon juice and the cream. Pass the mousse through a fine-mesh strainer set over a bowl, pressing it through the mesh with a rubber spatula or the back of wooden spoon. Cover the bowl with plastic wrap and refrigerate for 30 to 45 minutes to chill the mousse and give it some body. (The mousse can be made up to 2 days in advance of serving.)

Line the bottom and sides of a 3½ x 6½ x 2½-inch terrine mold with smoked salmon slices, allowing excess slices to drape over the top of the terrine with enough surplus to overlap and enclose the terrine once it is filled. Use a small offset spatula to spread a ⅛-inch-thick layer of salmon mousse along the bottom of the terrine. Top the mousse with 1 tablespoon of the caviar, spread across the length and width of the terrine. Cover the caviar with a single layer of sliced salmon. Repeat the layers—mousse, caviar, sliced salmon—3 more times. It may be necessary to chill the terrine in between layers as it is being built so as to keep the caviar from blending into the salmon mousse. Fold the draped salmon slices over the last layer to enclose the terrine top. Wrap the terrine well with plastic wrap and refrigerate for at least 2 hours or up to 2 days.

Cut the terrine into 8 equal slices and place a slice on each of 8 plates. Put a scoop of granita in a ramekin alongside the terrine on each plate. Serve the toast points from a passed plate or add them to the plate with the terrine and granita.

Duo of Tartares with Golden & Red Beets

I'm not one to bring ingredients into a dish for the sake of their presentation value, but every once in a while, happy coincidences occur and, in conceiving a new dish, you end up with a visually striking one. That was certainly the case here, as pairing two types of tuna with two varieties of beets led to a kaleidoscopic array of red, white, and golden hues. As lovely as this is, you can make it with all red beets and tuna and it will still be delicious.

Whenever you are serving raw fish, be sure to procure sushi-grade pieces from a reputable source. To further ensure the fish is kept as cold as possible, I recommend chilling the plates for a half an hour before serving. Be sure to have a very sharp knife on hand for thinly slicing the raw fish.

This recipe calls for white soy sauce, a traditional Japanese product fermented and brewed like regular (dark) soy sauce, but with a higher proportion of wheat to soy, which gives it a paler color and a more intense salty flavor. It is often used with fish.

Preheat the oven to 325°F.

Place each type of beet in a separate covered ovenproof pan and sprinkle with a little olive oil, salt, and pepper. Pour water into each pan to a depth of about 1 inch, then roast, shaking the pans occasionally, until the beets are very tender to a knife tip, about 2 hours, depending on size.

Let the beets cool until you can handle them, then, taking care to keep them separate, so that the red color doesn't leech onto the golden, slip off their skins and slice the beets ⅛ inch thick. Set aside 16 of the nicest slices of each color of beet, covered. Finely dice the remaining beets, still keeping the colors separate, and set aside. (The diced beets can be refrigerated overnight.)

To prepare the tartares: For the red tuna and golden beets, in a medium bowl, whisk together 2 tablespoons of the scallions, the lemon juice, white soy sauce, and 1½ tablespoons of the sesame oil. Finely dice the red tuna by hand, then toss it with half the dressing. Toss the remaining dressing with the diced golden beets.

For the yellowtail and red beets, in a medium bowl, whisk together the remaining 2 tablespoons scallions and 1½ tablespoons sesame oil, the regular soy sauce, and vinegar. Finely chop the yellowtail tuna by hand, then toss it with half the dressing. Toss the remaining dressing with the diced red beets.

On each of 4 plates—ideally round, oval, or rectangular—place 2 slices of golden beet and 2 of red, alternating colors. On each plate, top 1 slice of golden beet with red tuna tartare and the other with the diced red beets. Top 1 slice of red beet with the yellowtail tartare and the other with the diced golden beets. Garnish the red tuna with wasabi tobiko, if desired, and the yellowtail with red tobiko, if desired, and serve at once.

2 large red beets (about 8 ounces each), scrubbed and trimmed

2 large golden beets (about 8 ounces each) or an additional 2 red beets, scrubbed and trimmed

Extra-virgin olive oil, for drizzling

Coarse sea salt or kosher salt

Black pepper from a mill

¼ cup chopped scallions (white and light green parts)

1 tablespoon freshly squeezed lemon juice

1 tablespoon plus 1 teaspoon white soy sauce (see Headnote)

3 tablespoons toasted sesame oil

8 ounces sushi-grade tuna

1 tablespoon plus 1 teaspoon soy sauce

1 tablespoon plus 1 teaspoon balsamic vinegar

8 ounces sushi-grade yellowtail (hamachi)

¼ ounce wasabi tobiko (optional)

¼ ounce red tobiko (optional)

SERVES 4

Duck Terrine with Pistachios & Armagnac

Two 5-pound Muscovy ducks, skin removed from the breasts but left on the legs, the livers and hearts cut into large chunks

1 large garlic clove, minced

1 large shallot, minced

¼ cup ruby port

½ cup Armagnac

1 pound French or Canadian duck foie gras, in one piece, plus 6 ounces French or Canadian duck foie gras, cut into chunks

Pinch of pink curing salt (optional)

Kosher salt

1 cup Sauternes or other sweet wine, such as Muscat

1 large egg

½ teaspoon freshly grated nutmeg

½ teaspoon ground allspice

¼ teaspoon ground mace

¼ teaspoon freshly ground black pepper

¼ cup shelled unsalted pistachios

1 pound caul fat or pork fat back

5 bay leaves, preferably fresh

Duck Aspic (optional; recipe follows), coarsely chopped or cubed

SERVES 10

Classically terrines are made with a variety of ingredients that steal attention from what is supposedly its focus. (Our sommelier's father once said of a pheasant terrine that the taste of the bird was so faint that it was as if "the pheasant merely flew over it.") When I make a duck terrine, I want it to taste as ducky as possible, which is why this one is made with duck fat instead of the traditional pork (although the terrine itself is still lined with caul fat). I like to serve this along with cornichons and olives, and perhaps a simple salad.

Note that you will need a meat grinder with chilled fine- and medium-hole disks, cheesecloth, caul fat or very thinly sliced fat back, and a 3¼ x 11½-inch terrine dish with a 5-cup capacity.

Put the ducks, garlic, shallot, port, Armagnac, and the 6 ounces of the foie gras chunks in a large bowl, stir very gently, cover with plastic wrap, and refrigerate for 24 hours.

On a clean, dry surface, use a paring knife to carefully remove the veins that run through the remaining 16 ounces foie gras (see page 47). Put the cleaned foie gras in a large bowl, sprinkle it with the pink salt (if using) and 1 tablespoon kosher salt, and submerge it in ice water, gently agitating to dissolve the salts. Allow the foie gras to soak for about 1 hour.

Drain the foie gras, place it in a medium bowl, and pour in the Sauternes. Cover with plastic wrap or cheesecloth and refrigerate overnight.

When ready to proceed, drain the foie gras and transfer it to a dry, clean kitchen towel.

Finely grind half of the chilled marinated duck mixture, along with any remaining marinade, in a meat grinder. Place in a large bowl. Grind the remaining mixture to a medium grind. Add to the same bowl along with the egg, nutmeg, allspice, mace, pepper, pistachios, and 5 teaspoons kosher salt. Stir together with a rubber spatula or wooden spoon, cover with plastic wrap, and keep cold in the refrigerator.

Drain the Sauternes-marinated foie gras. Shape it into a cylinder by rolling it in cheesecloth and twisting the ends gently, as if wringing a towel.

Line the terrine dish with the caul fat, allowing the excess to flop over the sides (it will later be used to encase the terrine). Press the forcemeat mixture into the bottom of the mold, to a height of ½ inch. Remove the cheesecloth from the foie gras roll, place the roll into the mold over the first layer, and hold it centered as you press the remaining forcemeat over and around it. Arrange the bay leaves on top and enclose with the dangling caul fat.

Preheat the oven to 325°F.

Cover the dish with aluminum foil and set it in a roasting pan. Pour hot water into the pan until it comes halfway up the sides of the terrine. Bake until an instant-read thermometer inserted into the center registers 130°F, about 1½ hours.

Remove the roasting pan from the oven and carefully remove the terrine from the pan. Let cool at room temperature for 30 minutes. Weight the terrine down with an empty terrine dish and chill in the refrigerator overnight.

To serve, carefully unmold the terrine onto a plate and cut it into ½-inch-thick slices. Serve with the duck aspic mounded attractively on each slice.

Duck Aspic

Because it's often bland and rubbery, many believe aspic exists for purely visual reasons, but if made with a high-quality stock such as the homemade duck stock here, it can make a powerful flavor statement in its own right. Serve this very traditional garnish with duck terrine or as an accompaniment to foie gras.

Put the stock, egg whites, vinegar, onions, and carrot in a large heavy-bottomed saucepan over medium heat and slowly bring to a simmer, stirring occasionally, until a "raft" of egg whites forms on top, about 25 minutes. Stop stirring and cook the broth until reduced to 4 cups, another 20 minutes. Use a spoon to skim off the raft and discard it.

Strain the broth through a cheesecloth-lined strainer set over a bowl. Stir in the gelatin until it dissolves. Stir in the port and season generously to taste with salt. (Bear in mind that the aspic will be served chilled, so it should be assertively seasoned; cold temperatures tend to dull the palate.)

The finished aspic can be cut into whatever shapes you like, so chill it in an appropriate vessel: For thin shapes, choose a rimmed baking sheet or other shallow tray-like pan, and for thicker shapes, choose a smaller container with more depth.

Cover the aspic with plastic wrap and refrigerate until cold and set, at least 8 hours. It will keep in the refrigerator for up to 3 days.

Cut into decorative shapes and serve alongside the duck terrine.

8 cups Duck Stock (page 296), reduced to 6 cups in a simmering pot and fully chilled

3 large egg whites

1 teaspoon red wine vinegar

1½ medium Spanish onions, coarsely chopped

1 medium carrot, unpeeled, coarsely chopped

4 teaspoons powdered gelatin

1 tablespoon ruby port, plus more to taste

Kosher salt

MAKES ABOUT 4 CUPS

Potato Risotto with Sautéed Foie Gras

1 cup balsamic vinegar

Kosher salt

2 tablespoons unsalted butter

1 cup thinly sliced cremini mushroom caps (from about 5 mushrooms)

2 tablespoons finely diced shallot

1½ cups Yukon Gold potatoes cut into brunoise (from about 5 medium potatoes), held in cold water until needed

1 cup Mushroom Stock (page 290)

3 tablespoons freshly grated Parmigiano-Reggiano cheese

Black pepper from a mill

Wondra or all-purpose flour, for dredging

6 ounces duck foie gras (preferably New York State or Hudson Valley), cut into 4 equal slices

SERVES 4

This dish, one of Karen's all-time favorites, began with a simple observation: that the grains of rice in risotto are bound together by the starch they release when cooked. Considering this one day, it occurred to me to try making a "risotto" with finely diced potato. (In truth, I was also inspired by chef Charlie Trotter's recipe for butternut squash risotto.) The result worked so well that I built a composition around it, adding mushrooms (and using a mushroom stock for the risotto), sautéed foie gras, and a drizzle of balsamic reduction.

The most time-consuming part of the recipe is cutting the potatoes into the tiny cubes called *brunoise.* One good way to do this is to use a mandoline to cut the potato into thin strips (julienne) and then slice them crosswise into the smallest possible cubes.

While you could serve this without the foie gras, it really isn't complete that way; if you're looking for a less expensive or more user-friendly option, top the risotto with sautéed chicken livers.

Bring the vinegar to a boil in a small heavy-bottomed saucepan over medium-high heat, then reduce the heat to low and gently simmer until reduced to ¼ cup, about 20 minutes. Swirl in a pinch of salt, and set aside.

Put 1 tablespoon of the butter in a large heavy-bottomed sauté pan set over medium-high heat. When it is melted and hot, add the mushrooms and cook, tossing a few times, until softened, about 3 minutes. Add the shallot, then drain the potatoes and add them to the pan as well. Sauté for another minute or so, taking care not to let the vegetables brown. Add the stock, ¼ cup at a time, stirring frequently and allowing the potatoes to absorb the liquid, about 2 to 3 minutes, before adding more. (You should use all the stock.) When the potatoes are softened but still hold their shape, gently stir in the remaining 1 tablespoon butter and the cheese. Season to taste with salt and pepper and set aside, covered, to keep warm.

Put some flour in a shallow bowl or pan and dredge the foie gras slices through it to lightly coat both sides. Heat a medium heavy-bottomed sauté pan over high heat, letting it get very hot. Carefully place the foie gras slices in the pan and sear for 30 to 40 seconds per side, browning them well and warming them through. Remove from the pan and use a paper towel to blot any excess fat.

Divide the risotto evenly among 4 soup bowls or plates and place 1 foie gras slice on top of each serving. Drizzle some of the balsamic reduction decoratively over the dish and serve immediately.

Sautéed Foie Gras
with Hash Browns & Horseradish Jus

Highbrow meets down-and-dirty in this admittedly quirky-sounding starter that combines one of the most prized ingredients on the planet (foie gras) with my take on a diner staple (hash browns). What do these two components have in common? Decadence and enough presence to complement, not overwhelm, each other. Is it any wonder that this odd couple is sauced with a high-impact horseradish sauce, or that the hash browns are made by combining potatoes and onions cooked in duck fat? It's as obscenely rich as it sounds, which is why the portions are deceptively small.

Heat a large heavy-bottomed saucepan over medium-high heat. Add the wine and shallots and bring to a simmer. Stirring frequently, reduce the wine until almost completely evaporated, about 20 minutes. Add the vinegar, 1 cup of the grated horseradish, and the stock. Bring to a boil, then reduce the heat so the liquid is simmering and cook for 30 minutes. Strain through a fine-mesh strainer set over a medium heavy-bottomed saucepan. Bring to a boil and cook until reduced to 2 cups, about 20 minutes.

In a small bowl, knead together the butter and 1 tablespoon of the all-purpose flour until it forms a paste. Whisk this into the bubbling reduction and continue to reduce the sauce until it yields about 1 cup and has thickened slightly, about 10 minutes more. Season to taste with salt, remove from the heat, and keep covered and warm.

Meanwhile, put the potatoes in a medium heavy-bottomed saucepan. Season generously with salt and add enough cold water to cover them by several inches. Bring to a boil, then reduce the heat so the liquid is simmering and cook until the potatoes are tender to a knife tip but not entirely cooked in the center. Drain and set the potatoes aside to cool.

In small sauté pan over medium heat, melt the duck fat. Add the onion, cover, and allow it to sweat, stirring frequently, until very soft but not caramelized, 15 to 20 minutes. Remove from the heat.

Once the potatoes are cool enough to handle, peel and coarsely chop them, then transfer to a medium bowl. Add the onion, season well with salt and pepper, and toss to combine.

Arrange four 4 x 1-inch ring molds on a clean, dry surface and fill each with equal amounts of the hash brown mixture. While still molded, dust the hash browns on both sides with the remaining 3 tablespoons all-purpose flour. Heat a wide, deep, heavy-bottomed sauté pan over medium-high heat, add the oil, and heat it until a drop of water flicked into the pan sizzles on contact. Carefully place the 4 hash browns, *in their molds,* in the pan and cook until browned and crispy, 4 to 5 minutes per side. Transfer them to a paper towel–lined plate to drain. Once the ring molds are cool enough to handle, gently slide them off. (If necessary, the hash browns can be reheated in a 350°F oven.)

Heat a medium heavy-bottomed sauté pan over high heat. Dredge the foie gras slices in flour to lightly coat. Carefully place the foie gras slices in the pan and sear for 30 to 40 seconds on each side, browning the slices well and warming them through. Remove from the pan and blot any excess fat with a paper towel.

To serve, divide the horseradish sauce evenly among 4 plates. Place one hash brown in the center of the sauce and top with a slice of foie gras. Garnish with the remaining horseradish and serve immediately.

2 cups dry white wine

2 large shallots, coarsely chopped

1 tablespoon sherry vinegar

1 packed cup plus 1 tablespoon peeled and grated fresh horseradish

8 cups Veal Stock (page 294) or Duck Stock (page 296)

1 tablespoon unsalted butter

¼ cup all-purpose flour

Kosher salt

2 medium Yukon Gold potatoes, unpeeled

2 tablespoons rendered duck fat or unsalted butter

1 medium Spanish onion, cut into small dice

Black pepper from a mill

½ cup canola or other neutral oil

Wondra or all-purpose flour, for dredging

6 ounces duck foie gras (preferably New York State or Hudson Valley), cut into 4 equal slices

SERVES 4

Trio of Hot Foie Gras

1 cup balsamic vinegar

Kosher salt

2 tablespoons canola or other neutral oil, plus more for greasing the grill pan

2 medium onions, cut in half and thinly sliced into half moons

1 teaspoon sugar

1 teaspoon red wine vinegar

2 tablespoons dried currants

4 Savoy cabbage leaves

12 ounces duck foie gras (preferably New York State or Hudson Valley), cut into twelve 1-ounce slices

Black pepper from a mill

Wondra or all-purpose flour, for dredging

1 cup loosely packed mesclun greens

Fleur de sel

SERVES 4

This dish offers three of my favorite foie gras preparations: sautéed foie gras set atop a bed of greens and a drizzle of reduced balsamic vinegar; foie gras steamed in Savoy cabbage and seasoned with sea salt (a borrow from Alain Senderens); and grilled foie gras with caramelized onions and currants.

This trio is an ideal dish for people who like to pretend they're chefs at home, working a number of pans at once and plating a lineup of dishes just in time to be rushed out to waiting diners. If you fit this description, this is the dish for you. It requires a lot of focus and timing. I suggest that you read the recipe over several times and have all of your ingredients, equipment, and cooking appliances organized and ready to go so that you can move quickly and not have to refer back to the book too much, if at all. In the end, this is a fairly simple dish with complicated timing, so put your attention into that aspect of it and you should be fine.

Bring the balsamic vinegar to a boil in a small saucepan over medium-high heat, then reduce the heat to low and gently simmer until reduced to ¼ cup, about 20 minutes. Swirl in a pinch of salt, and set aside.

Heat a wide, deep, heavy-bottomed sauté pan over low heat. Add the oil and heat it. Add the onions and cook, tossing occasionally, until they have softened and released their liquid, about 10 minutes. Sprinkle with the sugar and cook until they have browned, about 20 minutes. Pour in the red wine vinegar and use a wooden spoon to scrape up the browned bits from the bottom of the pan. Toss in the currants, add ½ teaspoon salt, and warm the currants through, about 2 minutes. Set aside, keeping warm.

Meanwhile, bring a large pot of water to a boil. Fill a large bowl halfway with ice water. Carefully lower the cabbage leaves into the boiling water and blanch just long enough to wilt, about 15 seconds. Using tongs, transfer them to the ice bath to stop the cooking and preserve their color. Drain well on paper towels.

Arrange the foie gras slices on a clean, dry surface. Season on both sides with salt and pepper.

Prepare a bamboo steamer fit into a pan set over high heat and filled with an inch or two of simmering water. Carefully wrap a slice of foie gras in each of the 4 blanched cabbage leaves, using the weight of the foie gras to hold the wrap together at its seam. Trim the cabbage leaves to fit in the steamer, then set the cabbage-wrapped foie gras slices in it, cover, and steam for 2 minutes.

Dust 4 of the remaining slices of foie gras on both sides with the flour. Heat a large sauté pan over high heat, letting it get very hot. Add the foie gras and sear for 45 seconds on each side.

Meanwhile, heat a grill pan over medium-high heat and grease it with canola oil. Carefully set the last 4 foie gras slices in the pan and sear for 30 seconds on each side, turning them 90 degrees after 15 seconds on each side to create crosshatch grill marks.

To serve, drizzle each of 4 plates with 1 tablespoon of the balsamic reduction. Spoon a heaping tablespoon of caramelized onions on one side of the plate. Pile a few mesclun leaves on the other side. Rest the grilled foie gras on the caramelized onions, the seared foie gras on the lettuce, and the cabbage-wrapped foie gras on another part of the plate. Sprinkle the cabbage-wrapped foie gras with a scant pinch of fleur de sel. Serve immediately.

Terrine of Foie Gras
with Blond Raisins & Black Pepper

1 duck foie gras (about 1½ pounds),
preferably French or Canadian,
at room temperature

Pinch of pink salt
(potassium nitrate; optional)

Kosher salt

One 750 ml bottle Sauternes,
Muscat, or other sweet white wine

¼ cup golden raisins

Sugar

½ cup ground cracked black
peppercorns (available in
supermarkets already cracked
in the spice section)

8 to 16 slices brioche, toasted
and crusts removed

SERVES 8

There's a fair amount of fantasy involved in my kitchen thinking at Chanterelle, and one of the most outlandish imaginings I've ever engaged in was a daydream about foie gras carts. There's no such thing as a foie gras cart, of course, but there are so many irresistible preparations of this most luxurious of all ingredients that I found myself wishing that, rather than choosing just one or two for each month's menu, I could load up a little foie gras trolley with *all* my favorite ones year-round, and have a waiter roll it around the dining room, letting each guest choose the preparations that looked most appealing, the way they do desserts in some restaurants, and cheeses in others, including Chanterelle.

If such a thing existed, this is one of the preparations I would select from the trolley for my own foie gras course. The most successful treatments of foie gras offset its richness with comparably assertive flavors, usually sweet. Here blond raisins (our house way of referring to golden raisins) are marinated in dessert wine, which is often served as an accompanying drink with foie gras. The resulting plump, juicy raisins are layered into the terrine. A counterpoint to both the foie gras and the raisins is provided by a coating of coarsely ground black pepper, offering a gentle heat that cuts right through the creamy foie gras. There are fewer ingredients in this terrine recipe than you'll find in most, but these four ingredients carry the day, conjuring up all the complexity you could ask for.

This is presented simply here, with toasted brioche alongside. Duck Aspic (page 107) and/or a simple salad are also fine accompaniments.

Note that this recipe takes two days and requires two terrine molds.

Fill a large bowl halfway with ice water.

On a clean, dry surface, use a paring knife and your fingers to draw apart, but not entirely separate, the two lobes of the foie gras. Carefully remove the veins that run through the foie gras, dissecting the liver and opening it up to locate and pull them out as you go. Put the cleaned foie gras in a large bowl, sprinkle it with the pink salt (if using) and 1 tablespoon kosher salt, and submerge it in the ice water, gently agitating to dissolve the salts.

Allow the foie gras to soak for about 1 hour.

Meanwhile, put 1 cup of the Sauternes and the raisins in a small bowl.

Drain the foie gras, place it in a medium bowl, and pour in the remaining wine. Cover with plastic wrap or cheesecloth and refrigerate overnight.

When ready to proceed, drain the foie gras and the raisins. Transfer the foie gras to a dry, clean kitchen towel.

Preheat the oven to 200°F.

Evenly sprinkle a pinch of sugar and a generous pinch of salt in the bottom of a 3-cup terrine or casserole. Slice a third of the foie gras and place it in the terrine, pressing it down to cover the sugar and salt. Sprinkle the foie gras with half the raisins, another pinch of sugar, and another generous pinch of salt. Repeat with another third of the foie gras. Top with the last piece of foie gras and one final sprinkling of sugar and salt. (Don't be concerned if the foie gras rises above the terrine's top; it will shrink as it cooks.)

Cover the terrine with parchment paper, then with aluminum foil. Place it in a baking pan and carefully pour enough warm water into the pan to reach midway up the sides of the terrine. Transfer the water bath to the oven and bake for about 40 minutes, checking the temperature in the center of the foie gras at the 30-minute mark with an instant-read thermometer. Remove it from the oven when it registers 95°F in the center. Allow the terrine to cool for 15 minutes before weighting it down with a separate, clean terrine. Cover with plastic wrap and refrigerate overnight.

Dip the bottom of the terrine into a bowl filled with hot water for a minute or two, to loosen the foie gras from the sides. Run a knife around the inner edges, invert the terrine, and release the foie gras onto a large flat surface, allowing any accompanying fats and liquids to drain out of the dish and away from the foie gras. Line a small sheet pan with plastic wrap and sprinkle the entire tray with the cracked pepper. Gently lift the foie gras with a large metal spatula and transfer it to the pan, using your hands to cover it on all sides (but not the ends) with the pepper. (Don't roll it, or it may break.) Wrap the pepper-encrusted foie gras in the plastic and refrigerate it until ready to serve, up to 4 days.

Carefully cut the terrine into ½-inch-thick slices and serve with slices of toasted brioche.

Chanterelle Mushroom & Fingerling Potato Hash with Fried Quail Egg

Kosher salt

8 ounces fingerling potatoes

12 ounces chanterelle mushrooms, stems trimmed

½ cup (1 stick) plus 1 teaspoon unsalted butter

Black pepper from a mill

1 cup Mushroom Stock (page 290)

1 tablespoon Madeira

Juice of 1 lemon

4 quail eggs

8 sprigs fresh chervil

SERVES 4

A vegetarian take on one of the richest breakfast dishes of all time, corned beef hash, this starter finds diced fingerling potatoes and chanterelle mushrooms cooked in generous amounts of butter, topped with a heavily concentrated mushroom sauce, then a just-cooked quail egg that's meant to be broken over the hash. There is nothing subtle about this one: It is pure decadence.

You can find quail eggs at some gourmet markets, or order them from D'Artagnan (see Sources, page 298).

Fill a large pot with cold water. Salt it generously and add the potatoes. Bring to a boil, then reduce the heat to medium-high and cook until the potatoes are just tender when pierced with a knife, about 10 minutes. (Do not overcook or they will crumble when peeled and diced.) Drain in a colander, then turn the potatoes out onto a baking sheet to cool. When just cool enough to handle, peel the potatoes; the skin should come right off with the aid of a paring knife. When they're completely cool, cut them into ½-inch dice.

Put the mushrooms in a large bowl and run under a gentle stream of cold water, carefully submerging them to remove any debris. Drain well, then transfer to a clean kitchen towel to dry.

Melt 3 tablespoons of the butter in a large heavy-bottomed skillet over medium-high heat until foamy. Add half the chanterelles, so as not to crowd the pan, and season with salt and pepper. Cook until they have released much of their liquid, 3 to 4 minutes, then drain in a colander, reserving the liquid. Transfer the mushrooms to a bowl. Repeat with another 3 tablespoons of butter and the remaining chanterelles, draining and reserving their liquid (which should yield about 1 cup in total). Return the skillet to medium-high heat, return the mushrooms to the pan, and cook until dried and nicely browned, 5 to 10 minutes. Transfer to a bowl and carefully wipe out the pan.

Pour 1 cup of the reserved chanterelle cooking liquid, the stock, and Madeira into a medium heavy-bottomed saucepan over high heat and bring to a boil. Lower the heat to medium-high and reduce the sauce to ½ cup, 5 to 10 minutes; it should have a syrupy consistency. Season to taste with salt and a few drops of lemon juice.

Set the skillet you cooked the mushrooms in over medium-high heat and melt 2 tablespoons of the butter until foamy. Add the potatoes and mushrooms and sauté until they are crisp and brown, 12 to 15 minutes. Season to taste with salt and pepper.

Divide the mixture among 4 individual-size gratin dishes and spoon 2 tablespoons of the sauce over each dish.

Wipe out the skillet again and set it over medium heat. Melt the remaining 1 teaspoon butter until foamy. Carefully break the quail eggs into the pan, season with salt and pepper, and cook until just sunny side up, about 1 minute. (If the eggs run together while cooking, carefully separate them with the edge of a slotted spoon.) Carefully remove 1 egg at a time, topping each gratin dish with an egg. Garnish each serving with 2 chervil sprigs and serve immediately.

Squab Mousse
with Juniper & Green Peppercorns

I make my squab mousse by cooking the squab itself with all the other ingredients, processing it, and passing it through a strainer. The result is more of an emulsion than a mousse, loose enough that it has a tendency to separate. It isn't the prettiest dish; in fact, one critic referred to the quenelles of mousse as "ovoid gray blobs." But what it lacks in looks it more than makes up for in flavor, with the gamey squab well complemented by brandy, port, garlic, shallot, foie gras, and duck fat. It's based on a classic French dish made with little birds called *grive* that used to be served at Troisgros.

The mousse can also serve ten to twelve as an hors d'oeuvre, tightly packed into a ramekin or terrine, alongside the toast, so that guests may serve themselves.

Put the squabs, with their livers and hearts, in a large baking dish or bowl. Add the port, brandy, garlic, shallot, and foie gras. Cover the pan with plastic wrap, refrigerate, and let marinate for 24 hours.

When ready to proceed, melt the butter and duck fat together in a medium heavy-bottomed saucepan over medium-low heat. When completely melted, add the marinated squab and foie gras mixture, including all of the marinade. Add the bay leaves and juniper berries. Bring to a very gentle simmer and cook, stirring occasionally, until the foie gras melts almost completely and the meat turns a grayish color, about 20 minutes. Remove the pan from the heat and allow the meat to cool to room temperature, but do not drain. Remove and discard the bay leaves.

Transfer the cooled mixture to a food processor fitted with a steel blade and puree it, in batches if necessary, along with 1 teaspoon of the peppercorns. Pass this mixture through a fine-mesh sieve set over a bowl. (The mixture may appear to be "broken," meaning that the fat has separated somewhat from the mousse. This is normal.) Cover with plastic wrap and refrigerate until cool but still malleable, about 1 hour, but no longer.

Return the mousse to the food processor and puree it to reincorporate the fat. The mousse should be quite smooth. Season generously with salt and pepper, then fold in the remaining 2 teaspoons peppercorns. Transfer to a bowl, cover, and refrigerate until completely chilled, at least 2 hours and up to 2 days.

To serve, arrange the mousse in 3 tablespoon-size quenelles (see page 101) on each of 4 plates. Serve with the toast points alongside.

---

3 squabs (1 pound each), livers and hearts included, boned, skin intact (have the butcher do this for you; the bones can be saved for stock-making)

2 tablespoons ruby port

1 tablespoon brandy

1 tablespoon chopped garlic (about 2 cloves)

2 tablespoons minced shallot (1 medium shallot)

4 ounces duck foie gras (any variety) cut into ½-inch cubes

½ pound (2 sticks) unsalted butter

3 tablespoons rendered or store-bought duck fat

2 bay leaves, preferably fresh

20 juniper berries, finely ground

1 tablespoon canned green peppercorns, drained

Kosher salt

Black pepper from a mill

4 slices white bread, toasted, crusts removed, and quartered diagonally

SERVES 4

Cold Poached Beef Cheeks & Vegetables with Aromatic Aspic & Goat Cheese Cream

2 medium carrots, unpeeled, cut into 1-inch chunks

2 medium onions, unpeeled, cut into 1-inch chunks

3 garlic heads, in their skins, cut in half horizontally

1 large leek, cut into 1-inch chunks and washed well (see Prep Talk, page 53)

10 juniper berries

1 tablespoon black peppercorns

1 teaspoon coriander seeds

6 bay leaves, preferably fresh

1 tablespoon tomato paste

½ cup Madeira

1 cup dry white wine

1 cup coarsely chopped fresh flat-leaf parsley leaves and stems

1 teaspoon coarsely chopped fresh thyme

1 pound slab bacon (preferably with skin), cut into 2-inch chunks

12 cups Veal Stock (page 294)

1 pound beef cheeks, trimmed, outer cartilage removed

2 large carrots, peeled and cut into 12 small tourné shapes

continued on page 117

When I was a little kid, flipping through Time-Life books about classic French cooking, one of the things that most fascinated me was aspic: firm, gelatinous rectangles in which meats and vegetables were suspended. When we opened Chanterelle, one of the first things I put on the menu was an oxtail terrine, with pieces of deboned beef in a rich, aromatic aspic. I've explored this very old-fashioned idea in a number of ways over the years, and this house favorite is made up of braised beef cheeks topped with aspic and accompanied by tourné vegetables. One distinctly modern touch is the goat cheese cream; try to find a fresh, lemony *chevre,* like Montrachet, which will provide the greatest relief from all the rich, intense flavors.

PREP TALK

Tourné Vegetables

To cut a vegetable into a tourné shape means to sculpt it into a roughly oval shape (not unlike a football, but with flat rather than pointy ends). To do this, the vegetable must first be cut into a small rectangle, roughly the length and width that you want the tourné vegetable. Hold the piece in your hand and run a paring knife along one long side, cutting in a curving motion as though tracing the shape of a bow. Turn the vegetable slightly and make another lengthwise cut, half-overlapping the first cut. Continue in this manner until you have the desired size and shape.

If you don't want to cut vegetables into a tourné shape, cut them into medium dice and proceed with the recipe instructions.

Make the broth by putting the carrot and onion chunks, the garlic, leek, juniper berries, peppercorns, coriander seeds, bay leaves, tomato paste, Madeira, wine, parsley, thyme, bacon, and stock in a large heavy-bottomed stockpot. Bring to a boil, reduce the heat so the liquid is simmering, and cook, uncovered, for 2 hours, skimming any scum that rises to the surface. Strain the broth through a fine-mesh strainer set over a large bowl. (The broth may be cooled, covered, and refrigerated for 2 to 3 days, or frozen for up to 2 months.)

When ready to proceed, pour the broth into a clean, heavy-bottomed stockpot and set it over low heat. Add the beef cheeks and simmer until the meat is tender, about 2 hours. Transfer the beef cheeks to a bowl, leaving the broth in the pot.

Place the tourné carrots in the hot broth and cook until tender to a knife tip, about 2 minutes. Use a slotted spoon to transfer them to a bowl. Repeat with the turnips for 2 minutes, then the parsnips for 2 minutes. Add the pearl onions and cook for 3 to 4 minutes before adding them to the bowl with the other vegetables.

continued from page 116

2 large turnips, peeled and
cut into 12 small tourné shapes

2 large parsnips, peeled and
cut into 12 small tourné shapes

12 white pearl onions, peeled

1 medium carrot, cut into ¼-inch dice

1 medium onion, cut into ¼-inch dice

2 large egg whites

½ teaspoon red wine vinegar

Kosher salt

Black pepper from a mill

4 ounces fresh goat cheese,
ideally Montrachet

¼ cup cold water

1 bunch arugula, rinsed, dried,
and torn into 1-inch pieces,
or 1 bunch baby arugula, trimmed,
leaves left whole

SERVES 4

Fill a large bowl halfway with ice water. Pour the remaining few cups of broth into another bowl and set it in the ice water to chill quickly. (Alternatively, the beef cheeks, tourné vegetables, and broth can all be refrigerated, separately, overnight.)

Pour the cooled broth into a medium heavy-bottomed saucepan. Add the diced carrot and onion, egg whites, and vinegar and bring to a simmer over low heat, stirring occasionally, until the egg whites coagulate, collecting the broth's impurities, and form a "raft" on the broth's surface. Stop stirring, but continue to simmer the broth for 45 minutes, then use a slotted spoon to scoop up and discard the raft. Strain the broth through a cheesecloth-lined sieve set over a bowl. Season generously to taste with salt and pepper. Refrigerate the aspic to chill and gel completely, about 3 hours or overnight.

Just prior to serving, cut the chilled beef cheeks against the grain into ¼-inch-thick slices.

Put the goat cheese and water in a blender, season with salt and pepper, and pulse until combined. Divide the goat cheese cream evenly among 4 very shallow soup bowls. Divide the aspic into 4 servings, scooping it out into the center of each bowl. Arrange the slices of beef cheeks and the vegetables around and over the aspic. Garnish with the arugula and serve cold.

Grilled Asparagus with Black Truffles, Shaved Parmesan & a Poached Egg

Its name might suggest Italy, but in my mind, this dish took shape in Paris, during a visit Karen and I made there in the spring of 2002. When we got back to New York, I made this starter (also very appropriate for breakfast or brunch) to sum up my memories of our meals there. Not only did we seem to encounter asparagus—plump, impossibly perfect stalks fresh from the farm—everywhere we went, but outlandishly rich sauces, like hollandaise and black truffle sauce, were a part of just about every meal. Rather than include a hollandaise here, I decided to go with poached eggs; I've always been fond of them, especially the way the yolk becomes a kind of sauce in its own right.

This recipe makes more truffle sauce than you will need. The extra can be frozen for up to two months. It is delicious with a steak, roasted chicken, or, of course, poached eggs.

In a medium heavy-bottomed saucepan over medium heat, bring the truffle juice, truffles, Madeira, and stock to a boil, then lower the heat so the liquid is simmering and cook until the sauce is reduced by half, about 25 minutes.

Meanwhile, in a small bowl, knead the butter and flour together into a ball. Briskly whisk this into the reduced sauce and simmer just long enough to dissolve the flour and thicken the sauce slightly. Stir in the lemon juice. You should have 1 cup of sauce. Remove from the heat and keep the sauce covered and warm. (It can be refrigerated in an airtight container for up to 4 days; rewarm gently before proceeding.)

Trim each asparagus stalk to a 5-inch length, then use a vegetable peeler to trim the skin of the stalk to just below the bottom of the tip.

Bring a large pot of generously salted water to a boil. Fill a large bowl halfway with ice water. Gently blanch the asparagus in the boiling water for 1 minute, then use tongs or a slotted spoon to quickly transfer the stalks to the ice water to stop the cooking and preserve their color. Drain, pat dry with paper towels, and refrigerate until ready to serve.

Preheat a grill to high or preheat the oven to 350°F.

Lightly coat the asparagus with the olive oil and season with salt and pepper. Grill over high heat for 2 to 3 minutes to reheat and mark them, or place the stalks on a baking sheet and reheat in the oven for 2 to 3 minutes.

Poach the eggs by filling a wide, deep pan about halfway with water. Set the pan over high heat and bring to a simmer. Add the vinegar and very carefully crack the eggs, dropping them directly into the poaching liquid. Cook until they are just set with runny yolks, 2 to 3 minutes. Use a slotted spoon to remove the eggs, letting any excess water run off. (You can help keep the eggs from running together by setting 4 ring molds in the pan and breaking an egg into each mold. Remove the molds with tongs as soon as the eggs start to set.)

Arrange 5 asparagus stalks on each of 4 plates and drizzle each with ¼ cup of the black truffle sauce. Place an egg at the base of the asparagus on each plate. Season with salt and pepper. Use a wide vegetable peeler or a mandoline to shave some cheese over the egg and asparagus on each plate. Serve immediately.

One 7-ounce can black truffle juice

3 tablespoons minced fresh, flash-frozen, or canned black truffles

2 tablespoons Madeira

4 cups Chicken Stock (page 292)

1 tablespoon unsalted butter, softened at room temperature

2 teaspoons all-purpose flour

3 drops freshly squeezed lemon juice

20 stalks (about 2 pounds) jumbo asparagus

Kosher salt

About ¼ cup olive oil

Black pepper from a mill

1 tablespoon white wine vinegar

4 large eggs

One 2- to 3-ounce chunk Parmigiano-Reggiano cheese, for shaving (you will not use it all)

FISH & SHELLFISH

¶ "I didn't realize this was a fish restaurant." ¶ We hear that often at Chanterelle and we always receive it with amusement and understanding. The truth, of course, is that we are not a fish restaurant, but it's easy to mistake us for one because about half of our dishes are centered on fish or shellfish. ¶ There's a simple reason for this: I love cooking and eating seafood. And I'm not alone. Many chefs will tell you that they have a preference for fish and shellfish because the variety and possibility they offer is irresistible. That one club can include such disparate members as scallops, soft-shell crabs, Maine lobster, skate, halibut, salmon, and tuna is remarkable. The spectrum of flavors and textures stimulates my sense of fun and adventure, and has inspired some of the most original dishes ever to emerge from the Chanterelle kitchen. ¶ Generally speaking, techniques and ingredients have more of an impact on fish and shellfish than they do on poultry and meat; all seafood has its own flavor, of course, but most has the appealing ability to take on other flavors as well. This is why, for all of my classical leanings, I've never been especially beholden to classic thinking about cooking fish; I've always been as likely to fashion sauces for fish and shellfish with red wine as with white, and to use chicken or veal stock more often than fish stock. All of which is a roundabout way of saying that in these pages you'll find dishes to suit any flavor profile you seek.

Sautéed Bay Scallops with Duck Fat, Tomato & Basil

3 tablespoons rendered duck fat, at room temperature, or olive oil

1 pound dry bay scallops, preferably Nantucket or Peconic Bay

Kosher salt

Black pepper from a mill

3 medium garlic cloves, finely chopped

¼ cup dry white wine

3 tablespoons ripe plum tomato concassée (see Prep Talk, page 62)

1 cup Chicken Stock (page 292) or high-quality low-sodium store-bought chicken stock or ⅔ cup Thickened Chicken Stock (page 293)

1 tablespoon unsalted butter, softened at room temperature

About ½ teaspoon freshly squeezed lemon juice

2 tablespoons fresh basil cut into chiffonade (see Prep Talk, page 70)

SERVES 4

Some of my greatest delights as a chef have come from hitting upon seemingly illogical combinations that work. This dish is centered on such a pairing: Sautéing bay scallops in hot duck fat coats them with an addictively rich, viscous sauce that provides the perfect complement to the sweetness that's unlocked by cooking them. In essence a variation on scallops Provençal, with duck fat replacing the customary olive oil, the flavors here are rounded out with tomato concassée, garlic, and lemon juice, with a crucial lift from the last-second addition of basil.

I have a fondness for scallops and a particular affection for bay scallops, scarcely larger than pencil erasers and so delicate they almost look like miniature panna cottas that might collapse at the touch of a fork. The fact that bay scallops are seasonal, generally available from November through the end of March, only makes them more special.

Controlling the heat is very important in this recipe. To ensure that the ingredients do not stick or scorch, get the pan nice and hot before adding anything to it, then heat the duck fat well before adding the scallops.

I often serve this with a swirl of pasta, such as dried angel hair or dried or fresh fettuccine (about 1 ounce per person). The crisp texture of snow peas or sugar snap peas are an ideal contrast to the richness of the scallops and sauce.

Heat a wide, deep, heavy-bottomed sauté pan over high heat until very hot. Add 1 tablespoon of the duck fat and heat it, swirling the pan to keep the fat from scorching, for 30 seconds. Carefully add the scallops in a single layer and season lightly with salt and pepper. Cook the scallops, without shaking or tossing, until lightly browned, about 1 minute, then stir or toss to turn them and cook until lightly browned on the other side, about 1 minute more. (You can also use tongs to turn them over, but work quickly to ensure they all finish cooking at the same time.) Use tongs or a slotted spoon to transfer the scallops to a plate.

Discard the fat remaining in the pan and return the pan to high heat. (Do *not* wipe out the pan.) Add 1 tablespoon of the duck fat and immediately add the garlic. Cook, stirring, until the garlic is lightly browned, about 1 minute, taking care not to let it blacken or crisp. Quickly pour in the wine, stir with a wooden spoon, and bring to a boil, then reduce the heat so the liquid is simmering, scraping up any browned bits stuck to the bottom of the pan. If the scallops have given off any liquid while resting, add it to the pan, stir, and continue to simmer the mixture until it has almost completely evaporated, about 3 minutes.

Add the concassée and stock, bring to a boil, and reduce for 4 or 5 minutes (2 minutes if using Thickened Chicken Stock). Stir in the remaining 1 tablespoon duck fat, the butter, and lemon juice, and season with salt and pepper. Boil the sauce, stirring frequently, until it reduces and the fats have emulsified to the point that they generously coat the back of the wooden spoon, about 2 minutes or slightly less time if using Thickened Chicken Stock. (You want the sauce to be as reduced as possible without the fats separating or the liquid turning to syrup; the addition of the scallops, with their coating of duck fat, will reconstitute and finish the sauce.)

Return the scallops to the pan, swirling the pan to coat them with the sauce and warm them through, about 2 minutes. Gently stir in the basil, taking care not to crush the scallops, and adjust the seasoning to taste with salt and pepper and another drop or two of lemon juice, if necessary. If the sauce seems too intense, swirl in a few drops of hot water.

Divide the scallops and sauce among 4 dinner plates and serve immediately.

Soft-Shell Crabs with "Creamed" Corn & Chorizo Oil

1 cup olive oil

6 ounces fresh (uncooked) Spanish-style chorizo, cut into ¼-inch dice

½ teaspoon hot Spanish smoked paprika (pimentón picante)

½ teaspoon sweet Spanish smoked paprika (pimentón dulce)

3 tablespoons unsalted butter

1 cup finely diced yellow onion

2 tablespoons chopped garlic (about 3 cloves)

¼ cup dry white wine, plus more if necessary

1 teaspoon all-purpose flour, plus about 2 cups for dredging the crabs

2 cups Chicken Stock (page 292), high-quality low-sodium store-bought chicken stock, or water

2 cups fresh corn kernels (about 2 large ears)

Kosher salt

Black pepper from a mill

Pinch of sugar, if necessary

12 medium (hotel or prime size, 4 to 5 inches in width) soft-shell crabs, cleaned (see sidebar, facing page)

½ cup canola or other neutral oil

SERVES 4

As much as I love soft-shell crabs, the real standouts in this dish are the "creamed" corn and chorizo oil, each of which calls on clever technique to retain and maximize the flavor of its main ingredient. It's referred to as "creamed" corn because there's no actual cream in its preparation; instead, corn kernels are cooked in, and flavored by, a mixture of white wine, chicken stock, onion, and garlic, then a portion of the corn is processed to make the mixture creamy. The result is a component that acts as both vegetable and sauce. The flavor of fresh corn is essential in this dish, so do not substitute frozen.

Truth be told, my use of chorizo oil was born of a frustration I have with chorizo: When slowly rendered, much of its flavor leaches out into the pan along with its fat. So here, the slightly spicy, brick red oil itself is drizzled around the plate, with the chorizo serving as garnish.

This recipe calls for two Spanish paprikas that you will likely have to special-order or obtain from a very well stocked specialty market. If you don't want to do this, do *not* substitute other paprikas; instead, simply leave the paprika out of the dish.

You can expand each plate by mounding the crab on some wilted greens such as spinach or bok choy.

Put the olive oil and chorizo in a small heavy-bottomed sauté pan set over medium heat and cook, stirring occasionally, until the oil has taken on a reddish brown color and the chorizo crisps in the bubbling oil, about 20 minutes. Stir in the hot and sweet paprikas, and then, using a slotted spoon, transfer the chorizo to a small bowl. Pour the oil into a separate bowl. (The chorizo and chorizo oil may be cooled and refrigerated in separate airtight containers for up to 3 days; reheat the oil gently and let the chorizo come to room temperature before proceeding.)

Melt 2 tablespoons of the butter in a large heavy-bottomed saucepan over low heat. Add the onion and garlic and cook gently, stirring occasionally, until the onion is translucent but not browned, about 10 minutes.

(Add a scant splash of wine, if necessary, to keep the onion from browning.) Sprinkle with 1 teaspoon of the flour and continue to cook, stirring and not allowing the onion or flour to brown, for 3 minutes. Whisk in the wine and raise the heat to medium-high. Bring the wine to a boil, then whisk in the stock and bring back to a boil. Add the corn and, when the liquid returns to a boil, lower the heat slightly and simmer for 20 minutes.

Remove the pan from the heat. Puree about one-third of the corn either by using an immersion blender or ladling about one-third of the kernels into a regular blender, pureeing them, and stirring them back into the pot. This is the "creamed" corn sauce. Season to taste with salt and pepper and, if it lacks sweetness, the sugar. Cover and keep warm for up to 1 hour. (The corn sauce may also be cooled and refrigerated in an airtight container for up to 3 days; reheat gently before continuing.)

Line a large plate or platter with paper towels.

Put the 2 cups flour in a shallow bowl and dredge the crabs to lightly coat. Heat the canola oil in a wide, deep, heavy-bottomed sauté pan set over medium heat until very hot but not smoking. Add the crabs, shell side down. Add the remaining 1 tablespoon butter (it will help to crisp the crabs) and cook until they are crispy and browned, 4 to 5 minutes. Flip and cook until crispy and brown on the other side, another 3 to 4 minutes. Transfer the crabs to the paper towels to drain.

To serve, ladle the warm corn sauce evenly into the center of 4 large dinner plates. Drizzle each with 1 tablespoon of the warm chorizo oil, both over and around the corn. Sprinkle a little of the crisp chorizo pieces on each plate. Top with 3 crabs per serving. Serve immediately.

SOFT-SHELL CRABS

Soft-shell crabs are classified by the width of the shell covering the body. There are five sizes: whale, jumbo, prime, hotel, and medium. Whenever possible, I select crabs in the middle of the scale (prime or hotel) because they have the best ratio of shell to meat. I never season soft-shell crabs, as they have a natural salinity that more than suffices; when I have seasoned them, diners have inevitably found them salty. Be careful when cooking soft-shell crabs because their legs can "pop" when heat builds up inside them, causing them to spatter.

Soft-shell crabs should be purchased alive, as they come to us at Chanterelle. (I love ingredients that arrive this way because they serve as a powerful reminder of the source of our food.) You can have a fishmonger clean them for you, but only if you'll be cooking them almost as soon as you arrive home from the market. To clean a soft-shell crab, rinse it under gently running cold water and pat it dry with paper towels. Pull off and discard the feathery gills, located beneath the two sides of the shell. Turn the crab over and gently pull off the "apron," the flap that covers its underside. Use kitchen shears or scissors to snip off the front pincers and eyes.

Lobster with Sauternes & Curry

Don't be misled by "curry" in the name of this dish. I use curry the way some French chefs do: as a spice to be judiciously applied the way you would any other seasoning. Here, it offsets the sweet dessert wine Sauternes, with lime juice balancing and uniting the two. The technique is similar to the one used in the next recipe, but the result is completely different; as with that recipe, I sometimes add baby vegetables (carrots, turnips, pattypan squash, haricots verts) cooked in butter and water (or chicken stock), scattering them around the bowl.

Bring a large pot of salted water to a boil.

Kill the lobsters quickly by holding each one to face you, then driving a knife between the eyes and pulling it down through the head, like a lever. Using a heavy knife, split the lobster heads in half down the middle, then remove the heads, chop each one into 6 or 8 small pieces, and set the pieces aside. Separate the claws and tails from the bodies by twisting them, and discard the bodies or freeze them for another use. Put the claws into the boiling water and cook for 1 minute, then add the tails and cook for 1 minute more. Use a slotted spoon to remove them from the water and place them on a clean surface to cool. (You can put them in the refrigerator to speed the process if you like.) The lobster meat will appear quite underdone, but it will finish cooking later. Once it is cool, shell the lobster, splitting the tails and keeping the claw meat as intact as possible. Wrap the lobster meat in plastic wrap and refrigerate while you finish making the dish. Reserve the shells for the sauce.

Heat the oil in a large heavy-bottomed saucepan over medium-high heat until it is hot but not smoking. Add the lobster head pieces and reserved shells and cook, stirring a few times, for 5 minutes. (You should smell a potent oceanic aroma as the flavor is released.) Add the tomato paste, if using, and curry and stir for another 2 minutes.

Add the carrots, onions, garlic, and ginger and cook, stirring, for another 10 minutes. Remove from the heat and pour in the Cognac and Sauternes. Return to high heat and reduce by about two-thirds, until about 1 cup remains, 10 to 15 minutes. Pour in the stock and bring back to a boil. Reduce the heat to a simmer and cook for 1 hour. Season to taste with salt and pepper.

Strain the broth through a fine-mesh strainer set over a large bowl. Wipe out the pot and empty and rinse out the strainer. Line the strainer with cheesecloth, set it over the pot, and strain the broth again, back into the pot. Stir in the cream and bring to a boil, keeping a close eye on the pot so it doesn't boil over. Reduce the heat to medium and cook until slightly thickened and flavorful, about 30 minutes. Season to taste with lime juice and salt (keeping in mind that lobster is naturally salty). Remove any extra bits of lobster shell by straining the sauce through a fine-mesh strainer or cheesecloth set over a medium saucepan. Set the pan over medium heat and whisk in the butter. Add the lobster meat and reheat gently for 2 to 3 minutes.

To serve, place 2 claws and 1 whole tail in each of 4 shallow bowls, then spoon some sauce over each serving. Sprinkle with the basil and serve immediately.

Kosher salt

Four 1½- to 1¾-pound lobsters

1 cup canola or other neutral oil

1 tablespoon tomato paste
(omit if lobster stock is used)

2 tablespoons mild curry powder,
preferably Sun Brand Madras curry

3 medium carrots, unpeeled,
cut into 1-inch chunks

3 medium Spanish onions, unpeeled,
cut into large chunks

2 garlic heads, in their skins,
cut in half horizontally

4 ounces fresh ginger, unpeeled,
cut into ¼-inch-thick rounds

½ cup Cognac or brandy

One 750 ml bottle Sauternes or other
sweet wine, such as Muscat or Loupiac

8 cups Fish Stock (page 290),
Lobster Stock (page 292),
or Chicken Stock (page 292)

Black pepper from a mill

2 cups heavy cream, preferably
not ultrapasteurized

Juice of ½ lime, or more to taste

2 tablespoons unsalted butter,
softened at room temperature

2 tablespoons fresh basil (preferably
Thai) cut into chiffonade (see Prep Talk,
page 70) or ¼ cup fresh cilantro leaves

SERVES 4

Lobster with Cider & Apples

Kosher salt

Four 1½- to 1¾-pound lobsters

1 cup canola or other neutral oil

3 medium carrots, unpeeled, cut into 1-inch chunks

3 medium Spanish onions, unpeeled, cut into large chunks

2 garlic heads, in their skins, cut in half horizontally

½ cup Calvados or applejack

About 3 cups hard cider, preferably not too sweet (my favorite brand is Woodchuck®, from Springfield, Vermont)

12 cups Fish Stock (page 290), Lobster Stock (page 292), Chicken Stock (page 292), or high-quality low-sodium store-bought chicken stock

Black pepper from a mill

3 tablespoons unsalted butter, softened at room temperature

½ lemon, if necessary

1 medium crisp red apple, such as Cortland, peeled, seeded, cut into small dice, and tossed with 1 teaspoon lemon juice to prevent browning

2 tablespoons fresh chives cut into ¼-inch pieces

SERVES 4

I'll never forget the first time I made lobster bisque. The potent essence that's unlocked by cooking and processing lobster shells is something of a miracle to me, and the layering of flavors that occurs with wine, brandy, tomato, peppercorns, and everything else is the very pinnacle of the transformative power of cooking.

This recipe is an apple-themed variation of lobster bisque that replaces brandy with Calvados and wine with cider, then finishes the dish with apples as a garnish. As with the previous recipe, I sometimes expand this dish by cooking baby vegetables (carrots, turnips, pattypan squash, haricots verts) in butter and water (or chicken stock), and scattering them around the bowl, in the manner of a stew.

Bring a large pot of salted water to a boil.

Kill the lobsters quickly by holding each one to face you, then driving a knife between the eyes and pulling it down through the head, like a lever. Using a heavy knife, split the lobster heads in half down the middle, then remove the heads, chop each one into 6 or 8 small pieces, and set the pieces aside. (You can also process them in a food processor; the more broken up they are, the more flavor you will be able to extract from them.) Separate the claws and tails from the bodies by twisting them, and discard the bodies or freeze them for another use. Put the claws into the boiling water and cook for 1 minute, then add the tails and cook for 1 minute more. Use a slotted spoon to remove them from the water and place them on a clean surface to cool. (You can put them in the refrigerator to speed the process if you like.) The lobster meat will appear quite underdone, but will finish cooking later. Once it is cool, shell the lobster, splitting the tails and keeping the claw meat as intact as possible. Wrap the meat in plastic wrap and refrigerate while you finish making the dish. Reserve the shells for the sauce.

Heat the oil in a large heavy-bottomed pot over medium-high heat until it is hot but not smoking. Add the lobster head pieces and reserved shells and cook, stirring a few times, for 5 minutes. (You should smell a potent oceanic aroma as the flavor is released.) Add the carrots, onions, and garlic and cook, stirring, for another

10 minutes. Remove from the heat and pour in the Calvados and cider. Return to high heat and reduce the liquids by about two-thirds, until about 1 cup remains, 10 to 15 minutes. Pour in the stock and bring back to a boil. Reduce the heat so the liquid is simmering and cook for 1½ hours.

Strain the broth through a fine-mesh strainer set over a large bowl. Wipe out the pot and empty and rinse out the strainer. Line the strainer with cheesecloth, set it over the pot, and strain the broth again, back into the pot. Season to taste with salt and pepper. Bring the broth to a boil over medium-high heat and reduce by about one-third,

until about 2 cups remain, about 10 minutes. Whisk in the butter, taste, and adjust the seasonings if necessary. The sauce should taste of cider and be slightly sweet with a pronounced lobster flavor, but not excessively thick. If it doesn't taste at all sweet, add another teaspoon or two of cider; if it seems too sweet, add a few drops of lemon juice. If it has over-reduced, add a splash of hot water. Add the lobster meat to the broth and reheat gently for 2 to 3 minutes. Gently stir in the apple and chives.

To serve, place 2 lobster claws and 1 whole lobster tail in each of 4 wide, shallow bowls. Spoon some sauce over each serving and serve immediately.

Fricassée of Shellfish with Lemongrass & Lime Leaves

4 cups dry white wine

Juice of 1 lemon

Juice of 1 lime

10 wild lime leaves, thinly sliced

8 stalks lemongrass, tough outer layers removed and tender inner core very thinly sliced

4 scallions (white and green parts), cut into ½-inch pieces

One 2-inch piece fresh ginger, unpeeled, thinly sliced

1 garlic head, in its skin, cut in half horizontally

4 medium carrots, unpeeled, cut into 1-inch chunks

4 cups cold water

8 ounces mussels (about 12), scrubbed well under cold running water and debearded

12 ounces Manila clams or cockles (about 12), scrubbed well under cold running water

12 ounces jumbo or colossal shrimp (about 12, preferably with the heads on), shelled and deveined

continued on page 135

Much as I love outlandishly rich food, I have an equally abiding affection for light cuisine, especially dishes that use Asian ingredients such as lemongrass, lime leaves, and ginger. In addition to those high-impact aromatics, two of my favorite effects come into play here, with the mussels and clams imparting a briny flavor and a last-second hit of basil lifting and lightening the overall effect.

A nage is a dish in which fish or shellfish is served in the court bouillon in which it was poached. In the 1970s, chefs began adding a step to the tried-and-true tradition of nage-making, removing the fish from the poaching liquid, then reducing the liquid to concentrate its flavors and finishing it with butter. I decided to use this technique to introduce the flavors of Southeast Asian food.

I've also served this as a first course, and you can do the same by halving the recipe.

Put the wine, lemon and lime juices, lime leaves, lemongrass, scallions, ginger, garlic, carrot chunks, and water in a large, heavy-bottomed, nonreactive saucepan. Bring to a boil, reduce the heat so the liquid is simmering, and let gently bubble for 1½ hours. Strain through a fine-mesh strainer set over a large bowl and discard the solids. You should have about 6 cups of broth. If there is more than 6 cups, wipe out the pan, return the broth to the pan, bring to a boil, and reduce until 6 cups remain. (The broth can be cooled and refrigerated in an airtight container for up to 2 days; let come to room temperature before proceeding.)

Arrange the mussels and clams in a wide, deep, heavy-bottomed sauteuse (see page 145) with a tight-fitting lid so they are spread out in a single layer. Gently pour the broth over the shellfish, cover, and set over medium heat.

Cook, checking often, for about 4 minutes. As the shellfish open, transfer them to a bowl with a slotted spoon and keep covered and warm. (Discard any shellfish that have not opened after 5 or 6 minutes.) Add the shrimp and scallops to the broth and poach until just barely done, 2 to 3 minutes, then transfer to the covered bowl with the other shellfish. Remove the cover from the pan and continue to boil the broth over high heat until reduced by one-third, about 6 minutes. Stir in the fish sauce and sugar until well incorporated. Add the julienned vegetables, allowing them to wilt just slightly, about 2 minutes. Swirl in the butter to thicken and enrich the broth. Taste and season with more fish sauce, if desired.

Divide the shellfish among 4 wide, deep bowls. Stir the basil into the bouillon, spoon the bouillon over the shellfish, and serve immediately.

continued from page 134

12 ounces large dry sea scallops
(8 to 10), cut in half horizontally

1 tablespoon Asian fish sauce

Pinch of sugar

1 medium carrot, julienned
(3-inch-long pieces)

¼ cup julienned (3-inch-long pieces)
leek (white and light green parts)

¼ cup julienned (3-inch-long pieces)
zucchini skin

¼ cup julienned (3-inch-long pieces)
yellow squash skin

¼ cup peeled julienned (3-inch-long
pieces) daikon radish

4 ounces snow peas, stringed
and julienned (3-inch-long pieces)

½ cup (1 stick) unsalted butter,
cut into small pieces, softened at
room temperature

¼ cup fresh basil (green, purple,
and/or Thai) cut into chiffonade
(see Prep Talk, page 70)

SERVES 4

Striped Bass with Sage & Red Wine Butter

½ pound (2 sticks) unsalted butter, softened at room temperature

⅓ cup lightly packed fresh sage leaves

About 1 teaspoon freshly squeezed lemon juice

½ teaspoon kosher salt, plus more to taste

½ garlic clove, peeled

Four 6- to 7-ounce farm-raised striped bass or red snapper fillets, skin on, any pin bones removed

1½ cups Merlot or other soft red wine

2 tablespoons red wine vinegar

2 tablespoons ruby port

½ cup Veal Stock (page 294) or high-quality low-sodium store-bought veal stock

3 medium shallots, finely diced

½ pound (2 sticks) cold unsalted butter, cut into ½-inch cubes

Black pepper from a mill

About 2 cups Wondra or all-purpose flour, for dredging

½ cup canola or other neutral oil

20 Sage Potato Chips (page 252)

SERVES 4

Slipping ingredients under the skin of fish or fowl is one of those classic techniques that I love to call on in my cooking. Different ingredients produce different results: Black truffles dazzle the eye as much as the palate in a dish like Chicken Demi-Deuil (my version appears on page 170). Here, some butter under the skin melts and bastes the fish as it cooks. I suggest asking your fishmonger to cut the skin as directed in the recipe—he or she will have the proper knife and experience to do it very cleanly; if you opt to do it yourself, keep the blade as close to the skin as possible to avoid removing any of the flesh.

The sauce here is sort of a red beurre blanc that I used to use with a variety of fish dishes, but now only serve with this one because I think they really belong together. For the sauce, choose a wine that isn't excessively tannic, such as a Merlot or table wine. If possible, also use a wine with an unmistakably red color, as oppose to a purpley one.

I generally prefer the flavor of wild striped bass to the slightly muddy flavor of the farmed variety, but farmed striped bass happens to work better in this recipe—the thickness of the fillet is perfect and the skin crisps up very well.

Fresh green vegetables, such as snow peas, sugar snap peas, and haricot verts, are a perfect addition to this dish. Adding veal stock to the sauce will enrich it and guarantee a full mouth-feel.

To make the sage butter, put the softened butter, sage, lemon juice, ½ teaspoon salt, and the garlic in a food processor. Pulse to puree it as finely as possible, but bear in mind that it will not become completely smooth, as bits of sage will remain. Use a rubber spatula to transfer the sage butter to a small bowl. (This will keep, tightly wrapped, in the refrigerator for up to 5 days; let soften at room temperature for at least 1 hour before using.)

Set a fillet on a cutting board, skin side down. Using a very sharp knife, make a small horizontal incision between the skin and the flesh of the fish, about 1 inch from the thinner end of the fillet. Slide the knife toward the thin end, separating skin from flesh. Turn the knife around and cut toward the thicker end of the fish, pulling the skin as you do and stopping about ½ inch from the end so the skin remains attached at the end. Repeat with the remaining fillets.

Spread 2 tablespoons of the sage butter between the skin and flesh of each fillet. Lay the skin over the butter and wrap it over the thin end of the fish to hold it in place (after it's been loosened, the skin will exceed the length of the fillet). (The fillets can be prepared wrapped snugly in plastic wrap and refrigerated, skin side up, for up to 24 hours. Let come to room temperature before proceeding.)

To make the butter sauce, pour the wine, vinegar, port, and stock into a large, heavy-bottomed, nonreactive saucepan. Add the shallots and bring to a boil. Reduce the heat so the liquid is simmering and cook until the liquid is syrupy, yielding about 2 tablespoons, about 20 minutes. Periodically dip a clean, dry pastry brush into the liquid and brush the sides of the pan to return any shallots stuck to the sides to the liquid.

Reduce the heat to low and gradually whisk in the cold butter, a few cubes at a time, adding the next cubes only once the previous batch has become almost fully incorporated. Season with salt and pepper. For a very smooth emulsion, strain the sauce through a fine-mesh strainer set over a small saucepan. Keep the sauce warm, whisking occasionally to keep it from separating,

until ready to use. Put the flour in a wide, shallow bowl and dredge the fillets to coat lightly. Season with salt and pepper and set aside.

Heat a large, wide, deep-sided, heavy-bottomed sauté pan over medium-high heat until nice and hot. Add the oil and turn the pan to coat the bottom with the oil, letting it heat for a minute or two. Place the fillets in the pan, skin side down, and cook over medium heat. As they cook, drain off any fat that accumulates in the pan and continue to cook until the skin becomes nicely crisp, 6 to 8 minutes. Carefully turn the fish over and cook for 1 to 2 minutes more. Blot the skin side with paper towels.

To serve, spoon about 3 tablespoons of the butter sauce onto each of 4 dinner plates. Top with a fish fillet, garnish with 5 potato chips, and serve immediately.

Pan-Seared Arctic Char
with Grapefruit Butter & Savoy Cabbage

Zest of 1 large pink grapefruit, removed with a vegetable peeler (be sure to remove only the zest, not the white pith beneath) and julienned (3 inches long)

3 tablespoons sugar, plus more to taste

1 cup pink grapefruit juice (from 2 large grapefruit)

1 medium shallot, coarsely chopped

½ cup dry white wine

¼ cup heavy cream

¾ cup (1½ sticks) cold unsalted butter, cut into cubes, plus 2 tablespoons at room temperature

1 small head Savoy or green cabbage, cored and cut into very into thin strips

Kosher salt

Black pepper from a mill

Four 6-ounce Arctic char or salmon fillets, skin on, any pin bones removed

3 tablespoons canola or other neutral oil

2 tablespoon chopped fresh chives

SERVES 4

Like many fruits, grapefruit rarely shows up outside of breakfast or dessert. Here, both grapefruit juice and candied grapefruit rind make a main-course cameo. As fate would have it, tart grapefruit juice has a real affinity for many white- and pink-fleshed fish. In this case, Arctic char is paired with grapefruit butter, and the result is almost addictively satisfying. The dish is rounded out by buttery Savoy cabbage, which offers relief from the intense combination at its center, and by a scattering of candied rind over the finished plate. You can leave out the rind and this dish will still be delicious.

If you can find it, Tasmanian sea trout is a delicious alternative to the char.

Put the grapefruit zest in a small saucepan and cover with about 2 inches of cold water. Bring to a boil over medium-high heat, then drain the zest in a fine-mesh strainer. Repeat the process twice more, for a total of three times, to soften the zest and draw out some of its bitterness. After draining the zest for a third time, return it to the pan and add ½ cup water and the sugar. Stir together and cook over very low heat until the liquid is reduced to a syrup but is still loose and plentiful enough to cover the bottom of the pan, about 5 minutes. (You do *not* want to completely reduce the liquid, which would result in a cloyingly sweet and sticky rind. Taste a piece if you like; it should hold its shape but be easily chewable and slightly sweet.) If the liquid seems to be reducing too much, add a tablespoon or two of water to keep the zest from burning. Drain well and let cool on a baking rack. (The candied zest will keep in an airtight container at room temperature for up to 3 days.)

Put the grapefruit juice, shallot, and wine in a medium nonreactive saucepan over high heat and bring to a boil. Reduce the heat so the liquid is simmering and cook until reduced to about 3 tablespoons of syrupy liquid, about 15 minutes (be careful not to overcook or the natural sugars in the juice and wine will caramelize and discolor the sauce). Stir in the cream and let the sauce thicken over low heat for 2 to 3 minutes. (The reduction can be cooled, covered, and refrigerated for up to 24 hours; reheat gently before continuing.)

Reduce the heat to low and gradually whisk in the cold butter, a few cubes at a time, adding the next few cubes only after the previous batch has been well incorporated. Strain the sauce through a fine-mesh strainer set over a bowl and season with salt. You should have about ½ cup of sauce. Taste it; the sauce should be slightly sweet and tart. If you don't discern any sweetness, add a pinch of sugar. Keep the sauce covered and warm.

Melt the softened butter in a 10-inch sauté pan over medium heat. Add the cabbage and cook, tossing, until just slightly wilted, about 3 minutes. Add ¼ cup of water and season with salt and pepper to taste. Turn the heat up to medium-high and cook until most of the water has evaporated and the cabbage is cooked through but still a little crunchy, about 5 minutes. Drain any excess liquid.

Lay the fillets on a clean, dry surface and season both sides with salt and pepper. Heat the oil in a large heavy-bottomed sauté pan over medium-high heat until it is very warm (don't let it get really hot), then add the fillets, skin side down, and cook until the skin is crisp and browned, 3 to 4 minutes. (Keep a close eye on it because char burns easily.) Turn the fillets over and finish cooking the other side, 3 to 4 minutes more, depending on the thickness of the cut and the desired level of doneness. Blot the skin side with paper towels.

To serve, divide the cabbage among 4 dinner plates, placing a mound in the center of each. Evenly divide the grapefruit sauce, pouring it around the cabbage. Sprinkle the plates with the chives, then place a char fillet on top of each cabbage bed. Garnish with a sprinkling of the grapefruit zest and serve.

Poached Cod with Pig's Feet, Manila Clams & Fresh Herbs

1 large meaty pig's foot (try to get a long one, ideally with some of the hock attached), split and cut into 2-inch chunks (have the butcher do this for you)

2 cups dry white wine

4 cups Chicken Stock (page 292) or high-quality low-sodium store-bought chicken stock

3 bay leaves, preferably fresh

½ teaspoon coriander seeds

1 teaspoon black peppercorns

2 cups cold water, or more as needed

Four 6-ounce pieces cod, halibut, or grouper fillets, any pin bones removed

12 ounces Manila clams (about 20) or cockles, scrubbed clean

3 tablespoons finely diced leek (white and light green parts)

continued on page 145

I use pig's feet in my cooking more than any chef I know. I don't necessarily name them on the menu, or present them on the plate, but I appreciate and call on them for the gelatinous, lip-smacking, palate-coating quality they give sauces and stews.

In this dish, the pig's feet are present on the finished dish. Our guests are always surprised when they see this on the menu, but the combination of pork and clams isn't as outrageous as it may sound. In fact, two popular Portuguese dishes, *cataplana* and *porco a Alentejana,* are based on it. Making the combination a sauce for cod takes this out of the realm of casual home cooking and into something more sophisticated.

I like to intensify the flavor of the pig's feet by cooking them in chicken stock with wine and aromatics, such as coriander seeds, black peppercorns, and bay leaf. When the meat from the pig's feet is shredded and combined with the clams, the stew-like result may surprise you with its intensity.

Put the pig's foot, wine, stock, bay leaves, coriander seeds, and peppercorns in a large heavy-bottomed saucepan. Add the water. If the pig's foot isn't covered with liquid, add enough to submerge it. Set over high heat and bring to a boil. Cover, reduce the heat so the liquid is simmering, and cook until the pig's foot is very tender (prod it with a fork or knife to test), 1½ to 2 hours, periodically removing the cover and skimming any foam that accumulates on the surface with a kitchen spoon. Remove the pig's foot and allow it to cool. Strain the broth through a fine-mesh strainer set over a bowl and discard the solids. You should have about 4 cups of broth. (The broth can be refrigerated in an airtight container for up to 2 days; reheat gently before proceeding.)

Pull the meat (including skin and fat) from the bone of the pig's foot and dice it into ¼-inch cubes. You should have about 1 cup of diced meat. (The meat will keep in the refrigerator, well wrapped, for up to 4 days.)

Lightly butter the bottom of a sauteuse or other deep, flat pan with a tight-fitting lid. Pour in the broth, then add the cod, clams, and diced pig's foot meat. Set over high heat and bring to a boil. Reduce the heat to medium-high, cover, and cook for about 5 minutes, checking often and removing the clams with a slotted spoon as they open and the cod when it is just underdone (it will continue to cook on its own). Transfer the clams and cod to a covered plate and keep warm. Remove the top shell from each of the clams so they are on the half shell. Discard any clams that don't open.

Simmer the broth over medium heat until reduced by about one-third (about 2½ cups will remain). A small taste will feel sticky on your tongue, a result of the pig foot's natural gelatin. Reduce the heat to low, add the vegetables and lemon juice, and swirl in the butter to thicken and enrich the broth. Season to taste with salt and pepper. Just before serving, stir in the herbs.

Divide the cod and clams among 4 large shallow bowls. Spoon the sauce, vegetables, and diced pig's foot into each bowl. Serve immediately.

continued from page 144

3 tablespoons finely diced carrot

3 tablespoons finely diced zucchini skin (remove with a vegetable peeler before dicing)

3 tablespoons finely diced yellow squash skin (remove with a vegetable peeler before dicing)

About 1 teaspoon freshly squeezed lemon juice

3 tablespoons unsalted butter, softened at room temperature

Kosher salt

Black pepper from a mill

1½ teaspoons finely chopped fresh tarragon

1½ teaspoons finely chopped fresh chives

1½ teaspoons chopped fresh flat-leaf parsley

1½ teaspoons chopped fresh chervil

THE SAUTEUSE

If you don't already have one, I urge you to add a sauteuse to your kitchen equipment. A sauteuse is a round, lidded pan that is often used to sauté or braise a variety of foods. With short to medium outward-sloping sides, it's much deeper than a sauté pan and so is ideal for casseroles, stews, and pasta dishes, as well as for meat and poultry dishes. Common in European households, it usually has a small curved handle on each side, which facilitates lifting it, especially when it's relatively full and heavy. Sauteuses are typically available in sizes ranging from 2½ to 7 quarts.

Poached Halibut with Saffron, Leeks & Basil

I use a somewhat idiosyncratic poaching technique: Instead of submerging the fish into simmering or boiling liquid, I grease a pan with butter, sprinkle it with shallots, and lay the fillets over it. Then I cover the fish by about two-thirds with a combination of wine and fish stock, cover the pot, and bring it to a simmer. After a few minutes, I remove the pot from the heat and the fish from the pan. This technique—really a cross between steaming and poaching because half of the fish is exposed—makes it easy to monitor doneness and lets you use the same pan for reducing the broth and making the sauce.

The quality of the saffron is crucial to the success of this recipe. Not all saffrons are created equal. I use Iranian saffron. First add the scant quantity indicated in the recipe, then more as needed until you taste it clearly but not overpoweringly.

Rub 1 tablespoon of the butter over the bottom of a deep, heavy-bottomed 10- or 12-inch sauté pan. Sprinkle the shallot over the bottom of the pan and set the fillets on top without crowding them. Gently pour the wine and stock over and around the fish to come about two-thirds up their sides. Cover the pan tightly with a lid or aluminum foil, set over medium-high heat, and bring to a rolling boil, about 3 minutes. Reduce the heat to medium and cook the fish for another minute. Remove the lid, then use a fish spatula or regular spatula to carefully remove the fillets from the pan and transfer them to a large plate or platter. (They will be slightly undercooked, but will continue to cook via carryover heat.) Cover loosely with foil to keep them warm. (If you used foil to cover the pan, you can use the same foil to cover the fish.)

Reserve ½ cup of the poaching liquid and discard the rest. Return the liquid to the sauté pan, set over high heat, and bring to a rolling boil. Add the saffron and boil for 1 minute to reduce it and extract some flavor from the saffron. Add the lemon juice, salt, the remaining 1 tablespoon butter, and the leeks, and cook, stirring frequently, until the leeks are wilted and the sauce is slightly reduced, 3 to 4 minutes. Stir in the cream and continue to reduce over high heat until the leeks are softened but still *al dente* and the sauce just coats the back of a wooden spoon, about 5 minutes. Adjust the seasoning to taste with salt, more lemon juice if necessary, and a bit more saffron, if desired. Stir in the basil.

To serve, place a halibut fillet on each of 4 dinner plates, taking care to drain any juices that may have accumulated so as not to dilute the sauce. Spoon the leeks and sauce over the fish. Serve immediately.

2 tablespoons unsalted butter, softened at room temperature

1 large shallot, minced

Four 6-ounce halibut fillets, any pin bones removed

½ cup dry white wine

½ cup Fish Stock (page 290) or bottled clam juice

⅛ teaspoon high-quality saffron threads, plus more to taste

About ½ teaspoon freshly squeezed lemon juice

Pinch of kosher salt, plus more to taste

2 cups leeks (white and very light green parts only) cut into ¼ x 2-inch ribbons (from about 4 leeks)

1½ cups heavy cream

2 tablespoons fresh basil cut into chiffonade (see Prep Talk, page 70)

SERVES 4

Grilled Turbot with Peas, Pearl Onions & Pancetta

Kosher salt

2 cups shelled fresh peas
(from about 3 pounds peas in the pod)

1 cup loosely packed fresh spinach,
washed well

3 cups Chicken Stock (page 292)
or high-quality store-bought
chicken stock

20 pearl onions, peeled,
with the root left intact

About 1 teaspoon freshly squeezed
lemon juice

3 tablespoons unsalted butter,
softened at room temperature

1 tablespoon all-purpose flour

One 8-ounce slice pancetta
or slab bacon, cut into ½-inch dice

Pinch of sugar

Four 5- or 6-ounce turbot fillets,
any pin bones removed

Black pepper from a mill

SERVES 4

Sweet peas and salty bacon are an enduring combination that speaks to the power of simple, stark contrasts in cooking. Pancetta, often referred to as "Italian bacon," isn't smoked, like its American cousin, and has a more delicate flavor, even after it's been cooked. That said, a high-quality slab bacon can be used as well. The peas here are pureed into a sauce, with just a little spinach added to help ensure a beautiful, vibrant green color. (For this same reason, the puree should not be folded into the sauce until the last second.) While frozen peas are often a viable alternative to fresh, this recipe is not worth making with anything other than fresh, sweet peas.

Turbot, a delicate, white-fleshed fish with a tight, firm texture (it's similar to Dover sole), provides the perfect foil for these big flavors. It has a clean, unfishy character, so lets its fellow ingredients shine. I generally use farmed turbot because its quality is very consistent; you can substitute other mild white fish such as snapper or swordfish.

I like to serve roasted waxy potatoes with this dish, either fingerlings (whole or halved) or Yukon Golds cut into wedges.

Bring a large pot of salted water to a boil and fill a large bowl halfway with ice water. Add 1 cup of the peas to the boiling water and blanch until tender but still green, about 5 minutes. Add the spinach and let it wilt for just a few seconds. Drain the peas and spinach in a strainer, then quickly submerge them in the ice water. Once they are completely cold, drain them again and transfer to a blender. Puree, adding a little cold water if necessary to achieve a very smooth puree.

In a medium heavy-bottomed saucepan set over medium-high heat, bring the stock to a simmer. Add the pearl onions, a pinch of salt, and the lemon juice and cook until the onions are just tender, about 10 minutes. Use a slotted spoon to transfer them to a baking sheet to cool.

Knead 1 tablespoon of the butter and the flour together in a small bowl to make a paste. Stir this into the simmering stock, and cook, whisking occasionally, for about 10 minutes, until the liquid has thickened considerably and yields about 2 cups. Strain through a fine-mesh strainer set over a bowl. (The thickened broth can be cooled and refrigerated in an airtight container for up to 2 days; reheat gently before proceeding.)

Line a plate with paper towels.

In a small heavy-bottomed sauté pan set over low heat, cook the pancetta, stirring occasionally, until the fat is rendered and the meat is crisp, about 15 minutes, draining any excess fat as it accumulates. Remove the pancetta from the pan with a slotted spoon and transfer to the paper towels to drain.

Preheat a grill to high heat and lightly oil the rack.

Bring the thickened stock to a simmer over medium heat. Add the remaining raw peas and cook them for 5 minutes. Add the pearl onions, followed by the pancetta and the remaining 2 tablespoons butter, simmering for another 2 minutes. Just before serving, stir in the pea puree and heat the broth through, seasoning to taste with salt, additional lemon juice, and/or the sugar, if necessary.

Set the turbot on a clean, dry surface, and season it generously on both sides with salt and pepper. Put the fillets on the grill and cook until just done, about 2 minutes on the first side and 20 seconds on the other. Turn the fish 90 degrees after the first minute on the first side to create crosshatched grill marks. Take care not to overcook the fish, particularly if the fillets are thin.

Divide the sauce, peas, pancetta, and pearl onions among 4 dinner plates. Place a turbot fillet in the middle of each and serve immediately.

Osso Buco of Monkfish with Preserved Lemon

Referring to monkfish on the bone as osso buco wasn't my idea; a lot of chefs find that cross-sections of monkfish tail, when floured and browned, bear more than a passing resemblance to that Italian classic. It was, however, my idea to build on the visual similarity with a sauce of tomatoes. But the key ingredient in this recipe is really the preserved lemons. Traditionally a Moroccan condiment added to fragrant tagines of meat or vegetables, lemons preserved with salt and other spices like coriander make a tart, briny addition to recipes where you might otherwise add olives or anchovies. Rinse some of the salt off before using them.

Getting a 4-pound section of monkfish tail, with the bone in, requires some advance planning; call your fishmonger a day or two ahead to ask him or her to order or set this aside for you.

Put the shallots, garlic, coriander seeds, wine, and bay leaves in a large nonreactive saucepan set over medium-high heat. Bring to a boil, reduce the heat slightly, and simmer until reduced by about two-thirds (there will be about 1 cup remaining), about 15 minutes. Stir in the stock and tomato paste and bring to a boil again. Reduce the heat to medium and simmer until about 3 cups remain, about 1½ hours. Strain the liquid through a fine-mesh strainer set over a bowl. (The broth can be cooled and refrigerated in an airtight container for up to 1 week; reheat briefly before proceeding.)

Trim the monkfish tail, removing the slimy outer membranes and skin. Cut the tail crosswise into 4 equal portions with a sturdy knife or cleaver that can slice through the bone. Put the flour in a large shallow bowl and dredge each piece of the fish to coat lightly.

Heat the oil in a 12-inch sauté pan over medium-high heat until hot but not smoking. Add the monkfish to the pan and brown on all sides, about 10 minutes total. Transfer the fish to a plate and wipe out the pan with paper towels. Return the fish to the pan and add enough of the reduced broth to come halfway up the sides of the tails; reserve the remaining broth.

Set the pan over medium-high heat and bring to a boil. Reduce the heat to low, cover tightly with aluminum foil or a lid, and let simmer for about 15 minutes. The monkfish is done when it is tender but not falling off the bone. Carefully transfer the fish to a covered plate and set aside.

Return the broth in the pan to a boil. Add the vegetables, lemon juice, and preserved lemon rind and cook for about 15 minutes, until the liquid is reduced by half. The broth will be slightly thickened and the vegetables tender when done. If the broth is too thick, add some of the reserved broth and reduce to the desired consistency.

Swirl in the butter to mellow and slightly thicken the broth. Add salt and more lemon juice to taste. Return the monkfish to the broth for a moment to reheat.

Place one piece of the monkfish in each of 4 shallow bowls, standing it upright if possible. Spoon the sauce and vegetables over the fish, dividing them evenly among the bowls. Garnish with the cilantro leaves and serve immediately.

5 medium shallots, coarsely chopped

6 garlic cloves, coarsely chopped

2 tablespoons coriander seeds

3 cups dry white wine

3 bay leaves, preferably fresh

8 cups Chicken Stock (page 292) or high-quality low-sodium store-bought chicken stock

1 tablespoon tomato paste

1 large (about 4 pounds) bone-in monkfish tail

About 2 cups Wondra or all-purpose flour, for dredging

3 tablespoons canola or other neutral oil

1 cup finely diced carrot

1 cup finely diced leek (white and light green parts only)

½ cup finely diced yellow squash skin (remove with a vegetable peeler before dicing)

½ cup finely diced zucchini skin (remove with a vegetable peeler before dicing)

Juice of ½ lemon

2 tablespoons finely diced rind of preserved lemon, homemade (page 296) or store-bought

¼ cup (½ stick) unsalted butter, softened at room temperature

Kosher salt

¼ cup loosely packed fresh cilantro leaves

SERVES 4

Skate with Clams & Parsley on Angel Hair Pasta

10 garlic cloves, coarsely chopped

⅔ cup olive oil, plus 2 tablespoons for tossing pasta

1¾ pounds Manila clams (about 30), scrubbed clean

1 cup dry white wine

2 tablespoons unsalted butter, softened at room temperature

2 teaspoons all-purpose flour

1½ cups bottled clam juice

2 cups loosely packed fresh flat-leaf parsley leaves, large stems removed

4 anchovy fillets, preferably packed in olive oil (rather than salt)

4 ounces dried angel hair pasta

Four 5-ounce skate wing fillets (cut from 1 large wing), skinned and trimmed (fluke or turbot may be substituted)

Kosher salt

Black pepper from a mill

About 1 cup Wondra or all-purpose flour, for dusting

3 tablespoons canola or other neutral oil

About ½ teaspoon freshly squeezed lemon juice

SERVES 4

This main-course dish pairs delicate skate—a ray-like fish with faintly ridged flesh that's taken from its large pectoral fins in a shape that's referred to as a wing instead of a fillet—with a tangle of pasta based on the Italian *spaghetti alle vongole,* spaghetti with clams. My version ups all the qualities of the original with generous amounts of garlic and a clam sauce that's made by combining a white wine sauce with a parsley puree rather than just a scattering of chopped parsley. The pasta sauce makes such an impact that no further sauce is needed for the fish; simply lean the cooked fish against the angel hair and clams and serve.

Heat a large heavy-bottomed saucepan over low heat. Add the garlic and ⅓ cup of the olive oil and cook until the garlic softens and becomes somewhat translucent, allowing it to brown only slightly, 8 to 10 minutes. Add the clams and wine, cover tightly with a lid or aluminum foil, and raise the heat to high. Cook until the clams have all opened, 2 to 3 minutes. (Discard any that don't open.) Drain them in a colander set over a large bowl and reserve the liquids. When cool enough to handle, remove the clams from their shells and set aside. Discard the shells.

Knead together 1 tablespoon of the butter and the all-purpose flour in a small bowl until it forms a paste. Set aside. Strain the reserved clam liquid through a piece of cheesecloth (or a very fine sieve) set over a small saucepan. Add the bottled clam juice and bring to a boil. Whisk in the flour paste and continue to stir the sauce as it boils, allowing it to thicken slightly, about 5 minutes. Remove from the heat. (The sauce base can be cooled and refrigerated in an airtight container for up to 2 days; reheat gently before proceeding.)

Bring a large pot of water to a rapid boil and fill a large bowl halfway with ice water. Add the parsley to the boiling water and blanch until it is wilted and bright green, about 20 seconds. Swiftly drain the parsley and place it in the ice bath to stop the cooking process and preserve the parsley's

color. Transfer the parsley to a blender, add the anchovies, ⅓ cup of the olive oil, and an ice cube (to keep it from overheating and discoloring), and puree until very smooth. Set the puree aside. (It can be kept at room temperature for up to 2 hours.)

Bring a large pot of generously salted water to a boil. Add the pasta and cook until *al dente,* about 5 minutes. Drain well in a colander, return to the pot, and toss with the remaining 2 tablespoons olive oil.

Lay the skate fillets on a clean, dry surface and season with salt and pepper. Dust the fillets on both sides with the Wondra. Heat a large, wide, heavy-bottomed sauté pan over medium-high heat until hot. Add the canola oil and heat for a minute or two. Place the fish in the pan and cook for 3 to 4 minutes, then turn and cook the other side until nicely browned and just slightly undercooked, about 2 more minutes.

While the skate is cooking, reheat the clam sauce over low heat. Whisk in the remaining 1 tablespoon butter and, just before serving, add the clams and parsley puree to heat through. Swirl in the lemon juice, adding a few drops more to taste if necessary.

Divide the pasta evenly among 4 dinner plates. Drizzle the sauce and clams over the angel hair and top each with a skate fillet, leaning it against the pasta. Serve immediately.

Poached Salmon
with Basil Butter & "Succotash"

Kosher salt

1 cup mixed shell beans, such as cranberry, fava, lima, flageolets, and/or butter beans

3 tablespoons unsalted butter, softened

1 small onion, finely diced

1 cup fresh corn kernels (from about 1 large ear of corn)

1 cup Chicken Stock (page 292), high-quality low-sodium store-bought chicken stock, or water

Black pepper from a mill

1 large shallot, finely diced

Four 6-ounce wild salmon fillets, skin and any pin bones removed

½ cup Fish Stock (page 290)

½ cup dry white wine

1 teaspoon freshly squeezed lemon juice

⅓ cup heavy cream

½ cup (1 stick) cold unsalted butter, cut into ½-inch cubes

3 tablespoons fresh basil (preferably a mix of green and purple basil) cut into chiffonade (see Prep Talk, page 70)

SERVES 4

A great way to use beans and corn from your own garden or the farmer's market, this is the perfect dish for a warm summer's evening. Gently poached salmon, its flakes swollen and pillowy, is paired with a lightly glazed combination of fresh shell beans and corn. The poaching liquid is perked up with lemon juice, reduced, enriched with butter, and spooned over the fish to unite the salmon and the vegetables.

This dish is especially lovely with green and purple basil, another summer staple.

Bring a large pot of salted water to a boil and fill a large bowl halfway with ice water. Add the beans to the boiling water and blanch for 2 to 3 minutes, then drain, transfer to the ice water to stop the cooking and set the color, drain again, and set aside.

Heat a wide, deep, heavy-bottomed sauté pan over medium heat. Add 2 tablespoons of the softened butter and, when it has melted but not browned, add the onion. Cook until soft and translucent but not browned, 8 to 10 minutes. Add the corn and blanched beans and stir to heat through. Pour in the stock and raise the heat to high. Continue to cook until the liquid has almost completely reduced but enough remains to lightly coat the vegetables, about 5 minutes total. Be careful not to overcook the sauce, as the vegetables may discolor. Season to taste with salt and pepper and set aside, covered, to keep warm.

Rub the remaining 1 tablespoon softened butter over the bottom of a deep, heavy-bottomed 10- or 12-inch sauté pan. Sprinkle the shallot over the bottom of the pan and set the salmon fillets on top without crowding them. Gently pour the stock and wine over and around the fish to come about two-thirds up their sides. Cover the pan

tightly with a lid or aluminum foil, set over medium-high heat, and bring the liquid to a rolling boil, about 3 minutes. Reduce the heat to medium and cook the fish for another minute. Remove the cover and use a fish spatula or regular spatula to carefully remove the fillets from the sauté pan and transfer them to a large plate or platter. (They will be slightly undercooked, but will continue to cook via carryover heat.) Cover loosely with foil. (If you used foil to cover the pan, you can use that to tent the fish.)

Drain and discard all but ⅓ cup of the poaching liquid from the pan. Add the lemon juice and a pinch of salt. Place over high heat, bring to a boil, and cook until reduced by half, about 3 minutes. Stir in the cream, bring back to a boil, and continue to boil for 1 minute. Reduce the heat to medium and whisk in the cold butter, a few pieces at a time, incorporating each addition entirely before adding more. Season to taste with salt and pepper and keep warm. Stir in the basil just before serving.

To serve, drain the succotash in a strainer and divide it evenly among 4 dinner plates. Place the salmon on top and generously spoon over the sauce. Serve immediately.

Salmon with Chamomile & Crisp Artichokes

If you've ever wondered what to cook for those diners in your life who have eaten everywhere and tried everything, this might be a good place to start. A broth infused with chamomile tea is enriched with butter and cream and served with salmon and artichokes. It may take your guests a while to place the sauce's flavor as chamomile (if you want to have some fun, don't tell them what it is, at least not at first). The pan-crisped quartered artichokes look like little flowers, which I've always thought is an apt reflection of how special this dish is.

Roasted or sautéed potatoes make a fine addition to this dish.

Heat a medium, heavy-bottomed, nonreactive saucepan over medium heat. Add the wine and shallots, bring to a boil, and reduce until the pan is nearly dry, about 10 minutes. Add the stock and chamomile tea, bring to a simmer, and cook until about 2 cups remain, about 10 minutes.

Strain the broth through a fine-mesh strainer set over a small saucepan. Add the cream and butter, place the pan over medium heat, and cook at a low boil until thickened a bit, 15 to 20 minutes. Add 1 teaspoon of the lemon juice and season to taste with salt. Keep warm. (The sauce can be kept covered and warm for up to 1 hour; reheat gently and whisk to reincorporate the sauce just before serving.)

Bring a large pot of well-salted water to a boil. Add the artichokes and remaining lemon juice to the pot. Cook the artichokes until tender to a knife tip, about 20 minutes. Use a slotted spoon or tongs to transfer them to a rack to cool, then pull off the outer leaves and use a spoon to scoop out and discard the choke. Quarter the hearts.

Line a large plate with paper towels.

Heat a wide, deep, heavy-bottomed sauté pan over medium heat until hot. Pour in 1 cup of the oil and heat until very hot. Add the artichokes and cook, stirring occasionally, until well browned all over, about 6 minutes. Use a slotted spoon to transfer them to the paper towels to drain; season immediately with salt.

Meanwhile, arrange the salmon fillets on a clean, dry surface and season both sides generously with salt and pepper. Heat a wide, deep, heavy-bottomed sauté pan over medium-high heat. Add the remaining 3 tablespoons oil and turn the pan to coat the bottom with the oil, letting it heat for a minute or two. Add the fillets and cook for 3 minutes per side for rare or a minute or two longer for more well done.

To serve, divide the sauce evenly between 4 wide, shallow bowls. Place a salmon fillet on top of the sauce and arrange 6 pieces of artichoke around each fillet. Serve immediately.

2 cups dry white wine

3 large shallots, finely chopped

3 cups Chicken Stock (page 292) or high-quality low-sodium store-bought chicken stock

⅓ cup high-quality loose chamomile tea

1 cup heavy cream

1 tablespoon unsalted butter, softened at room temperature

Juice of 1 lemon

Kosher salt

6 large artichokes

1 cup plus 3 tablespoons canola or other neutral oil

Four 6- to 7-ounce wild salmon fillets, skin and any pin bones removed

Black pepper from a mill

SERVES 4

Cumin-Crusted Salmon with Citrus Butter & Chive Mashed Potatoes

I love the potent aroma of cumin, which will tease your senses before you eat your first bite of this dish. Paired with a complex citrus sauce featuring grapefruit, orange, lemon, and lime juices, it contributes to the vibrant quality of this composition. The chive mashed potatoes calm the dish down a bit and soak up any extra sauce.

If at all possible, use wild salmon, only because its flavor is more pronounced. Farmed salmon has fallen out of favor of late, but I consider it a perfectly viable alternative. For a special occasion, Scottish farmed salmon is also ideal here.

For a change of pace, using blood oranges in place of regular oranges will add another element to the flavor profile and make the sauce especially beautiful.

To make the citrus butter, combine the wine and all the citrus juices in a medium nonreactive saucepan over medium heat. Bring to a simmer and cook until reduced to ¼ cup of syrupy liquid, about 10 minutes. Take extra care to not burn the reduction, as the high sugar content can scorch easily. Stir in the cream and bring to a boil. Remove the pan from the heat and whisk in the cold butter, a few pieces at a time, thoroughly incorporating each piece before adding more. Season to taste with salt and, if it lacks sweetness, add sugar. Keep the sauce covered at room temperature for up to 1 hour. Reheat gently, if necessary, just before serving.

Lay the fillets out on a clean, dry surface and season both sides with salt and pepper. Coat the salmon on one side only with the cumin seeds, pressing them so they adhere. Heat a large, wide, heavy-bottomed sauté pan over medium-high heat until hot. Add the oil and turn the pan to coat the bottom with the oil, letting it heat for a minute or two. Add the fillets, cumin side down, and allow the fish to cook and the cumin to toast for 2 to 3 minutes (if the seeds appear to be toasting too quickly, lower the heat). Turn the fillets over and cook the other side, 3 to 4 minutes more depending on the thickness of the cut and the desired level of doneness.

Spoon a mound of mashed potatoes into the center of each of 4 dinner plates. Spoon some warm citrus butter around the potatoes on each plate and top the potatoes with a salmon fillet, cumin side up. Serve immediately.

½ cup dry white wine

⅓ cup freshly squeezed pink grapefruit juice (from about 1 grapefruit)

1 cup freshly squeezed orange juice (from about 3 oranges) or not-from-concentrate store-bought

2 tablespoons freshly squeezed lemon juice

1 tablespoon freshly squeezed lime juice

¼ cup heavy cream

½ pound (2 sticks) cold unsalted butter, cut into ½-inch cubes

Kosher salt

Pinch of sugar, if necessary

Four 6-ounce salmon fillets (preferably wild), at least 1 inch thick, skin and any pin bones removed

Black pepper from a mill

3 tablespoons canola or other neutral oil

¼ cup cumin seeds

Chive Mashed Potatoes (page 248)

SERVES 4

Olive Oil–Poached Yellowtail
with Saffron Orzo & Red Pepper Vinaigrette

3 medium red bell peppers

3 tablespoons plus ½ cup extra-virgin olive oil

¼ cup canned or bottled tomato juice

2 tablespoons sherry vinegar

1 small garlic clove, peeled

¼ cup water

Kosher salt

8 cups plus 2 tablespoons olive oil

1 cup coarsely chopped onion

1 cup orzo, preferably Greek or long-grain

¼ teaspoon saffron threads

2 cups Chicken Stock (page 292) or high-quality low-sodium store-bought chicken stock

Four 6-ounce yellowtail fillets or swordfish steaks, any pin bones removed

Fleur de sel or sea salt

Black pepper from a mill

1 tablespoon chopped fresh flat-leaf parsley

SERVES 4

When poached in olive oil, yellowtail—known to sushi lovers as hamachi—becomes quite luxurious. I have a penchant for buttery sauces, but the fish is so rich here that none is needed. This is intended as a summer dish, with the fish served warm rather than hot, and the other ingredients in perfect sync with the season: a lively, roasted red pepper vinaigrette and a saffron orzo, all of which bring to mind the Mediterranean and the seaside.

This recipe calls for a lot of olive oil. You can use the most inexpensive variety available; pomace is fine. You can reuse the oil, but it will take on the flavor of the fish, so should only be used for poaching or frying other fish.

To make the red pepper vinaigrette, preheat the oven to 425°F.

Cut the stem end off each pepper and remove the seeds. Place the peppers on a baking sheet, cut side down, and drizzle each one with 1 tablespoon of the extra-virgin olive oil. Transfer to the oven and roast until they are slightly charred and just starting to collapse, 20 to 25 minutes.

Transfer the peppers to a large nonreactive bowl, cover tightly with plastic wrap, and let steam in their own heat until cool enough to handle, about 15 minutes. Peel the peppers and place them, along with any juices that have accumulated in the bowl, into a blender. Add the remaining ½ cup extra-virgin olive oil, the tomato juice, vinegar, garlic, and water, and puree until smooth. Season to taste with salt. Set the vinaigrette aside or refrigerate in an airtight container for up to 2 days. (If it separates, reincorporate with an immersion blender or in a regular blender.)

Heat 2 tablespoons of the olive oil in a medium saucepan over medium heat. Add the onion and cook, stirring frequently, until softened but not browned, 8 to 10 minutes. Add the orzo and increase the heat slightly,

stirring to coat it with the oil and brown it slightly. Add the saffron and stir for another 2 to 3 minutes. Pour in the stock, increase the heat to high, and bring to a boil. Reduce the heat to low, add a generous pinch of salt, stir, cover, and cook until the stock is absorbed and the orzo is cooked through, about 20 minutes, adding more stock or water if necessary to keep the orzo from drying out. Season with more salt to taste and keep covered and warm.

Pour the remaining 8 cups olive oil into a large heavy-bottomed pot and heat over medium heat to a temperature of 100°F. Add the yellowtail and poach until it is just slightly underdone (it will feel firm but not excessively so), about 8 minutes. Carefully remove the fish from the oil using a metal spatula or slotted spoon. Drain each piece on paper towels and keep warm.

Divide the orzo evenly among 4 dinner plates. Place a fillet on top and season with fleur de sel and pepper. Drizzle each serving with red pepper sauce and garnish the plate with the parsley. Serve immediately.

Seared Tuna with Pistou

I've always had a fondness for pistou, the French version of pesto, a puree of basil, garlic, and olive oil. Here, I stir my version of this summery condiment, made luscious with butter, into a sauce based on minestrone, which I think of as a summer soup, the perfect place to show off fresh shell beans and zucchini in a lusty, garlicky broth. These two elements perfectly complement the seared tuna.

Heat ½ cup of the olive oil in a medium heavy-bottomed pot over medium heat. Add the carrot and onion chunks and garlic heads, and cook, stirring occasionally, until softened and lightly browned, about 10 minutes. Pour in the wine, raise the heat to high, and cook until the pan is almost dry, about 5 minutes. Add the stock, tomatoes, bay leaves, basil stems and any blemished leaves, and red chile flakes. Bring to a boil, then reduce the heat so the liquid is simmering and cook gently until about 5 cups remain, about 1½ hours.

Strain the broth through a fine-mesh strainer set over a medium heavy-bottomed saucepan. Bring the broth to a simmer over low heat. Add the diced carrots and cook until tender to a knife tip, about 4 minutes. Use a slotted spoon to transfer them to a large bowl. Repeat with the zucchini, cooking for about 2 minutes and adding it to the bowl, then the leeks (3 minutes), orzo (15 minutes), and, finally, the lima beans (8 minutes). Set the bowl with the vegetables and orzo aside. (The broth and vegetables can be prepared and refrigerated in separate airtight containers for up to 3 days; let come to room temperature before proceeding.)

To make the basil pistou, put the whole basil leaves, garlic cloves, the remaining ½ cup olive oil, and the butter in a blender and puree to a smooth paste. Transfer to a bowl, scraping down the sides of the blender with a rubber spatula to retrieve as much pistou as possible, and set aside at room temperature for up to 3 hours, but no longer or it will begin to discolor.

Lay the tuna out on a clean, dry surface, and generously season on both sides with salt and pepper. Heat a wide, deep, heavy-bottomed sauté pan over high heat until very hot. Add the canola oil and tilt the pan to coat the bottom with the oil. Add the tuna and sear for 2 to 3 minutes per side, turning the pieces as soon as each side is seared to maintain a rare interior.

Meanwhile, return the broth to a boil. Add all the vegetables, orzo, and beans back to the broth and reheat for 2 minutes. Add the lemon juice. Season to taste with salt and a few more drops of lemon juice, if necessary. Stir in the pistou, then taste and correct the seasoning, if necessary.

Ladle the vegetables and broth into 4 large shallow bowls. Set a piece of tuna in each bowl. Garnish with the basil chiffonade and serve immediately.

1 cup olive oil

3 medium carrots, unpeeled, cut into 1-inch chunks

2 large yellow onions, unpeeled, cut into 1-inch chunks

3 garlic heads, in their skins, cut in half horizontally

2 cups dry white wine

10 cups Fish Stock (page 290), Chicken Stock (page 292), or high-quality low-sodium store-bought chicken stock

2 cups canned tomatoes, with their juice, crushed by hand

3 bay leaves, preferably fresh

2 cups loosely packed fresh basil leaves, (set aside the basil stems and any blemished leaves for use in the broth)

¼ teaspoon red chile flakes

1 cup diced (¼-inch) carrots

1 cup diced (¼-inch) zucchini cut from the outer portion of the vegetable (so each piece has skin on one side)

1 large leek (white and light green parts), washed well and cut into ¼-inch dice

¼ cup orzo

1 cup shelled fresh or frozen lima or butter beans

2 garlic cloves, peeled

3 tablespoons unsalted butter, softened at room temperature

Four 6-ounce yellowfin or bigeye tuna steaks, ideally 1½ inches thick, any pin bones removed

Kosher salt

Black pepper from a mill

3 tablespoons canola or other neutral oil

About 1 teaspoon fresh lemon juice

2 tablespoons fresh basil cut into chiffonade (see Prep Talk, page 70)

SERVES 4

Peppered Tuna with Escarole & Sweet Wine Reduction

1¼ cups golden raisins

One 750 ml bottle sweet wine (Greek Muscat, if you can find it, is perfect for this recipe and inexpensive)

2 large shallots, coarsely chopped

5 cups Chicken Stock (page 292)

2½ tablespoons unsalted butter

½ tablespoon all-purpose flour

Juice from ½ lemon

Kosher salt

About 1 teaspoon honey (optional)

3 tablespoons olive oil

2 heads escarole, washed well, dried, and cut across into 1-inch-wide ribbons

Black pepper from a mill

20 ounces sushi-grade tuna, cut into 4 rectangles as uniform in shape as possible

Cracked black peppercorns

2 tablespoons canola or other neutral oil

Fleur de sel or fine sea salt (optional)

SERVES 4

This is an unusual treatment of tuna that pairs it with sweet and bitter flavors, specifically a reduction of sweet wine infused with raisins and shallots and offset by a simple sauté of escarole.

When cooking the tuna, the desired effect is a seared outside and a red-but-not-cold interior. To achieve this, careful timing is essential: Sear all but one side on the stovetop, then, after turning the tuna the final time, pop the pan in the oven so it warms through while the final side is seared.

I find that it's helpful to score tuna before cooking it and to use a very sharp knife; otherwise it may crumble when you slice it. One other note: Buy already cracked black pepper—sometimes sold as "butcher's grind"—for this dish. It's much more uniformly ground than any pepper you will crack at home.

A few hours before you plan to make the dish, soak ¼ cup of the raisins in ¼ cup of the wine.

Put the shallots, the remaining wine, and remaining 1 cup raisins in a large, heavy-bottomed, nonreactive saucepan. Bring to a boil and reduce the liquid by two-thirds, about 10 minutes. Add the stock, return to a boil, and then reduce the heat so the liquid is simmering and cook until the mixture is nicely thickened and has taken on the flavor of the raisins and shallots, 20 to 30 minutes.

Strain through a fine-mesh strainer set over a small heavy-bottomed saucepan on medium heat. In a small bowl, knead ½ tablespoon of the butter and the flour together into a paste and whisk this into the sauce. Cook, stirring and skimming occasionally, until the sauce is lightly thickened, with no flour taste whatsoever. You should have about 1 cup of sauce. Season with a few drops of lemon juice and salt. Depending on the wine you used, you might also want to add a little honey; the sauce should be sweet, but not cloyingly so. Keep the sauce covered and warm.

Preheat the broiler and position a rack in the center of the oven.

Heat the olive oil in a sauté pan over high heat. Add the escarole and cook, stirring, until just wilted but still *al dente,* 3 to 4 minutes. Drain well, season with salt and pepper, and set aside, covered, to keep it warm.

Lightly coat the tuna pieces all over with the cracked pepper and season with salt. Heat a large, wide, heavy-bottomed, ovenproof sauté pan over medium-high heat until hot. Add the canola oil and let it heat for a minute or two. Add the tuna and sear it on all sides, turning it with tongs. After turning the tuna onto its final side, pop the pan into the oven to just warm the tuna through about 30 seconds.

Gently reheat the escarole and/or sauce if necessary. Whisk the remaining 2 tablespoons butter into the sauce and adjust the seasoning if necessary. If the soaking raisins have not absorbed all of their wine, drain them.

Put a mound of escarole on each of 4 dinner plates and scatter some of the raisins about. Spoon some sauce around the escarole. Cut each piece of tuna into 3 or 4 slices and fan over the escarole. Sprinkle with fleur de sel, if using, and serve immediately.

A Mom-and-Pop Restaurant:
The Chanterelle Family

David and I often refer to Chanterelle as a mom-and-pop restaurant. We don't just mean that we try to bring a personal touch and hands-on approach to everything we do. We also mean that, although we have two dear children of our own, we think of ourselves as the mom and dad of the staff, providing a home for them to work and grow, encouraging them to pursue their other interests. We're always delighted to have staff return between other jobs, or after some time away from New York City...and what could be more mom-and-pop than that?

And, then, of course, there's the pleasure of watching them progress in their own pursuits. A perfect example is Adrian Murcia, who started with us as a waiter while he was establishing himself as a food writer and is now a maitre d'. Adrian is also a very passionate and ambitious cheese enthusiast: When we discovered the depth of his knowledge and knack for innovation, we made him our first *fromager*.

It's a tribute to the restaurant's environment that many of our employees stay with us for years, such as our dream sommelier Roger Dagorn (see page 237); our wonderful pastry chef, Kate Zuckerman, who's been with us since 1999; and my remarkable general manager for more than a decade, George Stinson, the perfect man for his job, impeccably groomed with a Fred Astaire grace on the service floor. There's Amy Ehrenreich, my officemate and the restaurant's special-events director supreme. In the kitchen, there's Steve Jackson, David's sous chef for nearly a decade and the consummate professional; in the dining room, the erudite Edward Easton, an eighteen-year veteran of the staff; and Randy Morey, a photographer in his other life, who waited tables at La Petite Ferme when David was the sous chef there all those years ago, then came with us to Chanterelle and never left.

Some of our employees come and go, like Keith Harry, who returns as sous chef between gigs as a chef in his own right, or the über-talented sous chef Daniel Rothstein, who worked with David for a time, then went on to manage another Tribeca institution, Montrachet, and came back briefly as our general manager before leaving the biz to get a Ph.D. in psychology.

One of our favorite sons is no longer with us: the composer Michael Bilunas, whose love of opera gave us a special connection. A true renaissance man, taking a serious interest in food and wine, he became my general manager, helping me keep the wine cellar in order and, in time, became our first sommelier. Michael was a riot: Once Frank Sinatra came in and spent the night smoking unfiltered cigarettes. Michael harvested the twisted, smashed butts from the ashtray, fixed them on a board with pushpins, framed it, and titled it "Frank Sinatra's Butts"—it's not the kind of thing most restaurateurs would encourage in their employees, but Michael wasn't just an employee.

None of them are.

—KAREN WALTUCK

Poultry & Rabbit

¶ Poultry and rabbit, which I group in a single category in my mind because I rarely serve both as part of the same meal, allow me to explore all facets of my fascination with food. Many of the most classic French dishes that first inspired me to cook are poultry based, and I've enjoyed a lifelong interest in Chinese cuisine, which has a major focus on chicken and duck with ambient flavors that couldn't be further removed from their western counterparts. ¶ This chapter makes room for both sides of my culinary personality, as well as some of my favorite game birds, such as quail and squab. What unites all of these dishes is that, whether they're based on classic French or Chinese formulas, they are all given the Chanterelle treatment, gussied up a bit to satisfy my tendency to romanticize food. So, a Chanterelle original such as Duck Breast with Fresh Chiles (page 191) looks as sophisticated and tastes as refined as the iconic Chicken Demi-Deuil (page 170). This is true even of the American staple chicken potpie, which is presented in our dining room, and in this book, as something special, cooked and served from a ceramic or cast-iron cooking vessel, turning the everyday into something beautiful and exciting.

Chicken Demi-Deuil

2 ounces fresh or flash-frozen black truffles (1 or 2 truffles)

2 tablespoons Madeira, plus more if necessary

Two 2½-pound chickens

Kosher salt

Black pepper from a mill

2 tablespoons unsalted butter, softened at room temperature

8 cups Chicken Stock (page 292)

One 7-ounce can black truffle juice

2 medium carrots, peeled

2 large leeks (white parts only)

2 medium zucchini

4 ounces haricots verts (about 1½ cups), ends trimmed

½ cup (1 stick) cold unsalted butter, cut into ½-inch cubes

½ teaspoon freshly squeezed lemon juice, plus more if necessary

SERVES 4

The name of this dish means "chicken in half-mourning," a reference to the veil-like appearance of the black truffles tucked beneath the skin of the chicken. It's a classic that I'd read about in cookbooks for years before first tasting it at La Pyramide. This is a quintessential Chanterelle dish that takes a time-honored recipe and really amps up the flavors. I let the prepared chicken rest overnight, giving the truffles a chance to permeate the meat, and the truffle theme is reinforced with reduced black truffle juice in the sauce. I also enhance this dish with assorted vegetables. You can alter the mixture; keep the carrots and leeks, but use turnips to replace some or all of the zucchini and thinly sliced snow peas for some or all of the haricots verts.

Slice the truffle very thinly using a mandoline or a very sharp, thin-bladed knife and a steady hand. Put the slices in a small bowl, add the Madeira, and let soak briefly to moisten the truffles (making it easier to slide them under the chicken skin and giving them some Madeira flavor). Strain the truffle in a fine-mesh strainer set over a small bowl. Reserve the liquid.

Moisten your hands under cold running water and loosen the skin on the chickens' breasts and thighs, carefully sliding your hands between the skin and meat. Slide the truffle slices under the skin of the chicken breasts to cover them, then slide a slice or two under the skin of each thigh. Finely chop the remaining truffle slices and set aside for use in the sauce. Truss the chickens, cover with plastic wrap, and refrigerate overnight to allow the truffles to flavor and perfume the chickens.

When ready to proceed, preheat the oven to 400°F.

Season the chickens generously with salt and pepper, then rub with the softened butter. Set on a rack in a roasting pan and roast for 40 minutes. (The chicken will be underdone.)

Pour the stock, truffle juice, reserved chopped truffle, and reserved Madeira into an ovenproof, flameproof casserole large enough to hold the chickens with some room to spare. Bring to a boil, then lower the heat so the liquid is simmering and cook until reduced to about 4 cups, about 30 minutes.

Remove the strings from the chickens and set them in the casserole, breast side up. Cover and braise at a simmer until fully cooked, about 20 minutes.

Meanwhile, cut the carrots and leeks into square segments, keeping them separate. Wash the leeks well (see page 53). Cut off the ends of the zucchini and cut out the center portion by slicing down its length to remove 4 rounded sides. Discard the rectangular center portion and cut the outer portions into 2½-x¼-inch-square segments.

Transfer the chickens to a large serving platter and cover with aluminum foil to keep warm.

Add the carrots, leeks, zucchini, and haricots verts to the braising liquid, raise the heat to high, and cook

continued

until the vegetables are heated through and the broth has reduced a bit, about 5 minutes. Swirl in the cold butter, one cube at a time, to thicken and enrich it. Taste and adjust the seasoning with salt, pepper, Madeira, and/or lemon juice.

Spoon some sauce and vegetables over the chickens on the serving platter and serve, or return the chickens to the casserole and serve from the casserole, carving the chickens at the table and serving the pieces in bowls, spooning vegetables and sauce over each serving.

Chicken with Verjus & Garlic Cloves

A variation on the classic chicken with forty cloves of garlic, this recipe makes great use of verjus. Once known almost exclusively to chefs, verjus—an acidic juice made from unripe wine grapes—has grown in popularity among home cooks in recent years. Here, it's the perfect complement to the garlic and chicken; the combination is so complete that very little technique is called for: the chicken is browned and finished in the oven and the sauce is made by lightly browning the garlic, deglazing with verjus, and finishing with butter.

I like to use California verjus in this and other dishes (my preferred brand is Fusion) because it has a more complex sweet-and-sour quality than French verjus, which is overwhelmingly sour.

Preheat the oven to 425°F.

Heat a large heavy-bottomed sauté pan over medium-high heat. Season the chicken on both sides with salt and pepper. Pour the oil into the hot pan. When it begins to smoke, add the chicken, skin side down, and cook until the skin is well browned, 7 to 8 minutes. Turn and cook the other side for 3 minutes. Transfer the breasts to a baking sheet, skin side up.

Pour all but 2 tablespoons of oil out of the pan. Reduce the heat to medium, add the garlic, and cook, stirring a few times, until the cloves are golden brown but no darker, about 5 minutes. Add the verjus, raise the heat to high, and scrape up any browned bits stuck to the bottom of the pan. Cook until the liquid is syrupy and slightly caramelized, about 5 minutes, but take care not to burn the sugars in the verjus. Pour in the stock, bring to a boil, and reduce by two-thirds, 10 to 15 minutes. Reduce the heat to medium-low and swirl in the butter, one cube at a time, to thicken and enrich the sauce.

Place the chicken breasts in the oven to finish cooking them and recrisp their skin, 4 to 5 minutes.

Meanwhile, taste the sauce and adjust the seasoning with salt and pepper. It should be sweet and sour, but more tart than sweet. Adjust with a few drops of lemon juice if necessary. Swirl in the parsley.

Place a chicken breast on each of 4 dinner plates. Top with a spoonful of sauce and serve immediately.

4 large boneless chicken breast halves, skin on, preferably "frenched" (first wing joint still attached)

Kosher salt

Black pepper from a mill

¼ cup canola or other neutral oil

1½ cups garlic cloves, peeled

2 cups verjus

2½ cups Chicken Stock (page 292)

3 tablespoons cold unsalted butter, cut into ½-inch cubes

Freshly squeezed lemon juice, if necessary

3 tablespoons coarsely chopped fresh flat-leaf parsley

SERVES 4

Steamed Chicken Breast Stuffed with Foie Gras in Leek Broth

12 large leeks

2 tablespoons unsalted butter

About 4 quarts Chicken Stock (page 292)

About 1 tablespoon dry white wine, if necessary

Kosher salt

Black pepper from a mill

2 bay leaves, preferably fresh

1 cup coarsely chopped fresh chives (about 1 ounce)

½ cup canola or other neutral oil

4 boneless, skinless chicken breast halves (about 6 ounces each)

Four ½-inch-thick slices duck foie gras (about 1 ounce each), preferably New York State or Hudson Valley

SERVES 4

There's a bit of a Trojan horse effect at work in this dish, which looks like a delicate, almost serene composition: steamed chicken breast and a variety of light green, onion-themed accompaniments (leek broth, chive puree). But when the breast is cut open, the delicate meat gives way to the oozing, decadent fat of foie gras, a rare but successful marriage of the subtle and the sensational.

While not absolutely essential, the chicken breasts are best cooked in a steaming basket large enough to hold a heatproof plate, so that you can catch the delicious juices from both the chicken and foie gras and incorporate them into the leek broth just before serving.

To make the leek compote, trim the greens off 4 of the leeks, setting them aside for use in the broth. Cut the white and light green portions in half lengthwise and then on the diagonal into 1-inch segments. Put the leeks in a large bowl filled with cold water and agitate to loosen any sand or dirt. Lift them out by hand and transfer to a colander to drain, leaving any sand and dirt in the bottom of the bowl. (Don't pour the contents of the bowl into the colander, or some dirt will catch in the leeks.)

Melt the butter in a large heavy-bottomed sauté pan over medium-low heat. When it has just melted, add the leeks and cook slowly, stirring occasionally, until they are very soft but not at all browned, about 20 minutes. If necessary, add a splash of chicken stock or white wine to keep them from scorching. Season with salt and pepper and keep warm. (The leek compote can be refrigerated in an airtight container for up to 3 days; gently reheat before proceeding.)

To make the leek broth, cut the remaining 8 leeks (green and white parts) into 1-inch chunks and wash well. Put them in a medium stockpot or soup pot. Add the greens trimmed from the leeks you used to make

the compote. Add the stock and bay leaves. Bring to a boil, then reduce the heat so the liquid is simmering and cook for 1½ hours; the liquid should be reduced and flavorful. Strain in a cheesecloth-lined colander set over a bowl. Press down on the leeks with the back of a ladle or wooden spoon to extract as much flavorful liquid as possible. If you have more than 3 cups, wipe out the pot, return the strained broth to the pot, bring to a boil, and reduce to 3 cups. If you have less than 3 cups, add enough chicken stock to yield 3 cups. Season with salt and keep warm. (The broth can be refrigerated in an airtight container for up to 3 days; reheat gently before proceeding.)

To make the chive puree, bring a large pot of salted water to a boil. Fill a large bowl halfway with ice water. Blanch the chives in the boiling water until wilted and bright green, about 10 seconds. Use tongs to transfer them to the ice water to stop the cooking and set the color. Drain and transfer to a blender. Add the oil and season with salt and pepper, then process to a pesto-like consistency. Cover and refrigerate for up to 3 hours.

When ready to cook and serve the dish, make an incision in each chicken breast on the thicker side, creating a pocket. Open it as wide as possible but don't tear the meat, and season inside with salt and pepper. Slide a piece of foie gras into the pocket of each chicken breast and close the incision by pressing it together firmly, taking care not to squeeze the foie gras.

Ideally, you will steam the chicken in a two-tiered, 12-inch steaming basket, but you can use a smaller basket, tiered or not, and steam in batches as necessary. If using a large enough steamer, set a heatproof plate in the bottom of each tier and set the chicken atop the plate. There should be space between the breasts and room around the edge of the plate for the steam to circulate freely. Fill a pot sized to hold the steaming basket(s) with 2 inches of water and bring to a boil.

Season the chicken with salt and pepper, then steam for 6 to 7 minutes; if using two steamers, carefully reverse them after 3 minutes to ensure even cooking. The chicken should be just cooked through and the foie gras warm. Turn off the heat and let the chicken rest in the covered steamer for 2 to 3 minutes.

To serve, stir the juices and fat from the plates holding the chicken into the warm leek broth. Divide the leek compote among 4 wide, shallow bowls. Cut each chicken breast in half and place two halves on top of the compote in each bowl. Ladle the broth (a little more than ¼ cup per serving) over and around the chicken in each bowl. Drizzle the chive puree around the chicken and serve immediately.

Chicken Breast with Black Trumpet Mushroom Coulis

There are two distinct ideas at work in this dish: The first is the steamed chicken breast. Cooking the meat in this way gives it a very full, voluptuous texture and clean flavor. The other is the black trumpet coulis. Black trumpets are thought of as a poor man's truffle in Europe, but I've always liked their earthy, nutty flavor, which I think deserves to stand on its own. They can be a little intense, and that's the surprise of this dish: The mushrooms are the star, the chicken is the relief.

Heat a large heavy-bottomed saucepan over medium-high heat. Add 1 tablespoon of the butter; when it's foamy, add the onion, garlic, and mushrooms. Cook, stirring a few times, until the onion and garlic are soft and translucent and the mushrooms have released most of their liquid, about 5 minutes. Pour in the stock, bring to a boil, and reduce until 1 cup remains, about 20 minutes. Let cool slightly, then transfer to a blender and puree until very smooth, leaving out the center piece of the blender cover to allow steam to escape and covering the top with a kitchen towel to keep hot liquid from escaping.

Wipe out the saucepan and pour the puree back into it. Set over low heat and whisk in the remaining 1 tablespoon butter, the Madeira, lemon juice, and kosher salt. If the puree looks too thick and pasty, thin it with additional stock or water to achieve a sauce consistency.

Keep warm until ready to serve, or refrigerate in an air-tight container for up to 2 days and reheat, whisking, just before serving.

(You may need to do the following in batches, or in two steamers.) When ready to serve, set a steamer basket snugly over a large pot filled one-third with water. (If the steamer basket doesn't fit snugly, line the edge of the pot with aluminum foil to help seal it and hold the basket in place.) Bring the water to a rapid simmer over high heat. Season the chicken on both sides with salt and pepper and set the pieces in the steamer. Steam until the breasts are almost cooked through, about 5 minutes. Transfer to a plate or platter and cover with foil; the carryover heat will finish cooking them.

To serve, spoon some sauce onto each of 4 dinner plates and top with a chicken breast. Season with sea salt to taste and serve immediately.

2 tablespoons unsalted butter

½ small onion, coarsely chopped

1½ medium garlic cloves, coarsely chopped

5 ounces black trumpet mushrooms, stems trimmed, cut in half lengthwise, and washed well in several changes of cold water (discard any slimy mushrooms)

2 cups Chicken Stock (page 292) or high-quality low-sodium store-bought chicken stock

½ teaspoon Madeira

½ teaspoon freshly squeezed lemon juice, plus more to taste

Kosher salt

4 boneless, skinless chicken breast halves (about 6 ounces each)

Sea salt

SERVES 4

Chicken Breast with Crayfish

One 750 ml bottle dry white wine

½ cup freshly squeezed lemon juice (from 3 to 4 lemons)

4 cups water

Kosher salt

18 live crayfish, cleaned if necessary (see sidebar on facing page)

½ cup (1 stick) unsalted butter

2 small shallots, finely chopped

1 small garlic clove, finely chopped

1 tablespoon tomato paste

4 boneless chicken breast halves, skin on, preferably "frenched" (first wing joint still attached)

Black pepper from a mill

¼ cup canola or other neutral oil

2 tablespoons good-quality brandy

½ cup heavy cream

Dash of Tabasco sauce

Finely chopped fresh tarragon

SERVES 4

To be honest, this dish is really all about the sauce. The chicken is just the vehicle to get it from the plate to your mouth. It's a terrific combination that entices many of our guests who wouldn't usually order chicken. You could also use this sauce on pasta or with fish.

Pour the wine, lemon juice, and water into a large pot, bring to a boil, and season with plenty of salt. Add the crayfish and blanch until bright red, about 5 minutes. Drain and lay them flat on a baking sheet to cool.

Twist off the crayfish heads, and twist and pull off their middle tail fins, taking out the dark vein with them (if the vein is stubborn, split the bodies lengthwise to remove it). Cut the tail meat into ½-inch-thick slices and set aside, along with any meat you can extract from the bodies. Reserve the heads and shells, and discard the veins.

In a wide sauté pan, melt the butter and add the crayfish shells and heads, shallots, and garlic. Season with salt and cook, stirring, over medium-low heat without browning, until most of the moisture has evaporated, about 8 minutes. Add the tomato paste and cook and stir for another minute. Transfer to a blender or food processor fitted with a steel blade and process into a coarse puree.

Return the puree to the pan and cook and stir, preferably with a heatproof rubber spatula, over medium-low heat until all the moisture has sizzled out, but the mixture has not browned, about 5 minutes more. Press the crayfish shell mixture through a fine-mesh strainer set over a bowl.

Season the chicken on both sides with salt and pepper. Heat the oil in a very large sauté pan over medium-high heat. Add the chicken, in batches if necessary, and cook until well browned and almost cooked through, about 6 minutes per side. Transfer to a platter and tent with aluminum foil to keep warm.

Wipe out the pan and add the crayfish puree (use 1 to 2 tablespoons per chicken breast). Heat until sizzling, then add the reserved crayfish meat. Cook over medium heat until warmed, about 3 minutes. Add the brandy and simmer for 1 minute. Add the cream and simmer until thickened, about 2 minutes. Season with Tabasco, salt, and pepper. Pour the sauce over the chicken breasts, garnish with tarragon, and serve immediately.

CRAYFISH

Known in France as *écrevisses* and served gratinéed, these small, lobsterlike shellfish are sold in this country as crayfish, crawfish, or crawdads, and are particularly favored down South. If your crayfish seem dirty, as they often are, wash them in a large bowl of cold water before cooking. Like shrimp, crayfish have a dark central intestinal vein that should be removed. Some older French cookbooks advocate twisting and pulling the heads off of live crayfish in such a way as to pull out the vein at the same time, but I've found the task to be nearly impossible. Instead, I blanch the crayfish first, then drain them and let them lie flat as they cool. Once cooked and cooled, it is easier to remove the vein by twisting and pulling off the middle tail fin (if the vein doesn't come along with the fin, split the body lengthwise and simply lift it out). If you can't find fresh crayfish, use frozen whole ones. Just avoid those from China, which are flavorless.

Kosher salt

8 baby carrots, peeled

8 baby yellow beets or baby turnips, peeled

¼ cup (½ stick) unsalted butter, softened at room temperature

1 pound chanterelle or other wild mushrooms, such as morels, stems trimmed and washed

Black pepper from a mill

Two 2½- to 3-pound chickens

7 cups Mushroom Stock (page 290)

2 medium carrots, unpeeled, cut into 1-inch chunks

1 medium onion, unpeeled, cut into 1-inch chunks

1 garlic head, in its skin, cut in half horizontally

1 tablespoon chopped fresh tarragon

½ teaspoon freshly squeezed lemon juice, plus more to taste

2 tablespoons Madeira, plus more to taste

4 ounces haricots verts, ends trimmed

¼ cup fines herbes (1 tablespoon each coarsely chopped fresh flat-leaf parsley, chives, tarragon, and chervil)

4 sheets frozen puff pastry, defrosted in the refrigerator

1 large egg

2 tablespoons milk

SERVES 4

Chicken Potpie with Chanterelles

Rooted in American comfort food, Chanterelle's chicken potpie is one of the true head-turning dishes in our dining room, where it's presented in its cooking vessel at the table, then "carved" tableside by a server who artfully arranges pieces of puff pastry, succulent chicken, and steamed vegetables, topped with an aromatic mushroom sauce, on the plate. It's a deconstructed take on a classic; in fact, it's literally deconstructed right before your eyes.

Much of this recipe can be prepared in advance; actually, it's essential that all of the components be cold when you assemble the potpies, or else the puff pastry will melt before the dish goes into the oven. So if you make the components just before assembling the pies, be sure to chill them.

This recipe is nicely adaptable—you can change the vegetables, substituting baby zucchini or baby corn for the carrots or beets, and, if you don't want to roast a whole chicken, you can buy and roast bone-in thigh and breast pieces. The result won't be as juicy, but it will still be good.

Note that you will need four ceramic or cast-iron dishes, such as soufflé dishes, with a 4-cup capacity, ideally 6 inches in diameter and 3 inches high.

Bring a large pot of salted water to a boil. Fill a bowl with ice water. Add the baby carrots to the boiling water and blanch for 5 minutes. Use a slotted spoon to transfer them to the ice water to stop the cooking, then transfer to a cutting board. Add the beets to the boiling water and blanch for 5 minutes, then transfer them to the ice water, and then to the cutting board. Halve the carrots, quarter the beets, and set aside separately.

Melt 2 tablespoons of the butter in a large heavy-bottomed sauté pan over medium heat. Add the mushrooms and cook until they have given off enough liquid that they are swimming in juice, about 5 minutes. Drain in a colander set over a small bowl and reserve the mushrooms and juice separately. Return the mushrooms

to the pan and set over medium-high heat. Cook, tossing or stirring gently, until they are dry and beginning to brown, 8 to 10 minutes. Season with salt and pepper and set aside to cool. (The mushrooms and liquid can be refrigerated in separate airtight containers for up to 3 days.)

Preheat the oven to 425°F.

Truss the chickens and rub each with 1 tablespoon of the remaining butter. Season them all over with salt and pepper. Set on a rack in a roasting pan and roast for 40 minutes. (The chickens will be slightly undercooked.) Remove from the oven and let cool completely.

Carve the chickens, removing the breasts, legs, and thighs. Separate the wings from the breasts. You will use only the breasts and thighs for the potpies; save the legs, wings, and carcasses for stock or soup. (The chicken will keep, wrapped in plastic wrap in the refrigerator, for up to 2 days.)

To make the sauce, pour the stock into a large heavy-bottomed saucepan and add the reserved mushroom cooking liquid. Add the carrot and onion chunks, the garlic, and tarragon, and bring to a boil. Reduce the heat so the liquid is simmering and cook until reduced to 3 cups, about 1 hour. Strain through a fine-mesh strainer set over

a bowl. Taste and season with salt, the lemon juice, and Madeira, then remove from the heat and let cool. (The sauce can be refrigerated in an airtight container for up to 3 days.)

To prepare the potpies for baking, divide the chanterelles among the 4 individual casseroles. Set a chicken breast and thigh in each dish. Divide the baby carrots, beets, haricots verts, and sauce evenly among the dishes and

continued

sprinkle 1 tablespoon of the fines herbes over the top of each. The filling of the potpies must be at least ¾ inch below the top of the dishes to keep the puff pastry from touching the filling, otherwise the pastry will remain raw and gummy after cooking.

On a lightly floured work surface, roll each pastry sheet out until ⅛ inch thick, then cut a 10-inch round from it. Beat the egg and milk together in a small bowl and use a pastry brush to brush the edge of each round with some of it. Reserve the remaining egg wash. Set a pastry round, egg-wash side down, on top of each casserole. There should be 1½ to 2 inches hanging over the sides. Gently press, but do not crimp, the overhanging pastry against the side of the casserole to hold it in place, but don't seal it. Chill the potpies in the refrigerator for at least

10 minutes or up to 1 hour to firm up the pastry. Don't let the pies touch each other or the pastry tops will stick together. Meanwhile, preheat the oven to 400°F.

Just before baking, crimp the pastry all the way around the top of the casserole, pressing it with your fingers to completely seal the contents inside. Brush the pastry with the remaining egg wash. Bake for about 20 minutes; the pastry will rise to form a dome and should be golden brown. (You can let the finished pies rest for up to 10 minutes and they will remain hot; the puff pastry will not fall.)

To serve, cut around the top of the potpies and place each pastry on a dinner plate. Spoon out the contents of the potpie over about half of the pastry, leaving the rest crisp and dry.

CHANTERELLES
(& OTHER WILD MUSHROOMS)

Every fall, one of my favorite purveyors appears at our door with a basket of new mushrooms. It's one of my favorite moments in the year, a reminder of our early days, when, because of our name, farmers and purveyors we'd never met would show up trying to sell us mushrooms. Karen often turns the first wild mushrooms of the year into an artful arrangement for the dining room; it's one of the few times anything other than flowers is displayed there.

Back when Chanterelle began, our namesake fungi, as well as cèpes (porcini), morels, black trumpets, and other wild mushrooms weren't as easy to find as they are today; they were almost a luxury item because they were so rare. Today, the mushroom industry has become a big business, which sounds great but has a downside: Larger companies focus on the most popular varieties, at the expense of lesser-known but very desirable ones. It makes me very grateful to have cultivated a network of trusted and valued purveyors over the years, people who are as passionate about growing and foraging for ingredients as I am about cooking them.

Roast Squab with Red Wine–Braised Porcini

Porcini mushrooms require loving attention, because their potential must be coaxed out during long, slow cooking, which pays off with a powerful, meaty depth of flavor. All mushrooms have a lot of moisture, which must be carefully managed when cooking, but this is especially true with porcini. But the payoff is worth the effort—the braised porcini are so intense you could almost serve them on their own, but I enjoy pairing them with the roasted squab.

Separate the porcini caps from their stems. Cut the stems crosswise into ½-inch-thick slices. If the caps are especially large, cut them in half. If the pores on the underside of the caps seem very soft, remove them.

Heat the oil in a large heavy-bottomed sauté pan over medium heat. Add the porcini and cook very slowly, stirring occasionally and very gently, until they are cooked through and not at all wet, about 45 minutes. Raise the heat to high and brown them lightly, about 5 minutes. Transfer to a plate. (If cooking them more than 1 hour in advance, cover tautly with plastic wrap and refrigerate for up to 24 hours.)

To make the sauce, put the shallots, wine, port, coriander, peppercorns, juniper berries, and bay leaves in a large nonreactive saucepan. Bring to a boil, then reduce the heat so the liquid is simmering and cook until reduced by about two-thirds, about 30 minutes. Pour in the chicken and mushroom stocks, raise the heat to high, and bring to a boil, then reduce the heat so the liquid is simmering and cook for 1 hour. Strain through a fine-mesh strainer set over a bowl, pressing down on the solids to extract as much flavorful liquid as possible. Wipe out the saucepan and

return the strained liquid to it. Bring to a simmer and let reduce and thicken until you have about 1½ cups of sauce.

Knead 2 tablespoons of the butter and the flour together in a small bowl to make a smooth paste. Whisk this into the sauce and cook at a simmer, whisking a few times, until reduced to about 1 cup. Season with salt and a dash of vinegar. Add the porcini and warm through. Remove from the heat and keep covered and warm while you roast the squabs.

Preheat the oven to 500°F. Position a rack in the top third of the oven.

Place the squabs on a rack in a roasting pan, with some space between them. Season well with salt and pepper. Smear 1 teaspoon of the softened butter over the breast of each squab, then roast for 10 to 12 minutes. They should be well browned and the breasts should be medium-rare to medium. Remove from the oven and let rest for 3 or 4 minutes. Carve the squabs, removing the legs and thighs and slicing the breast meat into 4 or 5 slices per breast.

To serve, divide the sauce and porcini among 4 dinner plates. Top with the pieces of one squab per plate and serve immediately.

12 ounces fresh, firm porcini mushrooms, stems trimmed if dry or dirty

2 tablespoons olive oil

5 large shallots, coarsely chopped (about 1 cup)

4 cups medium-bodied red wine

½ cup ruby port

½ teaspoon coriander seeds

1 teaspoon black peppercorns

6 juniper berries

2 bay leaves, preferably fresh

4 cups Chicken Stock (page 292)

4 cups Mushroom Stock (page 290)

3 tablespoons plus 1 teaspoon unsalted butter, softened at room temperature

2 tablespoons all-purpose flour

Kosher salt

Few drops of red wine vinegar

4 squabs (about 1 pound each)

Black pepper from a mill

SERVES 4

Roast Squab with Garlic Sauce & Pea Ravioli

Squab is one of my favorite game birds, largely because it's one of the very few that's available year-round. This dish came about when I decided to try to contrast the dense, gamey quality of squab with something unmistakably springlike. I ended up pairing it with pea ravioli and garlic sauce.

I like squab breasts medium-rare; this does risk the legs and thighs coming out slightly underdone. If this happens, simply return the other parts to the oven for a few minutes to cook further after carving the squab.

Heat the oil in a wide, heavy-bottomed sauté pan over medium heat. Add the garlic cloves and brown them, stirring, 10 to 15 minutes. Sprinkle with the sugar, stir, and brown a little more, about 3 minutes. Pour in the wine and scrape up any browned bits stuck to the bottom of the pan. Raise the heat to high, bring to a boil, and cook until the pan is dry, about 5 minutes. Pour in the stock, add the bay leaves, and bring back to a boil, then reduce the heat so the liquid is simmering and cook until the garlic cloves are very soft to a knife tip, about 30 minutes.

Preheat the oven to 500°F. Position a rack in the top third of the oven.

Strain the sauce through a large fine-mesh strainer set over a medium saucepan, pressing the garlic cloves out of their skins and through the strainer into the sauce.

Bring to a simmer and cook until reduced to about 1 cup, about 30 minutes. Wipe out the first pan you used and strain the sauce back into it. Season to taste with salt and pepper and 2 or 3 drops of lemon juice. Set over high heat and whisk in the cold butter, a few cubes at a time.

Place the squabs on a rack in a roasting pan, with some space between them. Season well with salt and pepper. Smear 1 teaspoon of the softened butter over the breast of each squab, then roast for 10 to 12 minutes. They should be well browned and the breasts should be medium-rare to medium. Remove from the oven and let rest for 3 or 4 minutes. Carve the squabs, removing the legs and thighs and slicing the breast meat into 4 or 5 slices per breast.

To serve, arrange the pieces of one squab on each of 4 dinner plates. Spoon some sauce over the squab, arrange several pea ravioli alongside, and serve immediately.

2 tablespoons canola or other neutral oil

4 garlic heads, separated into cloves, in their skins

1 teaspoon sugar

1 cup dry white wine

8 cups Chicken Stock (page 292)

2 bay leaves, preferably fresh

Kosher salt

Black pepper from a mill

Few drops of fresh lemon juice

2 tablespoons cold unsalted butter, cubed

4 squabs (about 1 pound each)

1 tablespoon plus 1 teaspoon unsalted butter, softened at room temperature

SERVES 4

Guinea Hen with Red Wine & Black Olives

Two 2½- to 3-pound guinea hens

¼ cup plus 3 tablespoons canola or other neutral oil

2 medium onions, unpeeled, cut into 1-inch chunks

2 medium carrots, unpeeled, cut into 1-inch chunks

3 garlic heads, in their skins, coarsely chopped

½ cup ruby port

2 tablespoons brandy

One 750 ml bottle red wine

1 cup brine from olives (preferably kalamata), plus ¼ cup pitted and slivered olives

6 cups Chicken Stock (page 292)

2 bay leaves, preferably fresh

Kosher salt

Black pepper from a mill

3 tablespoons unsalted butter

Fettuccine with Crème Fraîche & Lemon Zest (page 258)

SERVES 4

I like guinea hen as a more flavorful, gamier alternative to chicken; it's also easier to find an exceptional guinea hen than an exceptional chicken. While a roasted whole hen is always appealing, the legs can be a little tough, so I focus on the thighs and breast here, using the rest of the bird in the sauce. It's an intense concoction that should be carefully reduced and seasoned; there's a fine line between its being either delicious or overpowering. For the same reason, the fettuccine is essential, providing fresh, creamy relief to the big flavors on the plate.

Remove the legs and thighs from the guinea hens, then the breasts, leaving a wing joint attached to each. Chop off the tips of the wing joints and clean the bones. Cut apart the legs and thighs and remove the thigh bones. Chop the carcasses and legs into 2-inch pieces for use in the sauce.

Heat 3 tablespoons of the oil in a large heavy-bottomed saucepan over medium-high heat. Add the hen trimmings and carcasses, onions, carrots, and garlic. Cook over high heat, stirring from time to time, until the vegetables and bones are browned, about 15 minutes. Pour in the port, brandy, wine, and olive brine, bring to a boil, and cook until reduced by about two-thirds, about 15 minutes. Add the stock and bay leaves. Bring back to a boil, reduce the heat so the liquid is simmering, and cook for about 30 minutes, skimming the fat from the surface a few times.

Strain the sauce through a fine-mesh strainer set over a small saucepan. You should have about 2 cups. Set over medium-high heat and boil until reduced to 1 cup. Keep warm, or let cool and refrigerate in an airtight container for up to 24 hours; reheat gently before proceeding with the recipe.

Preheat the oven to 400°F.

To cook the hens, heat a large heavy-bottomed sauté pan over high heat. Add the remaining ¼ cup oil and heat until very hot but not smoking. Season the hen breasts and thighs with salt and pepper and place them, skin side down, in the hot oil. Cook until well browned and crisp on one side, about 5 minutes, lowering the heat if necessary to avoid scorching the skin. Drain and discard the oil from the pan, turn the hen pieces over, and put the pan in the oven to finish cooking, 8 to 10 minutes (it may still be a little pink at the bone, which is okay).

When the hen is done cooking, whisk the butter into the warm sauce. Taste and adjust the seasoning, if necessary. Stir in the sliced olives.

To serve, spoon some sauce in the center of each of 4 dinner plates. Set a hen breast and thigh on top, arrange some fettuccine alongside, and serve immediately.

Grilled Quail with Star Anise

One 3-inch piece fresh ginger, peeled and coarsely chopped (about ¼ cup)

6 scallions (white and green parts), coarsely chopped

5 dried shiitake mushrooms

¼ cup soy sauce

2 ounces rock sugar or ¼ cup lightly packed light brown sugar

½ cup whole star anise

½ stick cinnamon

1 large piece dried orange or tangerine peel

5 cups Chicken Stock (page 292)

1 tablespoon unsalted butter, softened at room temperature

2 tablespoons all-purpose flour

8 boneless quail (about 4 ounces each), wings removed, leaving only the first joint

Kosher salt

Black pepper from a mill

SERVES 4

The method of preparing the quail for grilling here is called *en crapaudine,* which refers to butterflying and flattening the bird in order to expose as much of the skin and meat as possible to the heat. The name of the technique refers to how it makes the bird look like a toad (*crapaud*) or—according to some—a toad that's been run over by a car. I also like to weigh the quail down to ensure even cooking, but I use a heavy skillet.

Put the ginger, scallions, shiitakes, soy sauce, sugar, star anise, cinnamon, orange peel, and stock in a large heavy-bottomed pot, bring to a boil, reduce the heat so the liquid is simmering, and cook for 1 hour; it should be reduced by about half. Strain through a fine-mesh strainer set over a small saucepan. Bring to a boil.

Meanwhile, knead the butter and flour together in a small bowl to make a smooth paste. Whisk this into the sauce and cook over high heat, whisking occasionally, until the sauce is thick enough to coat the back of a wooden spoon, about 15 minutes.

To prepare and cook the quail, preheat a grill to high. Put the quail, breast side down, on a cutting board and use a large heavy knife to split down the back of the bird, prying it open and flattening it with your hand. Make a diagonal slit at the tail end of each breast, about thigh high, and wrap the legs around to fit into each slot. Season with salt and pepper on both sides, then grill 2 to 3 minutes per side, weighing the quail down with a heavy sauté pan or skillet to help crisp the skin.

To serve, arrange 2 quail on each of 4 dinner places, spoon some sauce over and around the quail, and serve immediately.

Braised Duck Legs & Seared Duck Breast with Dried Cherries & Red Wine Sauce

The usual accompaniment to duck is something sweet or tart to offset its rich flavor and texture. That tradition is applied to the max here, with duck legs braised in a mixture of wine and port, with dried cherries added. The legs are served with seared duck breast and a sauce made by reducing the braising liquid and infusing it with even more cherry flavor.

Remove the legs and thighs (in one unit) and the breasts from the duck, following the instructions for the first duck on page 194. Score the skin of the breasts with a very sharp, thin-bladed knife, making slashes to help render the fat but without cutting through to the meat. Season the legs with salt and pepper.

Heat 1 tablespoon of the oil in a large heavy-bottomed sauté pan over medium-high heat. Add the duck legs, skin side down, and cook for 6 to 7 minutes, pouring off the fat as it accumulates in the pan, until the skin is nicely browned. Turn and cook until the meat side is golden brown, 3 to 4 minutes. Transfer to a plate.

Heat a large heavy-bottomed saucepan over medium-high heat, then add 2 tablespoons of the oil and heat well. Add the onions, carrot, and garlic and cook, stirring often, until they have browned, about 10 minutes. Add the wine, port, and 1 cup of the cherries. Bring to a boil, then reduce the heat to medium-high and cook until reduced by half, 15 to 20 minutes. Add the stock and bay leaf and cook for another 30 minutes. Add the duck legs, submerging them in the liquid. Bring back to a boil, then reduce the heat so the liquid is simmering, cover, and cook until the meat offers no resistance when pierced with a knife, about 1¼ hours.

Transfer the duck legs to a baking sheet, brushing off any particles of carrot, onion, or cherry that might be stuck on them. Strain the sauce through a fine-mesh strainer set over a medium saucepan, pressing down on the solids to extract as much flavorful liquid as possible. You should have about 4 cups. (If possible, refrigerate the legs overnight in enough liquid to cover, and refrigerate the remaining liquid separately.)

Bring the liquid to a boil. Meanwhile, knead the butter and flour together in a small bowl to form a paste. Whisk this into the sauce and cook over medium-high heat, whisking occasionally, until the sauce reduces to 2 cups, about 20 minutes. Add the remaining ½ cup cherries and the duck legs to warm them through. Taste and adjust the seasoning with salt if necessary. Keep warm.

Heat a large heavy-bottomed sauté pan over medium-high heat. Add the remaining 2 tablespoons oil and heat until nearly smoking. Season the duck breasts on both sides with salt and pepper. Place in the pan, skin side down, reduce the heat to medium, and cook, pouring off the fat as it renders, until the skin is well browned but not blackened and quite a bit of fat has rendered, about 10 minutes. Turn the breasts over and cook for 5 minutes for rare. Transfer to a cutting board, tent with aluminum foil, and let rest for 5 minutes.

To serve, slice the duck breasts crosswise and the legs at the joint to serve each person half a leg and half a duck breast. Top each serving with a ladleful of sauce and serve.

One 5½- to 6-pound Pekin duck

Kosher salt

Black pepper from a mill

5 tablespoons canola or other neutral oil

2 medium onions, unpeeled, cut into 1-inch chunks

1 large carrot, unpeeled, cut into ¼-inch chunks

2 garlic heads, in their skins, cut in half horizontally

3 cups robust red wine, such as Côtes du Rhône

1 cup ruby port

1½ cups dried tart cherries

8 cups Duck Stock (page 296)

1 bay leaf, preferably fresh

1 tablespoon unsalted butter, softened at room temperature

1 tablespoon all-purpose flour

SERVES 4

Duck Breast with Fresh Chiles

The spicy sauce in this dish is based on a *sauce charcutiere,* made by adding chopped cornichons to a *sauce Robert,* a brown sauce with Dijon mustard whisked into it often served with pork chops. Here it's made with duck stock and enlivened with tomato, vinegar, and assorted chiles. I originally made this with magret duck breast, but now use Pekin duck, which is more tender; slowly rendering out the fat results in soft, succulent meat and crackling skin.

Heat a large heavy-bottomed saucepan over medium-high heat. Pour in 3 tablespoons of the oil and heat until nearly smoking. Add the onions, carrot, and garlic and cook, stirring often, until they have browned nicely, about 10 minutes. Pour in the wine and vinegar, bring to a boil, reduce the heat so the liquid is simmering, and cook until the pan is nearly dry, about 10 minutes. Add the stock, tomatoes, and bay leaf and simmer for 1 hour over medium-high heat.

Strain the contents of the pot through a fine-mesh strainer set over a bowl and discard the solids. You should have 3 cups of liquid. If you have less, add enough duck stock to make up the difference; if you have more, wipe out the pot, return the liquid to the stovetop, bring to simmer, and reduce further.

Add the peppers and chiles to the sauce and simmer over medium heat for 15 minutes.

Meanwhile, knead the butter and flour together in a small bowl to make a smooth paste. Whisk this into the sauce and cook over medium-high heat, whisking occasionally, until the sauce has thickened, about 5 minutes more. Taste and adjust the seasoning with salt, if necessary.

Heat a large heavy-bottomed sauté pan over medium-high heat. Add the remaining 2 tablespoons oil and heat until nearly smoking. Score the skin of the duck breasts with a very sharp, thin-bladed knife, making slashes to help render the fat but without cutting through to the meat. Season the duck on both sides with salt and pepper. Place in the pan, skin side down, reduce the heat to medium, and cook, pouring off the fat as it renders, until the skin is well browned but not blackened and quite a bit of fat has rendered, about 10 minutes. Turn the breasts over and cook for another 5 minutes for rare. Transfer to a cutting board, tent with aluminum foil, and let rest for 5 minutes.

Ladle some sauce into the center of each of 4 dinner plates. Cut the duck crosswise into ½-inch-thick slices and arrange the pieces of one breast over the sauce on each plate. Serve immediately.

¼ cup plus 1 tablespoon canola or other neutral oil

2 medium onions, unpeeled, cut into 1-inch chunks

1 large carrot, sliced ¼ inch thick

2 garlic heads, in their skins, cut in half horizontally

1 cup dry white wine

⅓ cup sherry vinegar

6 cups Duck Stock (page 296), plus more if needed

1 cup canned whole tomatoes, with their juice

1 bay leaf, preferably fresh

½ cup diced (⅛-inch) red bell pepper (1 medium pepper)

1 teaspoon seeded and diced (⅛-inch) fresh jalapeño chile (½ jalapeño)

1 teaspoon seeded and diced (⅛-inch) fresh serrano chile (1 serrano)

2 tablespoons unsalted butter, softened at room temperature

2 teaspoons all-purpose flour

Kosher salt

4 Pekin duck breasts, skin on

Black pepper from a mill

SERVES 4

Duck Breast with Hot & Sour Sauce

This is another Chanterelle take on Chinese food, with a big range of flavors and textures represented. At the restaurant, we serve this with Braised Duck Leg Spring Rolls (page 48), and I suggest you do the same. The pairing of the breast, seared and served with a sauce redolent of duck stock, shiitake mushrooms, and black pepper, and the rolls, with their deep, meltingly tender braised meat, is truly irresistible.

To make the sauce, put the ginger, shiitakes, stock, vinegar, and soy sauce in a large heavy-bottomed saucepan. Bring to a boil, then reduce the heat so the liquid is simmering and cook, uncovered, for 1 hour. Strain the sauce through a fine-mesh strainer set over a medium saucepan. Bring to a boil and reduce the sauce for 10 minutes.

Meanwhile, knead the butter and flour together in a small bowl to make a smooth paste. Whisk this into the sauce and cook over high heat, whisking occasionally, until the sauce is lightly thickened, about another 10 minutes. Add the pepper and cook for another 5 minutes over low heat. Strain through a fine-mesh strainer or cheesecloth-lined colander to remove all the pepper. (The sauce can be refrigerated in an airtight container for up to 3 days; reheat gently before serving, checking the seasoning.)

Heat a large heavy-bottomed sauté pan over medium-high heat. Add the oil and heat until nearly smoking. Score the skin of the duck breasts with a very sharp, thin-bladed knife, making slashes to help render the fat but without cutting through to the meat. Season on both sides with salt and pepper. Place in the pan, skin side down, reduce the heat to medium, and cook, pouring off the fat as it renders, until the skin is well browned but not blackened and quite a bit of fat has rendered, about 10 minutes. Turn the breasts over and cook for another 5 minutes for rare. Transfer to a cutting board, tent with aluminum foil, and let rest for 5 minutes.

To serve, slice the duck thinly crosswise. Spoon some sauce onto each of 4 dinner plates and arrange the pieces of one breast on top of the sauce on each plate. Set a duck spring roll alongside, if using, garnish with the scallions, and serve immediately.

One 2-inch piece fresh ginger (about 2 ounces), unpeeled, thinly sliced

15 dried shiitake mushrooms (also sold as "black mushrooms" in Asian markets)

2 quarts Duck Stock (page 296)

½ cup rice vinegar

½ cup soy sauce

2 tablespoons unsalted butter, softened at room temperature

2 tablespoons all-purpose flour

½ teaspoon finely ground black pepper, plus more to taste

2 tablespoons canola or other neutral oil

4 Pekin duck breasts, skin on

Kosher salt

4 Braised Duck Leg Spring Rolls (optional; page 48)

4 scallions (green parts only), thinly sliced at an angle

SERVES 4

MEATS & GAME

Americans, by and large, consider meat the main event of a meal, the course to which the entire event builds, and there's often a premium placed on size: The bigger the cut, the more special the occasion. My own orientation toward tasting menus puts it in a slightly different place, as just the last in a series of savory dishes, no more or less important than any of those that preceded it. I love a gargantuan, grilled ribeye as much as the next guy, but they're best left to the steakhouses that specialize in them and their equally decadent side dishes. For this reason, even when ordered à la carte, the meat dishes at Chanterelle aren't any larger than the fish or poultry choices on the menu. ¶ I also put the same emphasis on sauces and accompaniments in this category as I do in the others. So, you might find the cross section of recipes in this chapter surprisingly seasonal, given that the meats themselves are available all year long. By virtue of the cooking technique and components, for example, Braised Pork Belly with Apple Cider & Root Vegetables (page 223) belongs to fall, while the same factors make Grilled Marinated Lamb Chops with Goat Cheese & Thyme (page 211) a summer affair.

Beef Filet with Oysters & Wild Mushrooms

Sometimes, a flurry of related ideas can lead to a successful dish, as they did here: Having read a lot about food history, I found myself thinking one day about carpetbagger steak, a late nineteenth– or early twentieth–century dish in which a thick steak was split and stuffed with oysters and mushrooms so that it resembled a carpetbag. Oysters were so plentiful in the United States at that time that they were often used as a seasoning in sauces, which led me to think of Asian oyster sauce. The result—filet mignon served with oysters, oyster mushrooms, and an oyster sauce–flavored sauce—worked beautifully. It wasn't until we began serving it that I realized I had come up with a new spin on another American culinary tradition: surf and turf!

Melt the butter in a large heavy-bottomed sauté pan over medium heat. Add the mushrooms and sauté until they are nearly dry, about 10 minutes. Transfer to a bowl.

Preheat the oven to 400°F.

Arrange the beef filets on a clean, dry surface and season both sides generously with salt and pepper. Heat a large heavy-bottomed sauté pan over high heat until very hot. Add the oil and swirl it to coat the bottom, then add the filets without crowding them. Brown well, 3 to 4 minutes per side. Transfer the filets to a baking sheet. (Don't rinse the pan.) Place the beef in the oven, roast for 5 minutes, remove, and let the filets rest for a few minutes while you make the sauce.

Use a paper towel to carefully wipe the excess oil out of the sauté pan. Add the cooked mushrooms and set the pan over high heat. Pour in the reserved oyster juice, the mushroom stock, and oyster sauce. Bring to a simmer, then swirl in the cream. Reduce the sauce until it thickens considerably, about 5 minutes. Add the oysters and cook them just enough for them to plump and release their liquids into the reduction. Stir in the lemon juice just before serving.

Arrange a filet on each of 4 dinner plates. Divide the sauce and oysters evenly among the plates, topping the filets with them. Garnish with the scallions and serve immediately.

2 tablespoons unsalted butter

1 pound fresh oyster mushrooms or assorted wild mushrooms, stems removed

Four 6-ounce beef filets

Kosher salt

Black pepper from a mill

2 tablespoons canola or other neutral oil

12 fresh oysters (preferably a larger East Coast variety such as Wellfleet or Malpeque), shucked and drained (juice reserved and strained)

3 tablespoons Mushroom Stock (page 290) or high-quality low-sodium store-bought chicken stock

3 tablespoons oyster sauce

1½ cups heavy cream

1 teaspoon freshly squeezed lemon juice

2 tablespoons finely sliced scallion greens

SERVES 4

Calf's Liver Sauté with Onion Coulis & Caramelized Onions

6 medium Spanish onions, cut end to end into ¼-inch-thick slices

¼ cup (½ stick) unsalted butter

About ½ cup dry white wine

1 cup Chicken Stock (page 292) or high-quality low-sodium store-bought chicken stock

Kosher salt

Pinch plus 1 tablespoon sugar

½ cup canola or other neutral oil

2 tablespoons balsamic vinegar

1 cup Veal Stock (page 294) or high-quality low-sodium store-bought beef stock

Black pepper from a mill

Splash of red wine vinegar (optional)

Four 6-ounce slices calf's liver (about ⅜ inch thick)

Wondra or all-purpose flour, for dusting

SERVES 4

Every chef is entitled to an indulgence on his or her menu, and one of mine is an occasional cameo by calf's liver, which I've always loved. I know it will never be the most popular dish (in fact, I usually assume it will be the worst-selling one), but when fellow liver-lovers come in for dinner, they are positively giddy when they find it there. This dish takes liver and onions, an American diner classic, and gives it the Chanterelle treatment, pairing the rich liver with sweet sautéed onions and an onion sauce.

A perfect accompaniment to this is sautéed bitter greens such as escarole or broccoli rabe.

Put 4 of the sliced onions, 3 tablespoons of the butter, and the wine in a medium heavy-bottomed sauté set over medium-low heat. Cook the onions very slowly, stirring occasionally, until they are very soft and translucent, about 1 hour. (You are not trying to caramelize the onions; instead you are cooking them very slowly to make them as soft as possible and to concentrate their flavor, so add a little more wine if they seem like they might begin to brown.) Add the chicken stock, bring to a simmer, and cook until reduced by about half, another 20 minutes. Remove from the heat and let cool, then transfer the mixture to a blender and puree until very smooth. Season to taste with salt and a pinch of sugar, if necessary. (The onion coulis will keep in the refrigerator in an airtight container for up to 3 days; reheat it gently before serving.)

Heat ¼ cup of the oil in a medium heavy-bottomed sauté pan over medium heat. Add the remaining 2 onions and cook, stirring frequently, until just browned and softened, about 25 minutes. Add the 1 tablespoon sugar and cook, stirring frequently, until the sugar caramelizes, about another 10 minutes. Pour in the balsamic vinegar and scrape up any browned bits stuck to the bottom of the pan. Simmer until the vinegar has reduced by half, about 3 minutes, then add the veal stock and stir again, scraping up any remaining caramelized bits. Reduce over high heat until syrupy, about 5 minutes. Stir in the remaining 1 tablespoon butter and season to taste with salt, pepper, and a splash of red wine vinegar, if desired. Set aside.

To cook the calf's liver, heat a large heavy-bottomed sauté pan over high heat. Add the remaining ¼ cup oil and heat it until smoking. Season the liver slices generously with salt and pepper and lightly dust on both sides with flour. Carefully place the liver in the hot pan and sear for 2 to 3 minutes per side for medium-rare, or to your desired degree of doneness.

Divide the onion coulis evenly among 4 dinner plates or wide, shallow bowls and top with a piece of liver, then a few spoonfuls of caramelized onions. Serve immediately.

Beef Rib-Eye with Sun-Dried Tomato Coulis, Chiles & a Drizzle of Goat Cheese Cream

A culinary example of the adage "necessity is the mother of invention," this dish came about for a promotional event we hosted for sun-dried tomatoes at Chanterelle. I borrowed a little from my repertoire, pairing a sun-dried tomato sauce with the goat cheese sauce I use with the beef cheek terrine on page 116, blending water into the cheese to make it pourable. The contrast of the intense tomato and chile and the cooling, soothing goat cheese really makes this dish come alive. I use sun-dried tomatoes from California, which are sweeter than European brands.

Blacken the jalapeños on a grill or under a broiler, or over the flame of a gas stovetop burner, impaling them on a meat fork and carefully turning them directly in the flame, until blackened and blistered all over. Transfer the peppers to a heatproof bowl, cover with plastic wrap, and let steam in their own heat for 5 minutes. Remove the plastic and, when cool enough to handle, remove and discard the skins. Cut the jalapeños into thin strips, discard the seeds, and set aside.

Melt the butter in a medium heavy-bottomed saucepan over medium-low heat. Add the onion and garlic and cook, stirring, until softened but not browned, about 10 minutes. Pour in the wine, bring to a simmer over medium-high heat, and reduce until the vegetables are almost dry, then stir in the tomato puree. Add the stock and sun-dried tomatoes, bring to a simmer, and cook until the tomatoes are softened and the mixture begins to thicken, about 20 minutes. Remove from the heat and let cool.

Transfer the cooled sun-dried tomato mixture to a food processor fitted with a steel blade. Process until very smooth and set aside.

Blend the goat cheese and water together in a medium bowl with an immersion blender until a smooth sauce forms.

Arrange the steaks on a clean, dry surface, season generously on both sides with salt and pepper, and coat lightly on both sides with the canola oil. Heat two large, wide, cast-iron skillets over high heat on different burners (or work in batches in one skillet). Add the steaks and sear until charred and crispy, about 10 minutes per side for medium-rare. Transfer to a plate and let the steaks rest for a few minutes before serving.

Divide the coulis evenly among 4 dinner plates. Place a steak in the center of each and drizzle with goat cheese sauce. Garnish with the julienned jalapeños and cilantro leaves and serve immediately.

PREP TALK

Working with Chile Peppers

I recommend wearing latex gloves when working with chiles to keep them from irritating, or injuring, your skin or eyes. They are inexpensive and don't take up much room in a drawer; a small box will last for years.

---

4 fresh jalapeño chiles

3 tablespoons unsalted butter

2 cups coarsely chopped Spanish onions (about 2 medium onions)

2 tablespoons minced garlic

1 cup dry white wine

1 tablespoon tomato puree

4½ cups Chicken Stock (page 292) or high-quality low-sodium store-bought chicken stock

2 cups whole dry (not packed in oil) sun-dried tomatoes

5 tablespoons fresh goat cheese (about 3 ounces)

½ cup water

Four 8-ounce rib-eye steaks, preferably 1 inch thick

Kosher salt

Black pepper from a mill

2 tablespoons canola or other neutral oil

¼ cup loosely packed fresh cilantro leaves

SERVES 4

Beef Rib with Red Wine, Shallots & Marrow

One 8-inch-long beef marrow bone (about 1 pound), cut into four 2-inch lengths (have the butcher do this for you)

Kosher salt

1½ cups halved and thinly sliced shallots (6 to 8 shallots)

One 750 ml bottle Rhône-style red wine

¼ cup ruby port

4 juniper berries

1 teaspoon black peppercorns

3 bay leaves, preferably fresh

8 cups Veal Stock (page 294)

4 ounces slab bacon, skin on, cut into 1-inch chunks

1 tablespoon all-purpose flour

¼ cup (½ stick) unsalted butter, softened at room temperature

2 bone-in beef ribs (about 2 pounds each), cut from prime rib, each about 2 inches thick, outer fat trimmed and rib bones scraped clean

Black pepper from a mill

¼ cup canola or other neutral oil

SERVES 4

This is a very extravagant beef dish, with double portions of beef cooked on the bone, then sliced and served with a rich red wine and marrow sauce. Like many of my favorite preparations, it's founded on lots of butter and long, patient reductions. Serve this with Creamed Spinach (page 241) and roasted potatoes.

Put the marrow bones in a medium bowl, sprinkle with 2 tablespoons of salt, and cover with ice water. Let soak for 1 hour or up to 3 hours to draw out the blood and make it easier to remove the marrow from the bones.

When ready to cook and serve the dish, combine the shallots, wine, and port in a large saucepan over high heat. Bring to a boil, then reduce the heat to medium-high and cook until the shallots are nearly dry and about ¼ cup liquid remains, about 20 minutes.

Put the juniper berries, peppercorns, and bay leaves in a piece of cheesecloth, and make a sachet by tying the ends together. Add this to the pan, along with the stock and bacon. Return to a simmer and cook at a gentle simmer for 1 hour.

Use a slotted spoon to remove and discard the sachet and bacon pieces, then strain the sauce through a fine-mesh strainer set over a bowl, reserving the shallots.

Preheat the oven to 500°F.

Carefully wipe out the pan, return the liquid to it, and bring to a simmer over medium heat. In a small bowl, knead the flour and 1 tablespoon of the butter into a paste, then whisk this into the simmering sauce to thicken it. Continue to cook until the sauce has reduced to 1 cup, about 10 minutes. Remove from the heat and keep covered and warm.

Arrange the beef ribs on a clean, dry surface and season generously with salt and pepper. Heat a large, heavy-bottomed, ovenproof sauté pan over high heat until very hot and add the oil. Immediately set the ribs in the pan and sear until well browned and crusty, 4 to 5 minutes per side. Transfer to the oven and roast until an instant-read meat thermometer inserted into the thickest part of a rib reads 100°F, 8 to 10 minutes. Remove from the oven, transfer the ribs to a platter, and let them rest for 5 minutes.

Meanwhile, finish the marrow and sauce. Drain the ice water from the marrow bones, then run hot tap water over them until the marrow can be popped out by pushing on one side with a finger tip. Arrange the marrow on a cutting board and slice each piece into ¼-inch-thick rounds. Gently whisk the remaining 3 tablespoons butter into the warm sauce. Add the marrow and reserved shallots and heat through. Season to taste with salt and pepper.

Present the beef ribs at the table on a platter, cutting 8 to 10 lengthwise slices from each rib. Present the sauce in a small pitcher or sauceboat alongside, pouring sauce over the beef after it has been plated.

Butternut Squash Ravioli with Oxtail Ragoût, Sage Cream & Shaved Parmesan

3 pounds oxtail, trimmed of extra fat and cut into 1½- to 2-inch pieces (have the butcher do this for you, if necessary)

Five 750 ml bottles red wine (avoid thin, Rhône-style wines or Merlot)

3 bay leaves, preferably fresh

10 juniper berries

1 tablespoon black peppercorns

¼ cup plus 1 tablespoon olive oil

1½ cups finely diced Spanish onion (1 medium onion)

1 cup diced (¼-inch) carrots

1 cup diced (¼-inch) Smithfield ham or other dry-cured ham (about 4 ounces)

1 tablespoon minced garlic

1 tablespoon all-purpose flour, plus more for dusting the ravioli

2 tablespoons ruby port

About 5 cups Veal Stock (page 294)

1 tablespoon tomato paste

Kosher salt

continued on page 209

Oxtail and squash are a classic combination for a very good reason: The deep, beefy quality of the oxtail is effortlessly matched by the natural sweetness of the squash. Here, the pair is recast as the basis of a ravioli and sauce duo, rounded out with sage cream and Parmesan cheese. I serve this as a starter at Chanterelle but, because of all the work it involves, I recommend it as a main course at home. This is a time-consuming recipe, but the components may all be made in advance. You can make the ragoût up to three days ahead, and I recommend doing just that; the flavor will intensify greatly over that time. You can also serve the ravioli on their own as a starter, tossed with browned butter and chopped marjoram or sage.

Put the oxtails in a very large bowl, pour the wine over them, cover with plastic wrap, and refrigerate overnight.

When ready to proceed, put the bay leaves, juniper berries, and peppercorns in a piece of cheesecloth, gather up the ends, and tie them together to make a sachet.

Heat 3 tablespoons of the olive oil in a large heavy-bottomed pot over medium heat. Add the onion, carrots, ham, and garlic, reduce the heat to medium-low, and cook, stirring a few times, until the vegetables have softened and lightly browned, about 15 minutes. Add the flour and cook, stirring, until slightly browned, about 5 minutes. Add the oxtails and marinade and stir well to dissolve the flour. Add the port, stock, tomato paste, and spice sachet. Raise the heat to high, bring to a boil, then reduce the heat so the liquid is simmering and cook for 1 hour, stirring often to keep the vegetables from sticking to the bottom of the pot.

Cover and continue to simmer until the oxtails are very tender and the meat is falling off the bone, another 45 minutes, adding more stock or water, if necessary. The sauce should be reduced and thickened, the vegetables soft and barely maintaining their shape, and the flavor intense. Remove and discard the sachet. Transfer the oxtails to a bowl and set aside to cool.

Pull the meat off the bones and coarsely dice it. Return the meat to the sauce and season to taste with salt and pepper. (The ragoût can be refrigerated in an airtight container for up to 3 days; skim off any fat that rises to the surface and reheat gently before proceeding.)

To make the squash ravioli filling, preheat the oven to 350°F.

Put the squash, cut side up, on a sheet pan and drizzle with the remaining 2 tablespoons olive oil. Sprinkle with salt and pepper and roast in the oven until very tender but only slightly browned, about 1½ hours. Let cool, then scoop the flesh of the squash out of its skin and pass it through a food mill or mash it well with a potato masher. Transfer the puree to a piece of cheesecloth, gather up the edges, and wring it tightly, draining the squash's liquid from its pulp. Put the drained puree in a bowl, add the grated cheeses, nutmeg, and salt and pepper to taste, and stir to incorporate.

Roll the pasta dough out and feed it through a hand-crank machine or stand mixer fitted with the pasta attachment, set to the thinnest setting. Using a ravioli mold or ravioli cutters, make at least 24 ravioli containing

continued

continued from page 208

Black pepper from a mill

3 pounds butternut squash, cut in half lengthwise and seeded

½ cup grated Italian fontina cheese (about 2 ounces)

2 tablespoons freshly grated Parmigiano-Reggiano cheese, plus a few shards shaved with a vegetable peeler

Pinch of ground nutmeg

1 recipe Pasta Dough (follow instructions on page 297, using ¾ cup flour and 1 large egg)

1½ cups heavy cream

10 fresh sage leaves, very coarsely chopped, or 6 bay leaves, preferably fresh

½ teaspoon freshly squeezed lemon juice, plus more to taste

1 tablespoon coarsely chopped fresh flat-leaf parsley

SERVES 4

Rack of Lamb with Cumin-Salt Crust

This is a summery treatment of lamb that I've enjoyed serving for years. The average rack of lamb has about eight ribs, enough to feed two or three, depending upon what else you are serving. Make sure to note which side of the rack has the layer of fat before you coat it with the spice mixture. This is the side that needs to have contact with the bottom of the pan first to brown.

This is delicious with the couscous on page 254, which picks up the Greek theme and soaks up the sauce.

Fill a wide, deep bowl with cold water. Combine the cumin, salt, and pepper in a wide, shallow bowl. Dip the lamb in the water and remove it, letting the excess water run off, then roll it in the spice mixture to coat on both sides. Set the lamb aside until ready to roast or cover with plastic wrap and refrigerate for up to 24 hours.

Pour the stock and wine into a large heavy-bottomed saucepan, add the garlic and lamb trimmings, and bring to a boil. Reduce the heat to medium-high and let simmer until the garlic is very soft, about 1 hour. Strain through a fine-mesh strainer set over a bowl, using the back of a wooden spoon to press the garlic pulp through the holes. Return the sauce to the pan and reduce over high heat to about 1½ cups, about another 20 minutes.

Preheat the oven to 500°F.

Heat a 10 x 14-inch roasting pan in the oven until very hot, about 10 minutes. Add the oil, then the two encrusted lamb racks, fat side down. Roast for 15 minutes, then use tongs to turn the shanks over and roast for another 5 minutes, until an instant-read meat thermometer inserted into the thickest part of the rack (away from the bone) registers 145°F. Transfer the lamb to a cutting board to rest for 5 minutes while you finish the sauce. Carefully pour the fat from the pan into a bowl to cool before discarding it.

Pour the veal reduction into the roasting pan and set over medium-high heat, loosening the browned bits from the bottom with a wooden spoon. Add the lemon juice, then whisk in the butter. Strain the sauce through a fine-mesh or a cheesecloth-lined strainer.

Cut the rack of lamb between the rib bones to separate the chops. Divide the sauce evenly among 4 dinner plates and arrange the chops in the center of each plate. Garnish with the cilantro leaves and serve immediately.

½ cup ground cumin

⅓ cup kosher salt

2 teaspoons finely ground black pepper

2 racks of lamb (about 2 pounds each; 8 bones each), frenched (have the butcher do this for you) and trimmed, trim reserved

6 cups Veal Stock (page 294)

2 cups dry white wine

5 garlic heads, in their skins, cut in half horizontally

2 tablespoons canola or other neutral oil

1 tablespoon freshly squeezed lemon juice

1 tablespoon unsalted butter, softened at room temperature

20 fresh cilantro leaves

SERVES 4

Moroccan Roast Loin & Braised Shank of Lamb with a Gâteau of Lamb Shank & Eggplant

6 tablespoons olive oil

2 medium carrots, unpeeled,
cut into 1-inch chunks

1 medium Spanish onion, unpeeled,
cut into 1-inch chunks

3 garlic heads, in their skins,
cut in half horizontally

1 cup dry white wine

1 teaspoon tomato paste

8 cups Veal Stock (page 294)

Pinch of saffron threads

¼ teaspoon ground coriander

¼ teaspoon turmeric

¼ teaspoon ground cumin

2 bay leaves, preferably fresh

¼ cup plus 1 tablespoon canola
or other neutral oil

2 lamb shanks (about 1½ pounds each)

continued on page 215

In the kitchen, the challenge and joy of this dish is keeping a lot of very powerful flavors in balance. Braised lamb shank is diced and served in an eggplant gâteau rather than at the center of the plate, where a more refined lamb loin is presented, sauced with the braising liquid from the shanks. I guess this is my version of serving a meat "two ways," which has become popular in restaurants as a way of serving a braised cut of meat with a roasted cut alongside.

Heat 3 tablespoons of the olive oil in a large heavy-bottomed saucepan over medium-high heat. Add the carrots, onion, and garlic and cook, stirring a few times, until they are well browned, about 15 minutes. Pour in the wine and reduce until nearly dry, about 5 minutes. Add the tomato paste, stock, saffron, coriander, turmeric, cumin, and bay leaves, bring to a boil, reduce the heat to medium, and simmer for 20 minutes.

Meanwhile, heat a large heavy-bottomed sauté pan over high heat until very hot. Add ¼ cup of the canola oil, then sear the lamb shanks on all sides until well browned. Transfer the shanks to the simmering braising liquid, cover, and simmer over medium-low heat until the meat falls off the bones, about 2 hours.

Use a slotted spoon to transfer the shanks to a bowl to cool, then pull the meat off the bones and coarsely chop it. Set aside or refrigerate in an airtight container for up to 48 hours. Pour the braising liquid through a fine-mesh strainer into a medium saucepan, bring to a boil, and reduce to about 1½ cups, about 20 minutes. Strain the sauce twice through cheesecloth, then season to taste with salt and a few drops of lemon juice. (The sauce can be

cooled and refrigerated in an airtight container for up to 48 hours; reheat gently before serving.)

To make the eggplant gâteaus, preheat the oven to 350°F.

Drizzle 1½ tablespoons of the olive oil onto a baking sheet and arrange the eggplant strips next to each other in a single layer. Season with salt and pepper, and drizzle with the remaining 1½ tablespoons olive oil. Bake until the eggplant is soft and pliable but not browned, about 10 minutes. Set aside to cool. Turn the oven up to 425°F to cook the lamb.

Grease four 4-ounce disposable round aluminum ramekins with nonstick cooking spray or a drop of olive oil. Line them with the strips of eggplant, allowing the strips to come up and over the sides of the ramekins so that they can be folded over the filling. Put the diced lamb shank meat in a medium bowl, add ¼ cup of the sauce, and toss well. Season to taste with salt and pepper. Fill the eggplant-lined ramekins with the mixture and fold over the overhanging ends to make 4 neat packets.

Heat a wide, deep, heavy-bottomed, ovenproof sauté pan over high heat, then add the remaining 1 tablespoon canola oil. When it is smoking hot, add the lamb loin and sear well, about 3 minutes per side. Transfer to the oven and roast until an instant-read meat thermometer inserted into the thickest part of the loin registers 110°F for medium-rare, 3 to 4 minutes, or to your desired degree of doneness. Transfer to a cutting board and let rest for 3 minutes.

To serve, unmold the gâteaus onto each of 4 dinner plates and divide the sauce evenly among each serving. Slice the lamb loin thinly and divide the slices among the plates. Garnish with the cilantro leaves and serve immediately.

continued from page 214

Kosher salt

½ lemon

2 medium Chinese or Japanese eggplant, cut crosswise into 5-inch lengths, then sliced lengthwise ⅛ inch thick on a mandoline (making wide ribbons edged on both sides with the eggplant skin)

Black pepper from a mill

Nonstick cooking spray or more olive oil, for greasing ramekins

1¼ pounds lamb loin (from the eye of one side of a loin), trimmed of fat

¼ cup loosely packed fresh cilantro leaves

SERVES 4

Roast Leg of Lamb with Marjoram & Mini Moussaka

2½ cups olive oil

1 tablespoon plus ½ teaspoon minced garlic

¼ cup chopped onion

1 pound ground lamb

¼ cup tomato puree

Kosher salt

1 teaspoon plus 2 pinches of piment d'Espelette or Aleppo pepper (red chile flakes can be substituted, but use less; ½ teaspoon in the marinade and a scant pinch for seasoning the lamb and preparing the custard)

¾ teaspoon ground cumin

¼ teaspoon ground allspice

1 cup coarsely chopped fresh marjoram leaves and stems, plus a few sprigs for garnish

3 tablespoons freshly squeezed lemon juice plus more for the sauce (optional)

1 pound lamb top round, trimmed of fat

2 medium onions, unpeeled, cut into 1-inch chunks

continued on page 217

I began serving this dish in the summer of 2004, when Athens hosted the Olympics, which I took as a cue to pay a playful tribute to Greek food. It was a chance to call on some of the things I'd observed over years of eating in Greek restaurants in Hell's Kitchen. For our customers, the most surprising thing on the plate was probably the mini moussaka, my version of a dish that many Americans haven't eaten since they took their meals in the high school cafeteria. I replace the traditional oregano with marjoram partially because I find fresh oregano so overwhelming that I actually prefer it in dried form.

Put 3 tablespoons of the olive oil in a large heavy-bottomed sauté pan set over medium heat. Add ½ teaspoon of the minced garlic and the chopped onion and sauté until they are softened but not browned, about 4 minutes. Add the ground lamb and cook, mixing and breaking up the lamb with a wooden spoon until it is mostly cooked and gray in color. Add the tomato puree and cook, stirring, until the lamb is nearly all cooked, about another 3 minutes.

Transfer the cooked lamb to a colander to drain of excess fat and liquid. Season with salt to taste, a pinch of the piment d'Espelette, the cumin, and allspice, tossing everything together well. Let cool and set aside, or refrigerate in an airtight container for up to 3 days.

Put 2 cups of the olive oil, 1 tablespoon salt, 1 tablespoon of the minced garlic, 1 teaspoon of the piment d'Espelette, ½ cup of the marjoram, and the lemon juice in a very large bowl and whisk together well. Put the lamb top round in the bowl, turning to coat the meat well with the marinade. Cover and refrigerate for at least 4 hours and up to 24 hours.

Heat 3 tablespoons of the olive oil in a heavy-bottomed pot set over medium-high heat. When it is hot but not quite smoking, add the onion chunks, carrots, halved garlic heads, and lamb shank and cook, stirring occasionally, until the vegetables and lamb have browned, about 20 minutes. Add the wine, raise the heat to high, and bring to a boil. Cook until the wine has almost entirely evaporated, scraping up the browned bits from the bottom of the pot, about 5 minutes. Add the stock, bay leaves, and the remaining ½ cup marjoram. Bring back to a boil, then reduce the heat to medium-low and simmer for 1 hour.

Strain the broth through a fine-mesh strainer set over a small saucepan. Set it over medium heat and simmer until reduced to 1 cup, about 15 minutes. Season to taste with salt and pepper and a few extra drops of lemon juice, if desired. (The sauce can be refrigerated in an airtight container for up to 3 days; reheat and whisk gently before serving.)

To make the moussaka, preheat the oven to 350°F. Toss the eggplant rounds with the remaining 2 tablespoons olive oil in a large bowl, seasoning generously with salt and pepper. Arrange the slices on a baking sheet and bake

continued

continued from page 216

2 medium carrots, unpeeled, cut into 1-inch chunks

3 garlic heads, in their skins, cut in half horizontally

1 pound lamb shank, cut through the bone into ¾-inch-thick sections (have the butcher do this for you)

1 cup dry white wine

6 cups Veal Stock (page 294)

2 bay leaves, preferably fresh

Black pepper from a mill

2 medium Chinese or Japanese eggplant, unpeeled, cut into ¼-inch-thick rounds

1 large egg plus 1 large egg yolk

⅔ cup plain whole-milk yogurt

¼ cup whole milk

3 tablespoons freshly grated Parmigiano-Reggiano cheese

Nonstick cooking spray

1 tablespoon canola or other neutral oil

SERVES 4

until softened but not browned, about 10 minutes. Do not turn off the oven.

In a separate bowl, make the custard by whisking together the whole egg, egg yolk, yogurt, milk, Parmigiano, 1 teaspoon salt, and the remaining pinch of piment d'Espelette.

Use four 2-inch-diameter (2-inch-tall) ring molds to assemble the individual moussaka. Line the bottom of each ring with aluminum foil and coat the interior walls generously with nonstick cooking spray. Arrange the lined molds on a baking sheet.

Divide the eggplant rounds among the molds, placing 5 or 6 overlapping slices of eggplant in each. Place about 3 tablespoons of the ground lamb mixture in each ring mold, packing the meat in well. Pour the custard over the lamb to nearly fill the molds. Bake until the custard is set, about 40 minutes. (The moussaka can be baked 2 to 3 hours ahead of serving and reheated in the 400°F oven when you roast the lamb for a few minutes; take care to not let them dry out.)

When ready to serve the dish, preheat the oven to 400°F.

Drain the leg of lamb from its marinade and pat well with paper towels to dry. Season generously with salt and pepper. Heat the canola oil in an ovenproof sauté pan over high heat until it's smoking, then carefully place the lamb in the pan, turning it to brown well on all sides, about 10 minutes total. Transfer to the oven and roast the lamb until an instant-read meat thermometer inserted into the thickest part registers 110°F for rare to medium-rare, about 8 minutes, or to your desired degree of doneness.

Transfer the lamb to a cutting board and let it rest for 5 minutes before slicing.

To serve the lamb, divide the sauce evenly among 4 dinner plates and arrange the lamb slices on top of the sauce. Unmold the moussaka by removing the foil from the bottom and gently pushing from the top, placing a moussaka, custard side up, toward the side of each plate. Garnish with sprigs of marjoram and serve immediately.

PREP TALK

Ground Meats

To ensure the highest quality of ground lamb, purchase lamb pieces (shoulder is ideal) and grind it yourself. It's the only way to know exactly what your getting. The same is true of ground chicken and turkey as well.

Brined Roast Pork Loin with Fennel Jus & Fennel Flan

This is a Chanterelle classic that has evolved over the years with my own changing palate. I first made this dish with braised fennel and a fennel-pork sauce, but in time I replaced the braised vegetable with the more elegant flan. And, because I first served this in the days before heirloom, or artisanal, pork was available, I began brining the meat to give it more character—the process lends the pork a slightly sweet, almost hammy quality and lowers the risk of overcooking it. I also sometimes garnish the dish with fennel pollen, an ingredient that nobody had ever heard of until Mario Batali began using it at Babbo, which happens to be around the corner from my home.

This recipe requires a lot of advance work, but you can plan it to suit your schedule. With the exception of the actual roasting, all of the steps can be performed well in advance of cooking and serving the dish.

To make the brining liquid, combine the water, 2 tablespoons of the fennel seeds, the sugar, 3 tablespoons salt, the cloves, and bay leaves in a stockpot and bring to a boil. Remove from the heat and let cool before transferring to a bowl and refrigerating, cooling the brining liquid completely. (It will keep in an airtight container in the refrigerator for up to 1 week.)

Put the pork loin in the cold marinade, cover well, and refrigerate overnight or for up to 48 hours.

To make the fennel base for the flan, put half the fennel bulb, 6 cups of the stock, and the pastis in a medium pot over medium heat. Bring to a boil, then reduce the heat so the liquid is simmering and cook until the fennel is very soft, about 20 minutes. Drain through a fine-mesh strainer set over a bowl, reserving (and refrigerating) the liquid before using it in the sauce.

Transfer the fennel to a food processor fitted with a steel blade and process until smooth. Transfer the puree to a cheesecloth-lined colander set over a bowl. Gather the edges of the cloth over the puree to form a bundle, set a few plates on top of the cheesecloth to weight it down, and set the colander and bowl in the refrigerator overnight to extract as much liquid as possible from the puree.

Preheat the oven to 250°F. Grease four 4-ounce ramekins with the canola oil.

In a large bowl, whisk together the cream, whole egg, egg yolk, cayenne, and nutmeg, season with salt, then incorporate ⅔ cup of the drained fennel puree. Fill the ramekins evenly with the flan mixture (they should be about seven-eighths full) and place them in a roasting pan. Carefully add warm water to the pan so that it comes halfway up the sides of the ramekins, then cover the pan loosely with aluminum foil. Transfer to the oven and bake until the flans are just set (a knife inserted into the center should come out clean), about 1 hour, although it may take up to 1½ hours. (The flan can be made up to 2 hours in advance, kept covered with plastic wrap at room temperature, and reheated in a water bath, covered,

continued

8 cups water

3 tablespoons fennel seeds

¾ cup sugar

Kosher salt

4 whole cloves

3 bay leaves, preferably fresh

One 1½-pound pork loin, tied
(have the butcher do this for you)

2 pounds fennel bulbs, trimmed and
cut into 2-inch chunks, fronds reserved

8 cups Chicken Stock (page 292)

¼ cup pastis, such as Pernod or Ricard

¼ cup plus 2 tablespoons canola
or other neutral oil, plus more for
greasing ramekins

⅔ cup heavy cream

1 large egg plus 1 large egg yolk

Pinch of cayenne

Pinch of freshly grated nutmeg

1 large onion, unpeeled,
cut into 1-inch chunks

1 garlic head, in its skin,
cut in half horizontally

1 cup dry white wine

2 tablespoons unsalted butter, softened
at room temperature

Black pepper from a mill

½ lemon

SERVES 4

in a 250°F oven for 10 minutes. They can also be refrigerated overnight; let them come to room temperature before reheating.)

Heat 2 tablespoons of the canola oil in a medium heavy-bottomed sauté pan over medium-high heat. Add the remaining fennel bulb, the onion, and garlic and cook, stirring, until well browned, about 15 minutes. Pour in the wine and cook until almost dry, about 5 minutes. Pour in 4 cups of the reserved fennel braising liquid and the remaining 2 cups stock and 1 tablespoon fennel seeds. Bring to a boil, then reduce the heat so the liquid is simmering and cook until the sauce is reduced by about half, about 1 hour.

Strain the sauce through a fine-mesh strainer set over a medium saucepan. Bring to a boil and cook until the sauce has reduced to 1 cup, about 15 minutes. Whisk in the butter and season to taste with salt, pepper, and a few drops of lemon juice. (The sauce can be made up to

2 hours ahead and reheated gently just before serving; if reheating, whisk the sauce to reincorporate the flavors.)

When ready to serve, preheat the oven to 400°F.

Drain the pork loin, patting it dry and discarding the brine. Season lightly with salt and pepper. Heat the remaining 4 tablespoons canola oil in a wide, deep, heavy-bottomed, ovenproof sauté pan set over high heat. Add the pork and sear it on all sides, adjusting the heat so it doesn't scorch. Transfer to the oven and roast until an instant-read meat thermometer inserted into the thickest part of the loin registers 120°F degrees, about 20 minutes. Transfer the loin to a cutting board and let rest for 10 minutes before cutting into ¼-inch-thick slices.

To serve, divide the fennel jus evenly among 4 dinner plates. Arrange the pork loin slices in the center of each plate and unmold a flan to the side of each portion of pork. Garnish with the reserved fennel fronds and serve immediately.

Pork Chops with Ginger, Sauternes & Coarse Mustard

¼ cup peeled and coarsely chopped fresh ginger

2 cups Sauternes or Muscat

2 cups Chicken Stock (page 292) or high-quality low-sodium store-bought chicken stock

Four 10-ounce bone-in center-cut pork chops, trimmed of fat

Kosher salt

Black pepper from a mill

¼ cup canola or other neutral oil

1 tablespoon freshly squeezed lemon juice

3 tablespoons grainy mustard

¼ cup (½ stick) cold unsalted butter

SERVES 4

This dish takes a number of pork-friendly condiments and fuses them together into a powerful sauce reminiscent of honey mustard—it's sweet and hot, with a peppery undercurrent thanks to an infusion of ginger. There are not many ingredients here, but each one contributes a distinct and forceful flavor. This is delicious with Potato Spring Rolls (page 251).

Put the ginger and Sauternes in a medium heavy-bottomed saucepan, bring to a boil, reduce the heat to medium, and reduce, swirling, until it becomes caramelized and syrupy, about 15 minutes. Strain through a fine-mesh strainer set over a bowl and discard the ginger. Return the reduction to the pan and pour in the stock. Bring to a boil and reduce the sauce to 1 cup, about 30 minutes. Remove from the heat. (The sauce can be refrigerated in an airtight container for up to 24 hours.)

Preheat the oven to 400°F.

Heat a large, heavy-bottomed, ovenproof sauté pan over high heat until very hot. Season the pork chops generously with salt and pepper. Pour the oil into the hot pan, let it get hot, and add the chops. Brown the meat well, about 4 minutes per side. Drain and discard the oil, then place the pan to the oven for 5 to 7 minutes. Transfer the chops to a plate or platter and keep covered and warm while you finish the sauce.

Use a paper towel to carefully wipe any excess oil out of the sauté pan. Return the pan to high heat, pour in the Sauternes reduction, and bring to a boil. Add the lemon juice and mustard, then whisk in the butter, 1 tablespoon at a time.

Put a chop on each of 4 dinner plates and divide the sauce evenly among the servings, covering the chops. Serve immediately.

Braised Pork Belly with Apple Cider & Root Vegetables

Lunchtime at Chanterelle is a chance for me to honor the "other" French cuisine that I love—casual, bistro-style cooking. I've been serving and enjoying pork belly (the cut that becomes bacon when it's cured) for years, going back to when my father used to take me out for Chinese food in the Bronx. Here, the pork is braised in a cider-based liquid that imparts some lovely sweetness to the meat.

Heat 3 tablespoons of the oil in a large heavy-bottomed sauté pan over high heat. When it begins to smoke, add the pork belly, skin side down, reduce the heat to medium-high, and cook until golden brown, about 8 minutes per side. Transfer the pork belly to a plate and set aside.

Heat another 3 tablespoons of the oil in a large heavy-bottomed saucepan over medium-high heat. Reduce the heat to medium, add the onions, and cook, stirring a few times, until just translucent, about 10 minutes. Raise the heat to medium-high, add the Calvados, and scrape up any browned bits stuck to the bottom of the pan. Add 3 cups of the cider and simmer until reduced by half, about 15 minutes.

Nestle the pork belly into the pan, add the stock, peppercorns, coriander seeds, and bay leaves, and bring to a boil over medium-high heat. Reduce the heat to medium-low, cover, and simmer until the pork is tender and gives no resistance when pierced with a knife, about 2½ hours. Transfer the pork to a plate and cover with aluminum foil to keep warm. There should be about 1½ cups of braising liquid remaining. If there's more, keep reducing; if less, add enough stock to yield 1½ cups.

Heat the remaining 2 tablespoons oil in a large sauté pan over high heat until smoking. Add the vegetables and cook, stirring a few times, until lightly browned, about 5 minutes. Pour in the remaining 1½ cups cider and scrape up any browned bits stuck to the bottom of the pan. Simmer until the cider evaporates, about 10 minutes. Add the softened butter, tossing the vegetables to coat. Adjust the seasoning to taste with salt and pepper.

Heat the braising liquid over medium heat and whisk in the cold butter until it is fully incorporated and the sauce has a syrupy consistency. Strain through a fine-mesh strainer set over a bowl. Carefully wipe out the pan and return the sauce to it. Add the lemon juice and adjust the seasoning with salt and more lemon juice to taste. Add the pork belly and heat through.

Divide the vegetables evenly among 4 dinner plates and top each with a piece of pork belly. Ladle the sauce over the pork and serve immediately.

½ cup canola or other neutral oil

2 pounds pork belly, skin on, cut into 4 equal pieces

2 cups finely diced Spanish onion (about 2 medium onions)

3 tablespoons Calvados

4½ cups hard cider

5 cups Chicken Stock (page 292), plus more if needed

½ teaspoon black peppercorns

½ teaspoon coriander seeds

2 bay leaves, preferably fresh

1 small or ½ large celery root, peeled and cut into matchsticks ¼ x 2 inches long (about ¾ cup)

1 medium carrot, peeled and cut into matchsticks ¼ x 2 inches long (about ¾ cup)

1 medium turnip, peeled and cut into matchsticks ¼ x 2 inches long (about ¾ cup)

1 large parsnip, peeled and cut into matchsticks ¼ x 2 inches long (about ¾ cup)

2 tablespoons unsalted butter, softened at room temperature

Kosher salt

Black pepper from a mill

2 tablespoons cold unsalted butter

½ teaspoon freshly squeezed lemon juice, plus more to taste

SERVES 4

Braised Veal Shank with Glazed Vegetables & Creamy Orzo

¾ cup canola or other neutral oil

3 garlic heads, in their skins, cut into large chunks

4 medium carrots, unpeeled, cut into large chunks

2 large Spanish onions, unpeeled, cut into large chunks

2 tablespoons all-purpose flour

1 teaspoon tomato paste

2 cups dry white wine

¼ cup brandy

8 cups Veal Stock (page 294)

3 bay leaves, preferably fresh

2 whole veal shanks (4 to 5 pounds each), trimmed of excess fat

Kosher salt

Black pepper from a mill

3 tablespoons unsalted butter, softened at room temperature

½ teaspoon freshly squeezed lemon juice, plus more to taste

3 tablespoons fresh basil cut into chiffonade (see Prep Talk, page 70)

SERVES 4

Rustic home cooking, in the style of what the French call *grand-mere,* is probably more suited to a bistro than to the elegant setting of Chanterelle, but I have such a soft spot for it that I've found ways to make it work in our dining room, serving traditionally casual dishes in a formal way. One of my favorite examples is our veal shank, a huge cut of meat braised in stock and white wine, offered as a dish for two and presented in a copper pan at the table, where the waiter divides it between two plates. We serve this with Glazed Root Vegetables (page 247) and Creamy Orzo (page 256), and I suggest you do the same. You can also make this with tarragon in place of the basil.

Preheat the oven to 350°F.

Heat ¼ cup of the oil in a large heavy-bottomed pot over medium-high heat. Add the garlic, carrots, and onions and brown, stirring often, about 15 minutes. Add the flour and cook, stirring, for another 5 minutes. Add the tomato paste, stirring to coat the vegetables with it. Pour in the wine and brandy and scrape up any browned bits stuck to the bottom of the pot. Pour in the stock, bring to a rapid boil, then reduce the heat to medium-low and add the bay leaves. Let simmer while you brown the veal shanks.

Arrange the veal shanks on a dry, clean surface and season generously with salt and pepper. Heat the remaining ½ cup oil in a very large heavy-bottomed sauté pan over high heat. Add the shanks and brown all sides evenly, about 10 minutes total.

Transfer the shanks and the unstrained braising liquid to a deep roasting pan. The liquid should come halfway up the sides of the shanks. Cover tightly with aluminum foil, place in the oven, and braise until the meat begins to pull away from the bone and gather into a ball, about 3 hours.

Remove the shanks from the pan and set aside. Strain the cooking liquid through a cheesecloth-lined fine-mesh strainer set over a bowl. Press down on the solids to extract as much flavorful liquid as possible. Carefully wipe out the pot you originally cooked the braising liquid in and pour the liquid back into it. Bring to a boil and reduce to about 4 cups, about 10 minutes.

Pour the braising liquid into a bowl, cover tightly with plastic wrap, and refrigerate for up to 2 hours. Skim off the layer of fat that accumulates on the surface. Pour the skimmed liquid into a large heavy-bottomed pot set over medium heat. Add the shanks and heat to warm through, at least 20 minutes. Transfer the shanks to a cutting board and cut the meat from the bones, arranging the slices on a serving platter. Bring the broth to a boil. Whisk in the butter, 1 tablespoon at a time, to enrich the sauce. Stir in the lemon juice and season to taste with salt and pepper.

Just before serving, stir the basil into the broth and pour it over the shanks. Serve immediately.

Sweetbreads with Caramelized Leeks & Orange

2 pounds sweetbreads

1 tablespoon kosher salt, plus more to taste

Juice of ½ lemon

¼ cup plus 3 tablespoons canola or other neutral oil

2 large onions, unpeeled, cut into large chunks

2 large carrots, unpeeled, cut into large chunks

2 garlic heads, in their skins, cut in half horizontally

½ cup cubed fresh ginger, unpeeled (about 3 ounces)

¼ cup plus 1 tablespoon sugar

½ cup water

1¼ cups orange juice (not from concentrate)

2 tablespoons red wine vinegar

6 cups Veal Stock (page 294)

3 tablespoons soy sauce

3 large pieces dried orange peel

Black pepper from a mill

3 cups leeks (white parts only) cut into 3½- x ¼-inch ribbons and washed well (see Prep Talk, page 53)

1 tablespoon unsalted butter, softened at room temperature

SERVES 4

How do you transform classic New York City Chinese food like General Tso's Chicken or Crispy Beef with Orange into something that's right for Chanterelle? The answer was to make a sauce in that style, assertively flavored with ginger, orange, and soy, but to use French technique, beginning with a gastrique—dissolving sugar into water, adding vinegar and orange juice—then incorporating the other flavors into it and building it out with veal stock. The other adjustment was making the dish with a surprising choice of protein: sweetbreads. Truth be told, I was never really a fan of braised sweetbreads, but I loved the ones I ate at Troisgros years ago, which were broken into small pieces and gently browned. Cooked that way, they're the perfect vehicle for the sauce here, which becomes like a glaze when the two are tossed together in a hot pan just before serving.

If you like, garnish each serving with finely sliced scallions and serve with steamed or sautéed bok choy.

Put the sweetbreads in a large bowl or roasting pan. Sprinkle with 1 tablespoon salt, then pour in enough cold water to fully submerge the sweetbreads. Cover with plastic wrap and refrigerate overnight.

Drain the sweetbreads, transfer to a large saucepan, and pour in enough cold water to cover them. Add the lemon juice, bring to just below a simmer over medium heat, and cook for about 30 minutes.

Use a slotted spoon to transfer the sweetbreads to a cutting board. When they are cool enough to handle, peel away the membrane and remove the connective tissue and fat. Wrap the sweetbreads well in plastic wrap and place on a baking sheet. Press them down with a second sheet weighted with a large heavy can or skillet. Refrigerate like this overnight to give them a uniform shape and firmer texture.

Heat ¼ cup of the oil in a large pot over high heat. Add the onions, carrots, garlic, and ginger and cook, stirring frequently, until lightly browned, about 10 minutes.

Combine ¼ cup of the sugar and the water in a small heavy-bottomed saucepan over medium-high heat. Cook, stirring, until it boils, then stop stirring but continue to cook until the sugar caramelizes and turns a medium golden brown, about 5 minutes. Carefully (the caramel will sputter and spit when liquid is added to it) add 1 cup of the orange juice and 1 tablespoon of the vinegar and simmer (still over medium-high heat), stirring, until the hardened caramel has dissolved.

Add the caramel to the browned vegetables. Add the stock and soy sauce, then the orange peel, and bring to a slow, steady simmer. Cook until the sauce is flavorful and slightly reduced, about 50 minutes. Strain through a fine-mesh strainer set over a small saucepan. Bring to a boil over medium-high heat and cook until reduced to 1 cup, about 10 minutes.

Arrange the chilled, pressed sweetbreads on a cutting board and cut into 2-inch chunks. Season generously with salt and pepper. Heat a wide, heavy-bottomed sauté pan over medium heat, then add the remaining 3 tablespoons oil. Add the sweetbreads and brown well on all sides, 10 to 12 minutes total, being very patient; the sweetbreads must be allowed to brown slowly and evenly or else they may burn in spots. Transfer to a plate, cover with plastic wrap, and set aside. Don't rinse out the pan.

Put the leek ribbons and remaining 1 tablespoon sugar in the sauté pan over medium heat and toss together with the hot oil remaining from the sweetbreads until slightly browned and caramelized, 3 to 4 minutes. Raise the heat to high, pour in the remaining ¼ cup orange juice and 1 tablespoon vinegar, and cook, stirring to loosen any browned bits stuck to the bottom of the pan. Reduce until the pan is nearly dry. Add the sauce, the browned sweetbreads, and butter, turning the sweetbreads to coat them with the sauce and melted butter.

Divide the sweetbreads and sauce among 4 dinner plates and serve immediately.

Sweetbreads with Sherry Vinegar & Wild Mushrooms

This is another recipe that combines the technique of a professional kitchen with the primal satisfaction of home cooking. This is based directly on the sweetbread dish from Troisgros described on page 226. You can make this with chanterelles or another wild mushroom, or even an assortment—wherever the best available mushrooms lead you on the day you do your shopping.

This is delicious with spinach and/or potato side dishes.

Put the sweetbreads in a large bowl or roasting pan. Sprinkle with 1 tablespoon salt, then pour in enough cold water to fully submerge the sweetbreads. Cover with plastic wrap and refrigerate overnight.

Drain the sweetbreads, transfer to a large saucepan, and pour in enough cold water to cover. Add the lemon juice, bring to just below a simmer over medium heat, and cook for about 30 minutes.

Use a slotted spoon to transfer the sweetbreads to a cutting board. When they are cool enough to handle, peel away the membrane and remove the connective tissue and fat. Wrap the sweetbreads well in plastic wrap and place on a baking sheet. Press them down with a second sheet weighted with a large heavy can or skillet. Refrigerate like this overnight to give them a uniform shape and firmer texture.

Melt 2 tablespoons of the butter in a heavy-bottomed sauté pan over medium heat. Add the mushrooms and cook, stirring a few times, until browned and dry, about 5 minutes. (The exact cooking time may vary greatly based on mushroom variety.) Transfer to a bowl to cool.

In an 8- or 10-quart pot set over high heat, heat ¼ cup of the oil. Add the onions, carrots, and garlic and cook, stirring often, until browned, 10 to 15 minutes. Add the tomato paste and stir until everything is coated with it. Pour in the wine, ½ cup of the vinegar, and the stock,

then add the mushroom stems and bay leaves. Bring to a boil, then reduce the heat so the liquid is simmering and cook until the liquid has reduced to 2 cups, 30 to 40 minutes. Strain through a fine-mesh strainer set over small a saucepan. Bring to a boil and reduce to 1 cup, about 5 minutes.

Arrange the chilled, pressed sweetbreads on a cutting board and cut into 2-inch chunks. Season generously with salt and pepper. Heat a wide, heavy-bottomed sauté pan over medium heat, then add the remaining 3 tablespoons oil. Add the sweetbreads and brown well on all sides, 10 to 12 minutes total, being very patient; the sweetbreads must be allowed to brown slowly and evenly or else they may burn in spots. Transfer to a plate, cover with plastic wrap, and set aside. Don't rinse out the pan.

Put the cooked mushrooms in the sauté pan and set over medium heat, tossing to heat the mushrooms through. Add the remaining 2 tablespoons vinegar, stirring to loosen any browned bits stuck to the bottom of the pan, then add the sauce, the remaining 2 table-spoons butter, and the browned sweetbreads. Turn the sweetbreads to coat them with the sauce and melted butter and heat through.

Divide the sweetbreads, mushrooms, and sauce among 4 dinner plates and serve immediately.

2 pounds sweetbreads

1 tablespoon kosher salt, plus more to taste

Juice of ½ lemon

¼ cup plus 3 tablespoons canola or other neutral oil

¼ cup (½ stick) unsalted butter, cut in half

1 pound chanterelle or assorted wild mushrooms, washed and stems removed and reserved

2 large Spanish onions, unpeeled, cut into large chunks

2 large carrots, unpeeled, cut into large chunks

2 garlic heads, in their skins, cut in half horizontally

1 teaspoon tomato paste

1 cup dry white wine

½ cup plus 2 tablespoons sherry vinegar

6 cups Veal Stock (page 294)

2 bay leaves, preferably fresh

Black pepper from a mill

SERVES 4

Roast Saddle of Venison with Creamed Sauerkraut & Hungarian Paprika

¼ cup plus 2 tablespoons canola or other neutral oil

3 medium carrots, unpeeled, coarsely chopped

2 large Spanish onions, unpeeled, quartered

2 garlic heads, in their skins, cut in half horizontally

8 ounces slab bacon, cut into 1-inch pieces

2 cups dry white wine

8 cups Venison Stock (page 295) or Veal Stock (page 294)

3 tablespoons sweet Hungarian paprika

2 teaspoons hot Hungarian paprika

3 tablespoons all-purpose flour

1 tablespoon unsalted butter, softened at room temperature

Kosher salt

Black pepper from a mill

2 tablespoons cold unsalted butter

½ cup minced onion

2 cups heavy cream

1 pound sauerkraut, drained and squeezed dry

One 1½-pound venison saddle, trimmed of fat

SERVES 4

Years ago, when I lived on the Upper East Side of Manhattan, I ate regularly in little Czech and Hungarian restaurants and grew to love a lot of the food, especially pork goulash, sauerkraut, and dishes flavored with paprika and finished with sour cream. In time, I began serving some of these dishes to my staff for our nightly meal, and eventually I found a way to incorporate their influence into the dining room menu with this venison dish. It's perhaps more refined than the cuisine that inspired it, but I think it captures its bacony, oniony, smoky qualities. I also love the way the various sauces, creams, and spices run together on the plate, and then on the palate. To put it plain and simple, this dish makes me happy.

Do not use jarred or canned sauerkraut because these products have been cooked to extend their shelf life, making them mushy and robbing them of some sour flavor. Instead, choose sauerkraut sold in bags or a barrel, which retains all of its natural texture and flavor.

This is best served with roasted potatoes.

Heat 3 tablespoons of the oil in a large heavy-bottomed pot over high heat. When it just begins to smoke, add the carrots, quartered onions, garlic pieces, and bacon, reduce the heat to medium, and cook, stirring frequently, until the vegetables are browned and soft, about 8 minutes. Pour in the wine and use a wooden spoon to scrape up any browned bits stuck to the bottom of the pot. Cook until the wine evaporates, about 10 minutes. Add the stock and both types of paprika, bring to a boil, then reduce the heat so the liquid is simmering and cook until the flavor has developed nicely, about 45 minutes.

Strain the sauce through a fine-mesh strainer set over a medium saucepan, using a wooden spoon or rubber spatula to push on the solids to extract all of their liquid. Bring to a simmer over medium heat. Meanwhile, in a small bowl, knead together 1 tablespoon of the flour and the softened butter to form a paste, then whisk this into the sauce, breaking up any lumps. Bring to a boil, then reduce the heat to a simmer and cook to eliminate the floury taste and reduce the sauce to about 1 cup, about 5 minutes. Strain through a fine-mesh strainer set over a bowl and adjust the seasoning with salt and pepper to taste. Set aside and keep warm.

Melt the cold butter in a small heavy-bottomed saucepan over medium heat until foamy. Add the minced onion and cook, stirring, until softened but not browned, about 8 minutes. Raise the heat to medium-high, add the remaining 2 tablespoons flour, and cook, stirring, for 3 minutes to cook out the floury taste. Whisk in the cream and bring to a brisk simmer, then add the sauerkraut. Reduce the heat to medium and cook until the mixture has a just slightly thickened consistency, about 10 minutes. Keep warm until ready to use.

Preheat the oven to 500°F.

Season the venison saddle on all sides with salt and pepper. Heat a large, heavy-bottomed, ovenproof sauté pan over high heat, then add the remaining 3 tablespoons oil. When it's just smoking, add the venison, reduce the heat to medium-high, and sear the meat until browned, about 2 minutes per side. Transfer to the oven and roast the venison until an instant-read meat thermometer inserted into its thickest part reads 120°F for medium-rare, about 5 minutes, or to your desired degree of doneness. Transfer the venison to a rack set on a rimmed baking sheet and let rest for 5 minutes before slicing it crosswise against the grain.

Divide the sauerkraut evenly among 4 dinner plates, spooning the sauce around it. Arrange the venison slices on top and serve immediately.

Roast Saddle of Venison with Red Wine & Prunes

12 ounces pitted prunes, soaked overnight in water to cover at room temperature

One 750 ml bottle dry red wine

2 tablespoons plus 1 cup ruby port

¼ cup canola or other neutral oil

3 medium carrots, unpeeled, coarsely chopped

1 large onion, unpeeled, quartered

2 garlic heads, in their skins, cut in half horizontally

2 tablespoons brandy

8 cups Venison Stock (page 295) or Veal Stock (page 294)

1 tablespoon unsalted butter, softened at room temperature

1 tablespoon all-purpose flour

Kosher salt

Black pepper from a mill

Two 12-ounce pieces venison leg

SERVES 4

I've always enjoyed the combination of red wine and prunes, and they're a perfect pairing with venison, which has a strong flavor of its own. Prunes don't get much respect in the culinary world, but they become a gourmet player here. Serve this with Wild Rice (page 255).

Put 8 of the prunes in a small bowl. Add ½ cup of the wine and 2 tablespoons of the port to cover. Cover and macerate the prunes for 1 to 2 hours.

Heat 3 tablespoons of the oil in a large heavy-bottomed saucepan over high heat until it smokes. Add the carrots, onion, and garlic, reduce the heat to medium-high, and cook, stirring frequently, until they're browned and soft, about 10 minutes. Pour in the brandy, the remaining 1 cup port, and the rest of the wine, then scrape up any browned bits stuck to the bottom of the pan. Bring to a boil and cook until reduced by half, about 20 minutes.

Add the stock and remaining prunes to the pan and bring back to a boil over medium-high heat. Cook until the prunes are tender and falling apart and the liquid has reduced by half, about 35 minutes. Strain through a fine-mesh strainer set over a medium saucepan, using a wooden spoon to push down on the solids to extract as much flavorful liquid as possible. Bring the sauce to a simmer over medium heat.

In a small bowl, knead the butter and flour together until it forms a paste, then whisk this into the simmering sauce, breaking up any lumps. Raise the heat slightly to bring it to a boil before returning to medium heat and simmering the sauce just long enough to eliminate the flour taste, about 5 minutes. Strain through a fine-mesh strainer set over a bowl and season to taste with salt and pepper. Keep the sauce warm while you cook the venison.

Preheat the oven to 500°F.

Season the venison on all sides with salt and pepper. Heat a large, heavy-bottomed, ovenproof sauté pan over high heat until very hot, then add the remaining ¼ cup oil. When it's just smoking, add the venison, reduce the heat to medium-high, and cook until browned, about 2 minutes per side. Transfer to the oven and roast until an instant-read meat thermometer inserted into the thickest part of the leg (away from the bone) reads 120°F, about 5 minutes. Transfer the venison to a rack set on a rimmed baking sheet and let rest for 5 minutes. Slice the venison crosswise against the grain.

Divide the sauce evenly among 4 wide, shallow bowls. Top with a few slices of venison, then a few of the prunes, and serve immediately.

Our Wine Dreams Come True:
Roger Dagorn

When it comes to wine, Roger Dagorn was the answer to our prayers. Literally.

All of the great restaurants that inspired us to open Chanterelle were founded on the triumvirate of a great chef, a great front-of-the-house team, and a stellar sommelier. While it was always a given that David and I would fill two of those roles, the realization of the third took years to achieve. When we first opened the restaurant, I actually filled that role myself.

In time, we had a number of wonderful people who were our sommeliers. Once, after one left us, we followed a piece of advice we'd begun to hear in restaurant circles around town: "If you want to find great wine talent in New York City, ask Roger," referring to Roger Dagorn, who was working his magic at Tse Yang, a modern Mandarin restaurant with a famously well-stocked cellar. After suggesting two excellent people to us, both of whom went on to pursue other professions after being at Chanterelle for several years, the third time was the charm: When we called Roger to ask him for yet another candidate, he nominated himself.

I thought he was joking. He wasn't.

So, in 1993, Roger joined the Chanterelle family, and we've all lived happily ever after.

Roger epitomizes the Chanterelle ethic: He's a traditionalist at heart, with a rich understanding of great wine from France, which is not surprising given that he was born into a restaurant family from Brittany. Of course, his heritage doesn't quite explain his almost encyclopedic knowledge of the great wines of the world, and it makes his ability to think outside the box all the more remarkable. Roger was the first person to turn me on to so many new- and old-world wines from small, lesser-known producers. Our guests are always surprised and delighted when he pairs something nontraditional, like sake, with one of their courses. (Roger's great memory extends to languages, and he knows enough of many to get around the world and learn what he needs to know about the wines he discovers in his travels.)

Having shared all of this, I have to add—and I know it sounds like a cliché—that as impressive as Roger's credentials are, what has truly endeared him to us is his character. For all of his accomplishments, he remains exceedingly humble, always encouraging newcomers to his profession and never losing the thrill of uncorking that next bottle of wine.

—KAREN WALTUCK

SIDE DISHES & ACCOMPANIMENTS

¶ It might surprise you to learn that, as hard as I work to hone each new Chanterelle dish, I'm often very flexible about one component on the plate, varying the vegetable or starch from year to year. Sure, some compositions never change, but many of them do: I'll put new greens on a fish dish, or use a different potato preparation alongside beef. To put it another way, I treat side dishes at the restaurant the same way I treat them at home, as a means of maintaining spontaneity, even with familiar favorites.

¶ That's the spirit of this chapter: I've tried to hit all the marks, with recipes that range from green vegetables to potatoes and other starches, as well as including favorites from each season of the year. Where applicable, I indicate which main-course dishes we serve each side with at Chanterelle, but I also offer suggestions for how you might incorporate these accompaniments into your own cooking.

Haricots Verts & Other Green Vegetables, the Chanterelle Way

¼ cup Chicken Stock (page 292), high-quality low-sodium store-bought chicken stock, or water

½ cup (1 stick) cold unsalted butter, cut into ½-inch cubes

Kosher salt

Black pepper from a mill

8 ounces haricots verts or other green vegetables, ends trimmed

SERVES 4

This is the basic way we cook and serve green vegetables such as haricots verts, sugar-snap peas, and snow peas. You can adapt the method for baby carrots or turnips, tourné vegetables, potatoes, and so on, boiling each one in salted water until they are tender to a knife tip.

Any vegetable prepared this way can be cooked ahead of time, then reheated in the butter sauce; at the restaurant we always cook green vegetables to order, since they take only a few minutes. Starchy vegetables and roots are cooked in advance, and I suggest doing the same at home.

Bring the stock to a rapid simmer in a small heavy-bottomed saucepan over medium-high heat. Whisk in the butter, a cube or two at a time, to make a light emulsion just thick enough to coat the back of a wooden spoon. Season to taste with salt and pepper. Remove from the heat and keep covered and warm for up to 2 hours.

Bring a medium saucepan pot of salted water to a boil. Add the beans and cook until done but still a little crunchy, 2 to 3 minutes. Drain well, then toss with the butter mixture. Drain again and serve, either presenting family style at the table or plating them alongside fish or meat.

Creamed Spinach

This version of the American steakhouse classic gains extra flavor from steeping bay leaves in the half-and-half before making the béchamel. Serve it with grilled beef, roasted meats, or chicken.

Bring a medium saucepan of salted water to a boil. Fill a large bowl halfway with ice water.

Cook the spinach in the boiling water for 1 minute. Use tongs to transfer it to the ice water to stop the cooking and preserve the green color. Drain the spinach well in a colander, squeezing it by hand to extract as much water as possible.

Carefully wipe out the saucepan and pour in the half-and-half. Set over medium-high heat and bring to a boil. Immediately remove from the heat and add the bay leaves. Steep for 20 minutes to infuse the liquid with the flavor of the bay. Use tongs to remove and discard the bay leaves.

Melt the butter in a medium heavy-bottomed sauté pan over low heat. Add the onion and cook, stirring frequently, until softened but not browned, about 10 minutes. Sprinkle with the flour and cook, stirring, until the butter and flour come together into a paste, about 10 minutes; don't let it brown. Slowly pour in the infused half-and-half, incorporating it with a whisk and breaking up any lumps. Cook, whisking, until the mixture has thickened, about 15 minutes. Strain the béchamel through a fine-mesh strainer set over a medium sauté pan. (The béchamel can be cooled, covered, and refrigerated for up to 24 hours; reheat gently before proceeding.)

When ready to serve, set the pan over low heat and fold in the drained spinach, cooking for a minute or two to warm the spinach and meld the flavors. Season to taste with lemon juice, nutmeg, salt, and pepper. Transfer to a serving bowl, or spoon alongside meats or poultry, and serve immediately.

Kosher salt

12 ounces fresh baby spinach leaves, rinsed well and spun dry

4 cups half-and-half

2 bay leaves, preferably fresh

¼ cup (½ stick) unsalted butter

2 cups coarsely chopped Spanish onion (about 1 large onion)

3 tablespoons all-purpose flour

½ teaspoon freshly squeezed lemon juice, plus more to taste

Pinch or 2 of freshly grated nutmeg

Black pepper from a mill

SERVES 4

Braised Fennel

2 large fennel bulbs

1 tablespoon unsalted butter, softened at room temperature

Kosher salt

Black pepper from a mill

About 2 cups Chicken Stock (page 292) or high-quality low-sodium store-bought chicken stock

1 tablespoon pastis, such as Pernod or Ricard

½ teaspoon freshly squeezed lemon juice, plus more to taste

SERVES 4

In this powerfully flavored side dish, the anise flavor of fennel is amplified by a small amount of pastis in the cooking liquid. Serve it with pork, chicken, fish, or veal dishes.

Remove the tops of the fennel bulbs, trim the bottoms, and peel off any outer layers that are tough or discolored. Cut the bulbs in half lengthwise so that the root end is still intact and holding the layers together.

Rub the softened butter over the bottom of a medium heavy-bottomed sauté pan. Place the fennel halves, cut side down, in the pan. Sprinkle with salt and pepper. Pour the stock over the fennel and add the pastis and lemon juice. Set over medium heat and bring to a simmer. Cover and cook until the fennel is tender when pierced with a knife and the liquid is reduced and syrupy, 15 to 20 minutes, lifting the lid occasionally to make sure the liquid hasn't completely evaporated, which might cause the fennel to burn or scorch. (Add more stock or water if necessary.)

Transfer the fennel to a plate or platter and reduce the liquid further if it seems thin or the flavor isn't pleasantly intense. Taste and adjust the seasoning of the liquid with salt, pepper, and lemon juice as needed. (The fennel can be made up to 3 hours in advance and kept warm. Reheat, if necessary, in its liquid, in an aluminum foil–covered pan in a preheated 350°F oven, or on the stovetop, adding a little more stock or water to keep it from drying out.) Serve from a platter or alongside fish and meat dishes.

A Trio of Purees

Preparing three types of puree doesn't take much more time and effort than making one, but the result makes a big impression: The variety of colors is striking, and there's nothing like a restaurant-style flourish to make your guests feel special. These purees are a perfect match for the Venison Chop with Sauce Poivrade on page 231. They also pair well with duck.

I've separated the individual purees here; if you make all three, they will serve 4 people. To serve one puree only, triple each of the ingredients.

If you make the purees in advance, put each one in a heatproof container, cover loosely with aluminum foil, and set the containers in a roasting pan or large baking dish. Fill the pan halfway up the sides of the containers with warm water and keep in an oven preheated to 200°F for up to 2 hours.

To serve, form quenelles of the purees, arranging one quenelle of each puree on each plate.

Beet Puree

Preheat the oven to 375°F.

Wash the beets, pat dry with paper towels, and rub with the oil. Wrap them individually in aluminum foil, set them on a baking sheet, and bake until soft and easily pierced with a paring knife, about 2 hours.

Remove from the oven and let the beets cool. When cool enough to handle, remove the foil and peel the beets, scraping off the skin with the back of a knife or a clean kitchen towel.

Cut the beets into 1-inch chunks and puree in a blender, adding a little water if necessary to help the blade catch. Pass the puree through a fine-mesh strainer set over a small saucepan. Add the butter and heat the puree over medium heat, stirring to just melt the butter and warm the mixture. Season to taste with salt and pepper. If the puree still seems loose, cook, stirring, for 2 or 3 minutes more, until it becomes thick enough to hold together in a quenelle.

3 medium to large red beets
(about 1½ pounds total)

2 tablespoons canola
or other neutral oil

1 tablespoon unsalted butter,
softened at room temperature

Kosher salt

Black pepper from a mill

MAKES 1 CUP

Kosher salt

12 ounces parsnips (3 to 4 parsnips)

1 medium Idaho potato
(about 8 ounces)

1 tablespoon heavy cream

2 tablespoons unsalted butter,
softened at room temperature

White pepper from a mill

MAKES 1 CUP

2 large sweet potatoes
(about 2 pounds total)

2 tablespoons canola
or other neutral oil

2 tablespoons unsalted butter,
softened at room temperature

Kosher salt

Black pepper from a mill

MAKES 1 CUP

Parsnip Puree

Bring a large pot of salted water to a boil.

Peel the parsnips and potato and cut into 1-inch chunks. Add to the boiling water and cook until very tender, 20 to 30 minutes. Drain in a colander and let sit in the sink to steam and dry for 5 minutes.

Wipe out the pot and pass the parsnip chunks through a fine-mesh strainer into the pot. Add the cream and butter and heat over medium heat, stirring, to just melt the butter and warm the mixture, about 2 minutes. Season to taste with salt and white pepper.

Sweet Potato Puree

Preheat the oven to 375°F.

Wash the potatoes, pat dry with paper towels, and rub with the oil. Place on a baking sheet and bake until soft and easily pierced with a paring knife, about 1¼ hours. Remove from the oven and let the potatoes cool. Cut them in half lengthwise and scoop the potato from the skins. Discard the skins.

Pass the potato through a fine-mesh strainer set over a small saucepan. Add the butter and heat the puree over medium heat, stirring to just melt the butter and warm the mixture. Season to taste with salt and pepper.

Glazed Root Vegetables

This autumnal side dish gets along great with roast chicken and pork, and it is a natural for fall staples such as duck and venison.

Heat the oil in a wide, heavy-bottomed sauté pan set over high heat until it smokes. Add the celery, carrot, turnip, and parsnip and cook, stirring a few times, until they just begin to soften, about 5 minutes.

Pour in the cider and stir, scraping up any browned bits stuck to the bottom of the pan. Cook over medium heat until it evaporates, about 10 minutes. Swirl in the butter, tossing the vegetables to coat them. Season to taste with salt and pepper. Serve immediately.

2 tablespoons canola or other neutral oil

¾ cup celery root peeled and cut into 2-inch-long matchsticks

¾ cup carrot peeled and cut into 2-inch-long matchsticks

¾ cup turnip peeled and cut into 2-inch-long matchsticks

¾ cup parsnip peeled and cut into 2-inch-long matchsticks

1½ cups hard cider

2 tablespoons unsalted butter, softened at room temperature

Kosher salt

Black pepper from a mill

SERVES 4

Chive Mashed Potatoes

4 ounces fresh chives

4 medium Idaho or Russet potatoes, peeled and quartered

Kosher salt

About ½ cup heavy cream

3 tablespoons unsalted butter, softened at room temperature

Black pepper from a mill

SERVES 4

Beautiful green chives, added at the last second, bring a gentle onion flavor and visual flair to a taken-for-granted side dish. Serve these with fish as well as pork and steak.

Bring a large pot of water to a rolling boil. Fill a large bowl halfway with ice water. Add the chives to the boiling water and blanch for 30 seconds. Drain and quickly transfer to the ice water to stop the cooking and preserve the green color. Drain again, then coarsely chop. Transfer the chives to a blender, add 1 ice cube (to prevent over-heating and discoloration), and puree to a fine paste. Transfer the puree to a bowl and set aside. (The puree can be covered and refrigerated for up to 2 hours.)

Put the potatoes in a medium saucepan and cover with cold water. Generously salt the water and bring to a boil. Reduce the heat to medium, cover, and cook until the potatoes are tender to a knife tip but not falling apart, 15 to 20 minutes. Drain the potatoes in a colander and leave them in the sink for a few minutes to steam and dry.

Meanwhile, heat the cream and butter in a small saucepan over low heat until the butter has melted.

Put the potatoes through a food mill or ricer set over a large saucepan (you can use the same pot you cooked the potatoes in if you clean and dry it first). Pour in the hot cream mixture, set the pan over low heat, and, using a wooden spoon, mix the potatoes well, but do not overmix or they will become gummy. (The potatoes can be kept warm for up to 2 hours by covering and keeping them in a warm place, such as a turned-off back burner or in the top of a double boiler set over simmering water; reheat gently before proceeding, adding a splash of cream if they have dried slightly.)

Gently fold the chive puree into the mashed potatoes with a wooden spoon or rubber spatula. Season to taste with salt and pepper and serve immediately.

Olive Oil Mashed Potatoes

These relatively loose mashed potatoes are powerfully flavored with garlic and olive oil. Intended to stand in for aïoli in Red Snapper with Bouillabaisse Broth (page 150), they are also a good match with roast chicken or beef, or just about any meat.

Put the potatoes in a medium saucepan and cover with cold water. Generously salt the water and bring to a boil. Reduce the heat to medium, cover, and cook until the potatoes are tender to a knife tip but not falling apart, 15 to 20 minutes.

Meanwhile, put the oil and garlic cloves in a small heavy-bottomed saucepan and heat over medium heat until the oil is just shimmering. Reduce the heat so the liquid is simmering and gently cook the cloves until they are very soft to a knife tip, about 10 minutes. Remove from the heat.

Drain the potatoes in a colander and leave them in the sink for 5 minutes to steam and dry.

Meanwhile, heat the cream in a small saucepan over low heat.

Put the potatoes through a food mill or ricer set over a large saucepan (you can use the same pot you cooked the potatoes in if you clean and dry it first). Use a slotted spoon to transfer the garlic cloves to the mill or ricer and process them as well. (Do not discard the oil.) Add the hot cream and garlic-infused oil to the pan with the potatoes and garlic, set it over low heat, and, using a wooden spoon, mix the potatoes well, but do not overmix or they will become gummy. Season to taste with salt and pepper. (The potatoes can be kept warm for up to 2 hours by covering and keeping them in a warm place, such as a turned-off back burner or in the top of a double boiler set over simmering water; reheat gently before proceeding, adding a splash of cream or olive oil if they have dried slightly.)

Serve from a bowl or under or alongside fish or meat.

2 pounds Idaho potatoes, peeled and cut in half crosswise

Kosher salt

¼ cup olive oil

10 garlic cloves, peeled

1 cup heavy cream

Black pepper from a mill

SERVES 4

Potato Spring Rolls

These spring rolls are essentially a fun, pick-up-able way to serve mashed potatoes. We serve them with the duck dish on page 191. I also recommend them with dishes that have an Asian inflection or feature pungent flavors that won't be smothered by the potatoes. This recipe uses *feuille de brik,* a very delicate, thin spring roll–type wrapper from North Africa that attains a nice crispness without too much presence when fried. It can be mail ordered or purchased from well-stocked gourmet markets. You may also substitute spring roll wrappers.

Bring a large pot of generously salted water to a boil. Add the potatoes and cook until tender, about 10 minutes. Drain in a colander and leave them in the sink for 5 minutes to steam and dry.

Melt the duck fat in a large heavy-bottomed sauté pan over low heat. Add the onion and cook until softened but not browned, stirring a few times, about 15 minutes. Pass the potatoes through a food mill or ricer set over a bowl. Add the onion–duck fat mixture and season to taste with salt and plenty of pepper.

In a small bowl, whisk together the egg and water to make a wash for the wrappers. Cut each pastry circle in half and arrange them on a clean, dry surface. Using a pastry brush, brush the left and right edges of each half-circle with egg wash. Spoon 2 tablespoons of the potato mixture in the center of each half-circle, then fold in the right and left edges to square off the sides of the half-wrapper. Roll up the spring rolls and secure the ends with a dab more egg wash. (The rolls can be refrigerated in an airtight container for up to 24 hours.)

Pour 4 inches of oil into a deep pot set over high heat or an electric fryer and heat the oil to 350°F. Carefully place the spring rolls in the hot oil and fry until golden brown, about 3 minutes. Use a slotted spoon to remove the rolls from the oil, draining them on a paper towel–lined plate before serving.

Kosher salt

2 medium Russet baking potatoes, peeled and cut into large chunks

3 tablespoons rendered duck fat

1 cup finely diced Spanish onion

Black pepper from a mill

1 large egg

1 tablespoon water

4 *feuille de brik* pastry sheets, 12 inches in diameter each

Canola or other neutral oil, for frying

SERVES 4

Sage Potato Chips

2 large Idaho or russet potatoes,
peeled and cut in half lengthwise

20 large fresh sage leaves

Canola or other neutral oil,
for greasing baking sheet
or for frying

Kosher salt

These look nothing like potato chips that come out of a bag. There's no egg wash or other binding agent used; the starch of the potato does the trick. For this reason, be sure not to rinse or soak the slices as you make them or the starch will be rinsed off. I like to fry these chips but have also provided instructions for baking them. This recipe can be multiplied to serve as many people as you like and may also be made with other herbs, such as flat-leaf parsley, instead of sage.

At Chanterelle we serve these with the bass dish on page 140. They are also delicious with lamb chops or hamburgers.

Use a mandoline to slice the potatoes lengthwise into 40 paper-thin slices, laying each slice flat on a clean, dry surface as it is cut. Top 20 of the slices with a sage leaf, centering it on the slice, then cover with another potato slice, gently pressing the layers together.

Line a large plate or platter with paper towels.

To bake the chips, preheat the oven to 350°F, and generously grease a large baking sheet with oil. Set the sandwiched potatoes on the baking sheet so they don't overlap. Place a sheet of parchment on top of the chips and place another baking sheet on top of the parchment to weight the chips down. Bake the chips for 10 minutes, then remove the top baking sheet and the parchment. Return the chips to the oven for about 2 minutes.

They should be browned, but not burned, and crisp. Transfer the chips to the paper towels and season to taste with salt.

To fry the chips, pour oil into a wide, deep, heavy-bottomed pot to a depth of 2 inches and heat over medium-high heat to a temperature of 325°F. Carefully lower the chips into the hot oil and fry until very lightly browned and crisp, 2 to 3 minutes. Use tongs or a slotted spoon to remove the chips from the hot oil and drain on the paper towels. Season to taste with salt.

(The chips can be stored in an airtight container at room temperature for up to 4 hours; reheat briefly on a baking sheet in a preheated 200°F oven, if desired.) Serve warm or at room temperature.

P

Se
m
ex

Br
ha

3 r
co
tra
bl
of
th
th

us
pc
su
3 i

Fettuccine with Crème Fraîche & Lemon Zest

Kosher salt

12 ounces homemade (page 297) or store-bought fresh fettuccine

1 cup crème fraîche

1 teaspoon freshly squeezed lemon juice

2 teaspoons finely grated lemon zest

Black pepper from a mill

2 tablespoons minced fresh chives

SERVES 4

Serve this creamy, lemony pasta with the guinea hen dish on page 186 or alongside fish dishes.

Bring a large pot of salted water to a boil. Add the pasta and cook until *al dente,* 2 to 3 minutes.

Meanwhile, put the crème fraîche, lemon juice, and zest in a wide, deep sauté pan, season with salt and pepper, and heat over medium heat until the crème fraîche is just melted.

When the pasta is done, drain and add it to the pan. Toss and garnish with the chives. Serve family style from a serving bowl or alongside fish or meats.

The Cheese of Chanterelle

In retrospect, the evolution of cheese at Chanterelle since we first opened our doors in 1979 has tracked the evolution of cheese appreciation, and availability, in the United States during the same time.

Offering a cheese course in the late 1970s, even in New York City, was something of a rarity, but David and I always knew we were going to do it: So many of our ideas and opinions about what makes a meal great were formed in France, where cheese courses are an expected interlude between the savory and sweet in fancy restaurants and a delightful option at the end of a meal everywhere else.

Back then, there were just a handful of food shops in Manhattan where you could find imported cheeses, and most represented only one country. It was a stroke of luck that Giorgio DeLuca and Joel Dean's food mecca, Dean & DeLuca, was down the block on Prince Street, just close enough to procure each evening's offering and always in perfect condition.

Over the years, we have nurtured our cheese selection, delighted by the increasing availability of international cheeses in the United States. But perhaps the most exciting development has been the rise of what was once an oxymoron: the American artisanal cheesemaker and a discerning, cheese-adoring public. Today, many of our cheeses come from right here at home, and some even rival their overseas counterparts in taste, texture, and popularity. There is also now a whole community of cheesemongers and *affineurs*.

As all of these exciting developments took place, it became obvious that we would need a dedicated person, so we created a *fromager* position, a member of our team who selects, purchases, and trains fellow staff members in the fine art of describing and serving our constantly changing offerings.

Our cheese program has also grown by leaps and bounds. Sommelier Roger Dagorn delights in selecting just the right wine or liqueur to bring out the best in each table's cheese choices, and, for years, the pastry team has baked special breads expressly for serving alongside them, as well. More recently, our *fromager* has been exploring the world of artisanal honeys (delicious drizzled over certain cheeses), and pastry chef Kate Zuckerman produces impeccable compotes from whatever is in season and strikes her fancy, everything from kumquats to quince, bringing a deeply personal, house-made flourish to our cheese board.

Come to think of it, our cheese program is a bit of a metaphor for the evolution of Chanterelle itself: tethered happily to tradition but always looking forward.

—KAREN WALTUCK

DESSERTS

¶ Dessert at Chanterelle is a dining experience all its own, a progression that begins with the plated sweets themselves, then moves on to coffee and *petits fours,* and often concludes with an after-dinner drink sipped late into the evening. As a final flourish, one of our waiters appears tableside during the waning moments to offer house-made fruit gelées from a silver tray. ¶ When we opened in 1979, I made the desserts myself, even though I wasn't a trained pastry chef and my own tastes ran to the exceedingly simple. (Nine times out of ten, I'd choose a bowl of ice cream to end just about any meal.) Eventually, one of my prep cooks with a knack for desserts began to help me and, when we moved to Tribeca, I appointed him the pastry chef. ¶ Since those days, we've had a few bona fide pastry chefs, two of whom are represented in this chapter: Michael Klug and our current pastry wizard, Kate Zuckerman. Our pastry chefs have always more or less had free rein, especially Kate, whose desserts sound perfect and taste even better, if that's possible. This chapter offers a sampling of some of our favorites, from a smattering of *petits fours* to the stollen we give friends and family every December to something sweet for any season of the year. ¶ Note: Because of a few pastry peculiarities, such as the frequent use of eggs (which cannot be divided) and larger-form desserts meant to be sliced into a variable number of servings, not all of these recipes yield four portions.

Pumpkin Mousse with Crunchy Gingersnaps & Maple Crème Fraîche

1 tablespoon powdered gelatin

¼ cup cold water

4 large egg yolks

6 tablespoons grade A maple syrup

1½ tablespoons light or dark rum

½ teaspoon ground ginger

½ teaspoon ground allspice

¼ teaspoon ground cinnamon

¼ teaspoon ground cloves

Pinch of freshly grated nutmeg

¼ teaspoon salt

Pinch of freshly ground white pepper

½ cup plus 2 tablespoons canned solid-pack pumpkin

¾ cup heavy cream

2 large egg whites

⅛ teaspoon cream of tartar

2 tablespoons granulated sugar

continued on page 265

Pumpkin and ginger, both quintessential fall ingredients, come together here in a dessert that would be perfect for Thanksgiving, or for any celebration of the season. The recipe uses canned pumpkin, to which many chefs turn for its uniform consistency. The dish is decorated with a maple syrup–crème fraîche mixture, a sweet, tart, distinctly autumnal finishing touch.

TO MAKE THE MOUSSE:
Put the gelatin in a small bowl. Add the cold water and stir to dissolve.

Pour 1 inch of water into a medium heavy-bottomed saucepan and set over medium heat. Whisk the egg yolks and maple syrup in a medium stainless steel bowl that will fit over the boiling water, functioning as a double boiler. Whisk in the rum, spices, salt, and white pepper and place the bowl over the double boiler. Whisk briskly until the mixture has thickened, tripled in volume, and holds the lines of the whisk for 10 seconds, 5 to 10 minutes. Remove the bowl from the heat. Add the moistened gelatin and whisk until it melts into the mousse base. Whisk in the pumpkin.

In a medium bowl with an electric mixer, whip the cream on medium speed until it holds soft peaks. Clean and dry the beater, then, in another medium bowl, whip the egg whites on medium-high speed until they are frothy and no longer liquid. Add the cream of tartar, whip for another minute, then begin adding the granulated sugar, 1 teaspoon at a time. After each addition, whip for 30 seconds. After you have added it all, whip until the whites are shiny, smooth, voluminous, and hold firm but not dry peaks.

Scrape the whipped cream over the pumpkin mixture and fold them together with a rubber spatula or bowl scraper. Make sure you place your spatula in the center of the bowl, scrape the bottom, and bring the bottom over the top. Rotate the bowl 45 degrees and repeat this motion. Continue folding the mixture together until all the cream is incorporated. Add the whipped egg whites and repeat the folding technique until fully incorporated. Divide the mousse evenly among 4 martini or wine glasses and refrigerate for at least 3 hours or overnight.

TO MAKE THE GINGERSNAPS:
Using a stand mixer fitted with the paddle attachment or a hand mixer, beat the butter on medium speed for 1 minute. Add the brown sugar and cream it with the butter until the mixture lightens in color significantly and increases in volume, 6 to 8 minutes. Add the whole egg and beat until incorporated.

Toss the flour, baking soda, spices, and salt in a small bowl with a whisk. Using a rubber spatula, fold this, in one or two turns, into the egg-butter mixture. Once the mixture is partially folded together, mix on low speed for 1 minute until all the ingredients are thoroughly incorporated. Add the molasses and mix on low speed until it is incorporated. Cover or wrap the dough and refrigerate for at least 3 hours or up to 1 week.

A half an hour before baking the cookies, preheat the oven to 350°F.

Grease a baking sheet with butter or nonstick cooking spray or line it with parchment. Place the turbinado sugar in a small bowl. Pinch off 1½-inch pieces of dough and roll into balls. Drop the balls into the sugar and roll them around until fully coated. Place the cookies on the prepared baking sheet 2 inches apart and press your thumb in the center of each cookie to flatten it a bit.

Bake half of these cookies to make a crumb topping; bake these for 20 minutes but take the others out after 13 to 15 minutes. The cookies being used as crumbs should spread,

rise, fall, crack a bit, and take on a dark golden brown color. Once these cookies have cooled, grind them in a food processor. Enjoy the other gingersnaps at your leisure.

Whisk the crème fraîche and maple syrup together in a small bowl until the mixture holds the lines of the whisk, about 1 minute.

To serve, remove the chilled mousse from the refrigerator. Top each glass with a heaping tablespoon of the maple crème fraîche. Sprinkle over the gingersnap crumbs and serve immediately.

continued from page 264

FOR THE GINGERSNAPS:

½ cup (1 stick) plus 1 tablespoon unsalted butter, softened at room temperature

½ cup plus 2 tablespoons firmly packed light brown sugar

1 large egg

1 cup plus 2 tablespoons all-purpose flour

1 teaspoon baking soda

1 teaspoon ground ginger

¾ teaspoon ground cloves

¾ teaspoon ground cinnamon

¼ teaspoon salt

2 tablespoons molasses

½ cup turbinado sugar or Sugar in the Raw®

FOR THE MAPLE CRÈME FRAÎCHE:

¾ cup crème fraîche

3 tablespoons grade A maple syrup

SERVES 4

Fig & Goat Cheese Tart with Huckleberry Ice Cream

This tart variation of cheesecake uses goat cheese for a funkier, more interesting flavor than the classic. Against that backdrop, the figs and huckleberries come into high relief. Huckleberries can be a bit difficult to find, but they are worth seeking out for their currant-like intensity, bringing the qualities of wine and cheese to this dessert.

TO MAKE THE HUCKLEBERRY ICE CREAM:

Put the huckleberries and ½ cup of the granulated sugar in a small heavy-bottomed saucepan and cook over low heat until the sugar dissolves some of the liquid in the fruit. Turn up the heat and simmer for 5 minutes. Remove from the heat and chill the berry compote over a large bowl of ice.

In a large heavy-bottomed saucepan, heat the cream, milk, and ¼ cup of the granulated sugar. Once it begins to steam, take it off the heat. In a large bowl, briskly whisk together the egg yolks, whole egg, and the remaining ¼ cup granulated sugar for 30 seconds. Slowly, using a ladle, whisk some of the hot cream mixture into the egg mixture to warm it. Gradually pour the warmed egg mixture into the hot cream mixture, whisking the cream constantly as you pour. Cook over medium heat, continuously stirring and scraping the bottom with a rubber spatula or wooden spoon. Remove it from the heat once it thickens enough to coat the back of a spoon. Chill the custard over a large bowl of ice. Combine the cooled custard with the berry compote, cover, and refrigerate for a minimum of 2 hours before churning. This ice cream base will keep for up to 2 days in the refrigerator.

Churn the custard in an ice-cream maker according to the manufacturer's instructions. The ice cream is finished once it has increased in volume and holds the line of the stirring mechanism; it should mound like softly whipped cream. At this point, you must freeze the ice cream for 4 hours to attain a scoopable consistency. It is best served the day it is churned but does keep for up to 1 week in the freezer.

TO MAKE THE SWEET TART CRUST:

Using a stand mixer fitted with the paddle attachment or an electric hand mixer, beat the butter on medium speed for 1 minute to soften. Cream together the butter, confectioners' sugar, and tangerine zest on medium-high speed until it becomes fluffy and light in color (almost white), about 4 minutes. Add the egg yolk and beat for 30 seconds. Whisk the flour and salt together in a dry bowl and add them, all at once, to the butter-egg mixture. Use a rubber spatula to fold in the flour, giving it a few turns, then turn on the mixer and mix on low speed until the mixture becomes homogenous, 1 to 2 minutes. Scrape down the side of the bowl with the spatula and mix for another 30 seconds.

Fold plastic wrap around the dough, then press it down in the plastic to form a 1-inch-thick disk. Refrigerate for at least 2 hours or overnight. It can also be frozen for up to 1 week.

Roll the chilled dough out on a lightly floured work surface until it is ⅛ inch thick. Line an 8-inch fluted or

continued

FOR THE HUCKLEBERRY ICE CREAM:

2 cups fresh or frozen huckleberries (you may substitute wild blueberries or even cultivated blueberries)

1 cup granulated sugar

2 cups heavy cream

⅓ cup whole milk

8 large egg yolks

1 large egg

FOR THE SWEET TART CRUST:

½ cup (1 stick) unsalted butter, softened at room temperature

⅔ cup confectioners' sugar

Finely grated zest of 1 tangerine or small orange

1 large egg yolk

1 cup plus 1 tablespoon all-purpose flour

¼ teaspoon salt

FOR THE GOAT CHEESE FILLING:

2 large egg yolks

1 large egg

½ cup granulated sugar

3 tablespoons water

10½ ounces fresh goat cheese, at room temperature

½ cup plus 2 tablespoons crème fraîche

¼ teaspoon salt

FOR THE FIG GLAZE:

½ cup medium-sweet Madeira

½ cup granulated sugar

17 medium Black Mission figs

Juice of 1 lime

MAKES ONE 8-INCH TART, ENOUGH TO SERVE 4 TO 6

straight-sided tart pan with the dough and freeze for 30 minutes before baking. Preheat the oven to 350°F.

Remove the shell from the freezer and line it with parchment, aluminum foil, or a coffee filter. Fill the liner with pie weights or dried beans and bake for 30 minutes. Remove from the oven and let sit for 5 minutes before

removing the liner and weights. Place the tart shell back in the oven to toast until it is golden brown all over, another 10 to 15 minutes.

To make the goat cheese filling, place the egg yolks and whole egg in a large bowl and briefly whisk together with an electric mixer. In a small saucepan, mix together the granulated sugar and water with your index finger until all the sugar is moist. Cook the mixture over medium-high heat until it reaches 248°F on a candy thermometer. (If you don't have a thermometer, you can use this test to determine whether the temperature is right: Dip a fork into the sugar syrup and let it drip onto your work counter; at 248°F, sugar droplets should cool into pliable balls that scrape cleanly off the counter.) Pour the hot sugar syrup into the egg mixture in a slow, continuous stream, beating all the while with the mixer. Whip until the eggs are pale, have tripled in volume, and cooled. Gently whisk in the goat cheese until the mixture is almost completely homogenous. Add the crème fraîche and salt and give the mixture a few hard turns with the whisk. Store in the refrigerator until you are ready to assemble the tart, up to overnight.

To make the fig glaze, bring the Madeira to a boil with the granulated sugar in a small saucepan over medium-high heat. Simmer while you slice and chop 5 of the figs. Add the figs to the syrup and continue to simmer for 10 to 15 minutes. Stir in the lime juice and cook for 1 minute longer. Strain the fig syrup through a fine-mesh strainer set over a bowl and refrigerate until you are ready to assemble the tart or for up to 1 week.

To assemble the tart, slice the remaining 12 figs as thinly as possible. Scrape and smooth the goat cheese filling into the prebaked tart shell. Layer the sliced figs in an overlapping circular pattern over the filling. Pour the glaze over the sliced figs and even it out with a spatula.

Serve the tart with the huckleberry ice cream on the side.

Rose Petal–Infused Parfait with Cantaloupe Sorbet & Summer Raspberries

Once in a while, a chef will be inspired by a product, conceiving a dish he or she might otherwise never have imagined. That was the case with this dessert, which Kate Zuckerman devised to take advantage of dried rose petals, offered to us by the same purveyor from whom we purchase Iranian saffron. Kate used the petals to create a rose syrup with a potent, flowery aroma. The rest of the composition followed from there, an elegant tribute to summer featuring cantaloupe and fresh berries.

4 cups peeled and seeded ripe, juicy cantaloupe cut into 1-inch chunks

⅔ cup superfine sugar

Juice of 1 lime

2 cups heavy cream

2 tablespoons culinary dried rose petals or ¼ cup fresh rose petals (make sure you know they haven't been sprayed with pesticides)

1 teaspoon finely grated orange zest

5 large egg yolks

⅓ cup plus ¼ cup granulated sugar

3 tablespoons water

Pinch of salt

2 cups fresh raspberries, cleaned

SERVES 6 TO 8

TO MAKE THE CANTALOUPE SORBET:

Puree the cantaloupe, in batches, in a blender or food processor fitted with a steel blade. Transfer to a medium bowl, add the superfine sugar, toss, and let macerate for 5 minutes. Stir in the lime juice, cover with plastic wrap, and refrigerate for at least 2 hours or up to overnight.

Churn the sorbet in an ice-cream maker according to the manufacturer's instructions. The sorbet is finished once it has slightly increased in volume and holds the line of the stirring mechanism, 15 to 20 minutes depending on the machine. Transfer to a freezer container and freeze for at least 4 hours to attain a scoopable consistency. It is best served the day it is churned but will keep for up to 1 week in the freezer.

TO MAKE THE ROSE PETAL PARFAIT:

First infuse the cream by pouring it into a medium heavy-bottomed saucepan and heating over medium heat to just under a boil. Stir in the rose petals and orange zest. Turn off the heat, cover, and let the cream steep for 20 minutes. Strain through a fine-mesh strainer set over a stainless steel bowl. Set the bowl on ice and chill the cream on the ice in the refrigerator for at least 1 hour, until the cream is cold enough to whip.

Put the egg yolks in a large bowl, add 2 tablespoons of the granulated sugar, and beat with an electric mixer fitted with the whisk attachment at medium speed while you heat the sugar syrup. In a small heavy-bottomed saucepan, mix together ⅓ cup of the granulated sugar and the water with your index finger until all the sugar is moist. Cook the mixture over medium-high heat until it reaches 248°F on a candy thermometer. (If you don't have a thermometer, you can use this test to determine whether the temperature is right: Dip a fork into the sugar syrup and let it drip onto your work counter; at 248°F, the sugar droplets should cool into pliable balls that scrape cleanly off the counter.) Pour the hot sugar syrup into the egg yolks in a slow, continuous stream, beating all the while with the mixer. Whip until the yolks become pale, have tripled in volume, and are just slightly warm. Add the salt.

Using a whisk or electric mixer (make sure to wash and dry the beaters first), whip the cold infused cream to soft peaks. Add the whipped cream to the whipped yolks. Stick a rubber spatula in the center of the mixture and fold the two together by scraping and scooping the mixture out from the bottom onto the top of the cream, *continued* moving from the bottom center to the rim of the bowl and over. Repeat this folding technique while rotating the bowl after every fold until the mixture is homogeneous.

Pour the parfait into 6 small bowls or 8 parfait glasses and chill in the freezer for at least 4 hours or up to overnight.

When ready to serve, toss the berries with the remaining 2 tablespoons granulated sugar in a bowl

and let sit for 10 to 15 minutes, but no longer or the raspberries will release too much juice.

Meanwhile, remove the frozen parfaits and the cantaloupe sorbet from the freezer, allowing them to soften for 5 minutes. Top each parfait with a scoop of the sorbet, then sprinkle with 2 heaping tablespoons of raspberries. Serve immediately.

Cherry Vanilla Brioche Pudding with Maple–Star Anise Ice Cream

FOR THE MAPLE–STAR
ANISE ICE CREAM:

1⅓ cups grade A maple syrup

10 whole star anise

2 cups heavy cream

1 cup whole milk

6 large egg yolks

1 large egg

¼ teaspoon salt

FOR THE CHERRY COMPOTE:

40 to 45 fresh sweet cherries

1 vanilla bean

½ cup sweet port

½ cup granulated sugar

FOR THE PUDDING:

Eight ½-inch-thick slices brioche bread (about 11 ounces)

2 tablespoons unsalted butter, melted

1½ cups heavy cream

1½ cups whole milk

1 vanilla bean

⅔ cup granulated sugar

¼ teaspoon salt

3 large egg yolks

2 large eggs

1 tablespoon unsalted butter, softened at room temperature

SERVES 6

I've always been attracted to the idea of elevating home food, and this dish from Kate Zuckerman goes about as far as you can in that direction, exceeding my wildest expectations about the possibilities for bread pudding. (Then again, I remember the time my father took me to a Jewish deli that served bread pudding made with *onion* rolls, so, for me, the bar on bread pudding is pretty low.) Kate makes her bread pudding a refined affair by using brioche and a very custardy crème anglaise sauce. Keep in mind that brioche is baked into loaves of varying size; you can also use challah or any buttery egg bread for this dish. I use eight slices of bread that are roughly ½ inch thick.

To make the maple–star anise ice cream, bring the maple syrup to a boil with the star anise in a large heavy-bottomed saucepan over medium-high heat and cook until a candy thermometer registers reads 240°F. (If you don't have a thermometer, you can use this test to determine whether the temperature is right: Dip a fork in the mixture and let it drip on your work counter; at 240°F, once cooled, the sugar droplets should be somewhat gummy and firm, not sticking to your finger when you touch them lightly.)

Gradually whisk in the cream. Once incorporated, add the milk and heat to just under a boil. Meanwhile in a medium bowl, briskly whisk together the egg yolks, whole egg, and the salt for 1 minute. Slowly, using a ladle, whisk some of the hot cream into the egg mixture to warm it. Gradually pour the warmed egg mixture into the hot cream mixture, whisking the cream constantly as you pour.

Cook over medium heat, continuously stirring and scraping the bottom with a rubber spatula or wooden spoon, until the custard thickens enough to coat the back of a spoon. Strain through a fine-mesh strainer to remove the star anise. Set in a large bowl of ice to cool it to room temperature, then refrigerate for at least 2 hours and up to 2 days before churning.

Churn the custard in an ice-cream maker according to the manufacturer's instructions. The ice cream is finished once it has increased in volume and holds the line of the stirring mechanism. It should mound like softly whipped cream. At this point, you must freeze the ice cream for 4 hours to attain a scoopable consistency. It is best served the day it is churned but will keep for up to 1 week in the freezer.

To make the cherry compote, using a cherry pitter, remove the cherries' pits. Run a paring knife down the center of one of the vanilla beans and scrape the seeds into a medium heavy-bottomed saucepan; add the split pod as well. Add the port and sugar, bring to a simmer, and let cook for 5 minutes. Add the pitted cherries, bring to a boil, then reduce the heat to a simmer and cook for 10 minutes, making sure to stir the mixture gently 2 or 3 times. Chill the compote over a bowl of ice until cool.

continued

Combine the cream and milk in a small heavy-bottomed saucepan. Slice open the vanilla bean and scrape all the tiny seeds into the pan. Add the scraped pod and set over medium-high heat. When the cream is almost boiling, remove from the heat and cover for 20 minutes to steep the mixture.

Meanwhile, in a medium bowl, whisk together the sugar, salt, egg yolks, and whole eggs. Slowly, using a ladle, whisk some of the hot liquid into the egg mixture to warm it. Gradually pour the warmed egg mixture into the hot cream mixture, whisking the cream constantly as you pour. Don't cook the custard; set it aside until the next step. Remove the vanilla pod. (Wash and dry it over the oven for another use.)

You can bake this pudding in one 6 x 9-inch baking dish or in 6 individual ramekins. With the softened butter, grease the dish(es) you are using. If baking it in a single dish, spread the toasted bread over the bottom. Pick out about one-third of the cherries from the compote and intersperse them among the pieces of bread. Pour the warm custard over everything and leave the dish on the counter for 10 to 15 minutes, letting the bread soak up the custard. Bake until any bread chunks sticking out from the top are crispy and brown, 30 to 40 minutes. The center should not jiggle separately from the outside of the custard. If you push a piece of bread down in the center, it should have a very slight spring to it.

If you are baking individual ramekins, place 3 pieces of toasted bread in the bottom of each ramekin. Use 3 bread cubes to line the sides. Set 3 cherries in the center of each ramekin and top the cherries with one final cube of toasted bread. Pour the warm custard over the top to fill the ramekins. Bake for 20 to 25 minutes.

Serve the bread pudding warm. If you make it early in the day, reheat it in a preheated 300°F oven for 10 minutes. If you have baked it in a large baking dish, simply serve a portion on a plate with the cherry compote and a scoop of maple–star anise ice cream. If you are serving ramekins, pour some compote over the bread pudding and serve the ice cream on a side plate. You can also remove the pudding from the ramekins and serve on a plate with the cherry compote and ice cream.

(The compote will keep in an airtight container in the refrigerator for up to 3 days.)

To make the bread pudding, preheat the oven to 350°F.

Trim off the hard brown crusts of the brioche and cut each slice into about 6 rectangles measuring 1¼ x 1½ inches. Lay these rectangular pieces of bread on a baking sheet and drizzle the melted butter over them. Bake until the rectangles are a golden brown. Set aside. Reduce the oven temperature to 275°F.

Bartlett Pears Served Two Ways

Kate has always had a talent for roasting fruits, finding that perfect balance between natural sweetness and the more intense, caramelized variety unleashed by roasting. At Chanterelle, she often serves dessert trios on compartmentalized rectangular plates, showing the various treatments of one ingredient that are possible, but two treatments seem like plenty in a home setting. One preparation here features the simple combination of roasted pear and cool, creamy ricotta cheese; the other offers the pear in a beignet (fritter) topped with truffle honey.

Wrap the ricotta in cheesecloth or a clean dish towel and place it in a strainer set over a bowl to remove excess liquid. Leave it overnight in the refrigerator until 1 hour before you are ready to serve the dessert, then remove to allow it to come to room temperature.

To roast and glaze the pear halves, preheat the oven to 400°F.

Peel 3 of the pears. Slice a disk about ¾ inch in diameter off the bottom of each one to remove the fibrous core that sits on the bottom of the pears. Stand the pears up on a cutting board and slice them in half, leaving the long stem on one half or split between both halves. Using a melon baller, scoop out the seeds and fibrous stems, leaving a round cavity in each pear half. Lay the halves down, cavity side up, in a roasting pan just large enough to accommodate them all in a single layer. Pour the white wine and Muscat over them, drizzle with the honey, and sprinkle with 2 tablespoons of the sugar. Roast the pears for 30 minutes, then remove from the oven and, with the tip of a metal spatula, gently flip the pears over, cavity side down, and roast for another 20 minutes. Remove from the oven again, flip the pears over, cavity side up, and drizzle some of the cooking liquids over the top.

Raise the oven temperature to 425°F. Sprinkle the pears with 1 tablespoon of the sugar and bake for two more 20-minute periods, basting them with the roasting syrup and sprinkling them with the remaining 1 tablespoon sugar after the first 20-minute period. The pears should be tender when a sharp paring knife is inserted, reduced in size, shiny, and have some areas of caramelization. If you think they need more time in the oven, ladle the cooking liquid over the pears and bake for another 10 to 15 minutes. Allow the pears to cool in the roasting pan. Reduce the oven temperature to 350°F.

To roast the pear slices, peel the pears and slice a disk about ¾ inch in diameter off the bottom of each one to remove the fibrous core that sits on the bottom of the pears. Remove about 1 inch off the top of the pears, at the stem end. Use an apple corer to remove the center core. With a sharp knife, slice each pear into 4 equal doughnut-shaped cross sections. Lay out the slices on a greased or parchment-lined baking sheet and dot them with the butter. Sprinkle with the sugar and bake for 30 minutes. The pears are done when they are soft to the touch; there

continued

1 pound whole-milk ricotta cheese

**FOR ROASTING
THE PEAR HALVES:**

3 just-ripe Bartlett pears

¼ cup dry white wine

¼ cup sweet Muscat

3 tablespoons honey

¼ cup granulated sugar

**FOR ROASTING
THE PEAR SLICES:**

3 just-ripe Bartlett pears

2 tablespoons unsalted butter, cut into small pieces

2 tablespoons granulated sugar

FOR THE BEIGNET BATTER:

2 large eggs

¼ teaspoon salt

2 tablespoons vegetable oil

6 tablespoons light beer

¾ cup all-purpose flour

Pinch of cream of tartar

2 teaspoons granulated sugar

FOR FRYING THE BEIGNETS:

1½ cups vegetable oil

¼ cup granulated sugar

½ teaspoon ground cardamom

TO SERVE:

One 4-ounce jar truffle honey or other varietal honey

SERVES 6

Crispy Walnut Wafers (page 280), Candied Ginger (page 279), Tangerine Fruit Gelées (page 281)

Petits Fours

Petits fours have been a part of the Chanterelle experience from the very beginning. These little pastries, meant to be picked up by hand and consumed in one bite, are the bookend to the *amuses* that begin each meal. They are never ordered, but instead are sent out from the kitchen, a final gift from us to our guests.

Here is a sample of *petits fours:* candied ginger, crispy walnut wafers, and fruit gelées. You can serve all three, or just one on its own.

Candied Ginger

Slice any knobs off the ginger. Peel it with a sharp peeler or scrape the skin away with a spoon. Cut it in half so you have two 3-inch-long pieces. With a sharp knife, slice each piece lengthwise into 5 slabs. Slice the slabs into ⅜-inch-thick batons or sticks.

Bring a small saucepan of water to a boil, then add the ginger sticks and, once the water comes back to a boil, drain the ginger. Repeat the blanching process one more time.

Bring 1½ cups of the sugar, 1 cup of the water, and 2 tablespoons of the corn syrup to a boil in a small heavy-bottomed saucepan. Add the ginger and simmer over low heat until tender, 20 to 30 minutes.

Drain the ginger and discard the syrup. Rinse the ginger in warm water. Repeat this candying process in a clean saucepan with 1½ cups of the sugar and the remaining 1 cup water and 2 tablespoons corn syrup. Simmer until the ginger is very tender and the syrup reduces and becomes strongly flavored, 20 to 30 minutes. Drain and discard the candying syrup. Don't rinse the ginger the second time.

Lay out the sticky ginger sticks on a rack to dry for 2 hours, then roll them in the remaining ½ cup sugar. These will keep in an airtight container at room temperature for up to 1 month.

One 5-ounce piece fresh ginger, 5 to 6 inches in length, preferably young ginger if you can find it

3½ cups granulated sugar

1 cup water

¼ cup light corn syrup

MAKES ABOUT 100 PIECES

FOR THE WALNUT WAFERS:

2½ cups walnuts

¼ cup cornstarch

1½ cups plus 1 tablespoon
all-purpose flour

¼ teaspoon salt

¾ cup (1½ sticks) unsalted butter,
softened at room temperature

1 cup granulated sugar

1 large egg yolk

2 tablespoons brandy

FOR THE TOFFEE:

2 tablespoons unsalted butter

2 tablespoons granulated sugar

2 tablespoons dark brown sugar

¼ cup light corn syrup

¼ cup heavy cream

1 tablespoon brandy

MAKES 50 TO 60 WAFERS

Crispy Walnut Wafers

Two options are presented here: baking the wafers in a mold to create a perfect shape as we do at Chanterelle and baking them freeform for a more rustic appearance.

To make the walnut shortbread dough, in a coffee grinder or food processor, grind 2 cups of the walnuts with the cornstarch, processing it to a flour, but not a paste—you don't want the nuts to release their oils. Toss the ground walnut mixture with the flour and salt. Set aside. Grind the remaining ½ cup walnuts separately and set aside for garnish until you bake the cookies.

In the bowl of a stand mixer fitted with the paddle attachment or with an electric hand mixer, cream the butter for 1 minute. Add the granulated sugar and cream it with the butter on medium-high speed until it becomes fluffy and light in color. Add the egg yolk and mix for 1 minute. Add the flour mixture and mix on low speed for 1 minute. Add the brandy and beat on medium speed for 30 seconds.

Remove the dough from the bowl and shape it into two long logs. Wrap a piece of parchment or waxed paper around each one and continue to roll it until it is a nearly perfect log, 1 to 1½ inches in diameter if you plan to bake the cookies freeform. If you want all the cookies to be petite and uniform in size, you need molds or rings to bake the cookies (mini-muffin tins could work). If you are using a mold, roll the dough into logs with a diameter that is just smaller than the molds. Chill the dough in the refrigerator until firm enough to cut slices that will hold their shape (how long will depend on how cold your refrigerator is). (You can also freeze the dough for up to 1 week.)

Meanwhile, to prepare the toffee, in a small heavy-bottomed saucepan, bring the butter, both sugars, and

corn syrup to a boil. While whisking, let it boil for 1 minute. Remove from the heat and let cool for 20 minutes. Then, with a whisk, slowly incorporate the cream, 2 tablespoons at a time, then whisk in the brandy and refrigerate the toffee until chilled.

Preheat the oven to 350°F.

If you are using molds for a uniform look, cut the logs of dough into ⅛- to 3⁄16-inch-thick slices and place them in your molds. (Make sure the molds are nonstick or sprayed with oil.) With a spoon or a small piping bag, spoon or squeeze about ½ teaspoon of chilled toffee sauce on top of each cookie. Sprinkle some of the ground walnuts you set aside over each cookie. Bake the cookies until the toffee spreads and takes on a deep golden brown color, 10 to 15 minutes. If you underbake these cookies, they will not be crispy.

If you are baking the cookies freeform on a baking sheet, cut the dough a little thicker, ¼ to 5⁄16 inch thick. Lay out the disks on an aluminum foil– or parchment-lined baking sheet. Hold each disk with 3 fingers on one hand while you make a slight indentation in the center of the cookie with the index finger of your other hand. Squeeze or spoon the toffee sauce over the indented area. Sprinkle the ground walnuts over the cookies and bake until the toffee spreads and browns over the walnut shortbread, 10 to 15 minutes. Let cool before sealing in an airtight container, where they will keep for 2 to 3 days.

Tangerine Fruit Gelées

Here's a recipe for tangerine fruit gelées, which are known as *pate de fruit* ("fruit dough") in France. They can be made with almost any fruit, although the texture will vary depending on the natural pectin content and acidity level of individual fruits. Following the recipe are alternatives that can be made with the amount of pectin and sugar in this recipe.

You will need a 9 x 13-inch pan, lined with parchment paper to pour and set the jelly in. Using a rasp or grater, remove the zest from 5 of the tangerines. Juice all but 1 tangerine, catching the seeds in your hand, and juice the lemons as well, also catching the seeds. Slice the remaining tangerine into 8 wedges and use a paring knife to remove the seeds and the center white pith. In a blender, puree the juices with the tangerine wedges and zest. Do not strain the mixture.

Pour the juice mixture into a heavy-bottomed, stainless-steel pot, add 3½ cups of the sugar, and bring to a boil over high heat. Stir the juice mixture with a whisk once or twice as the sugar dissolves. While the mixture is coming to a boil, put ½ cup of the sugar and the pectin in a lidded container and shake it. Once the juice-sugar mixture has come to a boil, begin rapidly whisking it. With one hand, gently shake the sugar-pectin mixture into the pot while rapidly whisking with the other hand. Do not allow the pectin to clump in the pot. Cook this mixture over high heat, whisking constantly, until it has thickened significantly, about 10 minutes. (To determine if the mixture has gelled properly, drizzle a drop or two onto a dry counter. Allow it to cool for a minute and touch the drop with the tip of your finger. If the drop holds its shape and does not stick to your finger, it is done. If it seems like syrup and leaves a film on your fingertip, continue to cook it.) Once the jelly is done, pour the mixture into the prepared pan and allow it to cool at room temperature for least 4 hours or overnight.

Once the jelly has set, run a paring knife along the edge of the candy, where it meets the sides of the pan. Flip the pan over and unmold the jelly onto a cutting board. Peel off the parchment. If the jelly seems a bit moist or sticky, let it to sit out at room temperature, uncovered, for a day. Cut the jellies into squares or diamonds using a knife, or use a small candy cutter to punch out shapes. Put the remaining ¾ cup of sugar on a plate and roll the cut jellies in the sugar to coat them.

These candies keep for 2 weeks if they are wrapped or stored in a tin. If they are left uncovered they will dry out.

---

10 large tangerines

2 lemons

4¾ cups granulated sugar

3 tablespoons pectin

MAKES ABOUT 4 DOZEN CANDIES

NOTE:

You can vary the fruit to make other flavors by replacing the tangerines and lemons with the following alternatives. Puree fresh fruit for the purees; any seeds (such as raspberry) are optional—strain them out for a smoother texture.

Raspberry-lime: 3 cups raspberry puree and 1 cup freshly squeezed lime juice

Blackberry: 4 cups blackberry puree

Lychee: 3½ cups lychee juice (unsweetened) and ½ cup freshly squeezed lime juice

Red currant: 4 cups red currant puree

Apricot & Almond Crisps
with Apricot Pit Ice Cream

FOR THE APRICOT PIT
ICE CREAM:

10 small ripe apricots

½ lemon

1 cup heavy cream

1 cup whole milk

½ cup granulated sugar

4 large egg yolks

1 large egg

Pinch of kosher salt

2 tablespoons powdered skim milk

FOR THE SWEET TART CRUST:

½ cup (1 stick) unsalted butter,
softened at room temperature

⅔ cup confectioners' sugar

Finely grated zest of 1 tangerine
or small orange

1 large egg yolk

1 cup plus 1 tablespoon
all-purpose flour

¼ teaspoon salt

continued on page 283

I love the flavor of apricots, and this dessert of Kate's cleverly presents it not only in a crisp, but also in an ice cream that's infused by smashed apricot pits, which have a taste not unlike that of bitter almonds, giving the ice cream a marzipan-like flavor that's unique and compelling. I'll guess that nobody at your table will be quite able to place where it comes from, making this something of a conversation piece.

Note that you will need 6 individual stainless steel tart rings or entremets rings 2¼ to 3 inches in diameter and at least 1 inch high.

To make the apricot pit ice cream, slice the apricots in half and remove the pits. Squeeze the lemon juice over the halves and set them in the refrigerator. Place the pits in a small sealed sandwich bag.

On a hard, nonscratchable surface, using a hammer, meat tenderizer, or mallet, smash the apricot pits so they crack open. If the almond-like seeds inside break apart, that's okay. Make sure you have opened all the pits and exposed all the seeds. In a medium heavy-bottomed saucepan, combine the cream, milk, ¼ cup of the granulated sugar, and smashed apricot pits and allow the mixture to simmer over low heat for 5 minutes. Remove from the heat and set aside for 10 minutes.

Meanwhile, in a large bowl, briskly whisk together the egg yolks, whole egg, salt, powdered skim milk, and granulated sugar for 1 minute. Slowly, using a ladle, whisk some of the hot cream mixture into the egg mixture to warm it. Gradually pour the warmed egg mixture into the hot cream mixture, whisking the cream constantly as you pour.

Set the pan over medium heat and cook, continuously stirring and scraping the bottom with a rubber spatula or wooden spoon, until it thickens enough to coat the back of a spoon. Strain the custard through a fine-mesh strainer to remove the apricot pits and seeds.

Set the bowl with the ice-cream base over a larger bowl filled with ice until it cools to room temperature, then refrigerate for at least 2 hours and up to 2 days before churning it in an ice-cream machine according to the manufacturer's instructions. The ice cream is finished once it has increased in volume and holds the line of the stirring mechanism. It should mound like softly whipped cream. At this point, you must freeze the ice cream for 4 hours to attain a scoopable consistency. It is best served the day it is churned but will keep for up to 1 week in the freezer.

To make the sweet tart crust, using a stand mixer fitted with the paddle attachment or an electric hand mixer, beat the butter on medium speed for 1 minute to soften. Cream the butter with the confectioners' sugar and zest on medium-high speed until it becomes fluffy and light in color (almost white), about 4 minutes. Add the egg yolk and beat for 30 seconds.

Whisk the flour and salt together in a small bowl, then add it all at once to the butter-egg mixture. Use a rubber spatula to fold in the flour with a few turns before turning the mixer on at a slow speed. Mix the dough until it becomes homogenous, 1 to 2 minutes. Scrape down the sides of the bowl and mix for another 30 seconds. Shape the dough into a ball. Fold plastic wrap around it, then press it down in the plastic to form a 1-inch-thick disc. Let the dough cool in the refrigerator for at least 2 hours or up to 1 week.

Roll the dough out on a lightly floured work surface until it is ⅛ inch thick. Dust off any excess flour and use a cookie cutter slightly larger than the ring molds you are using to cut the dough into 6 circles. Lay out the circles of dough on a baking sheet and refrigerate for 10 to 15 minutes before baking.

Preheat the oven to 350°F. Grease the ring molds with butter or nonstick cooking spray.

Bake the circles of dough until they just begin to color, 10 to 14 minutes. Remove the sheet from the oven.

Take the greased ring molds and press them into the hot circles of parbaked dough, pushing down so that the dough forms a perfect circle lining the inside of the ring molds. Set these dough-filled rings on a baking sheet and set aside while you prepare the filling.

To make the almond streusel, in a food processor, grind the blanched almonds with 2 tablespoons of the flour until the almonds are evenly ground but not greasy. In the bowl of a stand mixer with the paddle attachment or in a stainless steel bowl with two knives, toss the almonds with the remaining 6 tablespoons flour, the brown sugar, granulated sugar, and salt. Cut the cold butter into ¼-inch cubes and add to the dry ingredients. Toss and mix the streusel until the butter chunks are coated and no larger than peas. Allow the streusel to sit out on the counter for 1 hour to dry out before baking.

To make the frangipane filling, in a stainless steel bowl, using a wooden spoon, beat together the granulated sugar, egg yolk, and almond paste until smooth. Add the egg white and smooth out the mixture with a whisk. Slowly, mix the flour, almond flour, and ⅛ teaspoon salt with a wooden spoon until well combined.

In a small heavy-bottomed sauté pan, melt the softened butter over medium-high heat until the foam becomes freckled and the butter smells like sweet roasted nuts, about 5 minutes. Immediately remove the butter from the heat and slowly drizzle it into the almond paste mixture, whisking constantly. Make sure that the butter is being absorbed into the batter. (If you add the fat too quickly, the frangipane will separate.) The frangipane can be refrigerated in an airtight container for up to 4 days; bring it to room temperature before using.

To assemble and bake the crisps, preheat the oven to 350°F.

Slice each apricot half into 4 pieces and mix them with the frangipane. Fill each of the dough-filled rings with the apricot filling, dividing it evenly among the molds. Sprinkle a generous amount of streusel over the filling, making sure you use enough streusel so that you cannot see the filling beneath.

Bake the crisps until the streusel browns, 30 to 40 minutes. Let cool in the rings for 30 minutes before trying to remove the rings. Run a paring knife along the inside of the rings, hugging the metal as much as possible.

To serve, put a crisp on each of 6 dessert plates. Top with some apricot pit ice cream and a dollop of crème fraîche and serve immediately.

continued from page 282

FOR THE ALMOND STREUSEL:

¾ cup (1½ sticks) unsalted butter, softened at room temperature

¼ cup blanched almonds

½ cup all-purpose flour

2 tablespoons firmly packed light brown sugar

2 tablespoons granulated sugar

¼ teaspoon salt

¼ cup (½ stick) cold unsalted butter

FOR THE FRANGIPANE:

6 tablespoons granulated sugar

1 large egg yolk

1 tablespoon almond paste

1 large egg white

3 tablespoons all-purpose flour

⅔ cup almond flour

⅛ teaspoon salt

¼ cup (½ stick) unsalted butter, softened at room temperature

TO SERVE:

¼ cup plus 2 tablespoons crème fraîche

SERVES 6

Chocolate Beggar's Purses
on Pineapple Slices with Coconut Sorbet

1 cup unsweetened shredded coconut

Two 13.5-ounce cans unsweetened coconut milk

Juice of 2 limes

One 15-ounce can crème de coconut, such as Coco Lopez®

6 ounces dark chocolate, coarsely chopped

3 large eggs

⅓ cup granulated sugar

½ cup (1 stick) unsalted butter

1 vanilla bean

20 sheets frozen Chinese spring roll wrappers

1¼ cups pineapple juice

Canola or other neutral oil, for frying

1 large golden pineapple (about 1½ pounds), peeled, cored, and cut crosswise into thin slices

SERVES 6

Before Michael Klug, and then Kate, joined the Chanterelle family, we rarely presented duos or trios for desserts, but Michael brought a level of sophistication to our menu with dishes like this one. The combination of different textures and temperatures—especially this warm, fried beggar's purse (crispy on the outside, molten and chocolatey on the inside) alongside cool, creamy coconut sorbet—is very pleasing. If you don't have an ice-cream maker, you can purchase a high-quality store-bought coconut sorbet.

To make the coconut sorbet, preheat the oven to 300°F.

Put the coconut on a baking sheet and toast until golden brown, about 5 minutes, shaking the pan occasionally to ensure even toasting. Remove from the oven and let the coconut cool. Set aside 2 tablespoons for garnish.

In a large bowl, combine the coconut milk, lime juice, and crème de coconut. Refrigerate for 1 hour, then churn in an ice-cream maker according to the manufacturer's instructions. The sorbet is finished once it has slightly increased in volume and holds the line of the stirring mechanism, 15 to 20 minutes depending on the machine. Transfer to a container and freeze for at least 4 hours to attain a scoopable consistency. It is best served the day it is churned but will keep for up to 1 week in the freezer.

To make the beggar's purses, melt the chocolate and butter together in the top of a double boiler set over simmering water.

Put the eggs and sugar in a medium bowl. Scrape out the seeds from the vanilla bean and whisk them into the mixture. Cut the scraped-out bean thinly lengthwise into 12 slices and wrap them tightly in plastic (you'll use them later to tie the beggar's purses). When the sugar is dissolved, pour in the melted chocolate mixture and incorporate. Cover the bowl with plastic wrap and refrigerate for at least 2 hours, until cool and set enough to pipe in a pastry bag. It will keep in the refrigerator for 1 week.

Defrost the frozen spring roll wrappers and set them under a damp paper towel to keep them from drying out, removing just a few at a time as you work. Trim 12 of the wrappers to make twelve 4-inch squares. Cut the remaining 8 wrappers into twenty-four 2- x 6-inch strips (3 strips per wrapper).

To make the first beggar's purse, lay out 2 strips in an "X" formation. Place a pastry sheet square in the center of the X. Spoon or pipe about 2 tablespoons of the stiff chocolate mixture into the center of each square. Fold the corners together and gather the strips into the center. Tie with a strip of vanilla bean and snip off the extra vanilla bean with scissors, so that the purse is tied with only a small knot. Cover a plate with a paper towel and place the purse on top. This will absorb additional moisture. Repeat for a total of 12 purses.

Make the sauce by bringing the pineapple juice to a boil over medium-high heat in a small, heavy-bottomed, nonreactive saucepan. Cook until reduced by about half, about 5 minutes. Remove from the heat and let cool.

Pour canola oil into a wide, deep, heavy-bottomed saucepan to a depth of 4 inches. Heat to a temperature of 380°F over medium-high heat.

Lay out a thin circle of pineapple slices on each of 6 dessert plates and spoon some sauce over the slices.

Deep-fry the beggar's purses, a few at a time, until golden brown, turning them with a kitchen spoon or tongs to ensure even cooking. Drain on paper towels and dust with the confectioners' sugar. Place 2 purses on each of the dessert plates, beside the pineapple and sauce, and scoop some coconut sorbet alongside. Garnish with the reserved toasted coconut and serve immediately.

Holiday Stollen

½ cup whole milk

2 tablespoons plus 1 teaspoon fresh bread yeast, or half as much envelope yeast

4½ cups all-purpose flour

2 cups raisins or dried currants

½ cup diced (¼-inch) candied orange peel (about 15 pieces)

½ cup diced (¼-inch) candied lemon peel (about 15 pieces)

½ cup finely chopped almonds

¼ cup light or dark rum

⅓ cup granulated sugar

1 large egg

¾ teaspoon salt

2 teaspoons ground cardamom

Pinch of freshly grated nutmeg

Finely grated zest of 1 medium lemon

3⅓ cups unsalted butter, softened at room temperature

2 cups vanilla sugar (made by grinding a dried vanilla bean with the sugar, then sifting it)

MAKES FOUR 8-INCH LOAVES

We once received a gift of holiday stollen from Gray Kunz when he was the chef of Lespinasse restaurant in New York City and found it to be an utterly charming gesture. Years later, when Michael Klug became our pastry chef, we were delighted to learn that he had been the pastry chef at Lespinasse and was the man who had baked the stollen we loved so much, from his grandmother's personal recipe, no less. We started making them as a holiday gift for friends and family of Chanterelle and continue to do so to this day. We think it's very much in the spirit of the season to have a house tradition like this and love handing out this little gift every year. If you'd like to do the same, start early, as stollen improve with time—an ideal time to bake them for Christmas is right after Thanksgiving.

Each stollen makes 10 to 12 slices, which are best enjoyed with a little butter spread on them and a cup of hot coffee alongside.

Heat the milk over low heat in a small heavy-bottomed saucepan until tepid. Remove the pan from the heat. Put the yeast in a large heatproof bowl and pour the milk over it. Whisk in ½ cup of the flour and let it set in a warm place until it bubbles. This is the starter.

Pour about an inch of water into the bottom of a double boiler and bring to a simmer. Put the raisins, orange peel, lemon peel, and almonds in the top of the double boiler and pour in the rum. Set the top of the double boiler over the simmering water and let marinate over medium heat while you prepare the dough.

Meanwhile, mix the starter with the granulated sugar, the remaining 4 cups flour, and the egg. Add 1⅓ cups of the butter and mix well. (If you have a stand mixer, use the dough hook for this.) Stir in the salt, cardamom, nutmeg, and lemon zest. Add the marinated fruit and incorporate, but don't mix for too long (if overmixed, the raisins will darken the stollen). Cover the bowl with a clean, damp towel or plastic wrap to keep it from drying out. Let proof in a warm place until doubled in size, about 1 hour.

Divide the dough into 4 pieces. On a lightly floured work surface, knead each one and roll it out to an oval shape ¾ inch thick. To shape the stollen, fold each oval lengthwise, letting the top portion be smaller than the bottom portion. Set them on a baking sheet (don't let them touch each other), cover with plastic wrap, and let proof until double in size, about 1 hour.

Preheat the oven to 300°F.

Bake the stollen until golden brown, about 30 minutes.

While the stollen are baking, put the remaining 2 cups (1 pound) butter in a saucepan and cook, swirling occasionally, over medium heat, until the fats separate and the butter begins to turn brown. Remove from the heat.

When the stollen are done, remove from the oven. Use a metal spatula to carefully transfer them to a wire rack and let rest for 10 minutes.

Briefly reheat the browned butter and use a pastry brush to brush it liberally over the stollen. Let rest for another 20 minutes.

Roll the loaves in the vanilla sugar and, once cooled completely, wrap with plastic wrap. Store the stollen in cool, dry place for up to 2 months. The flavor will develop and deepen over time, so making them several weeks in advance is recommended.

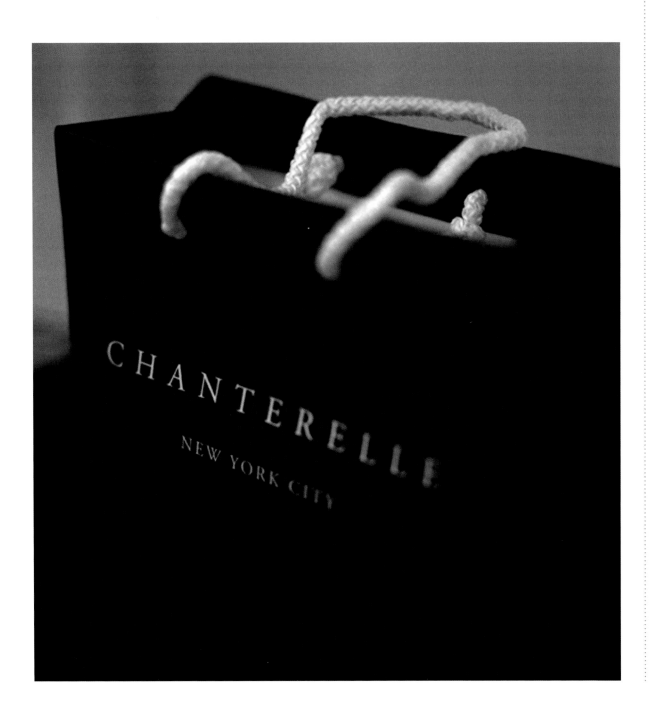

BASIC RECIPES

Most of the recipes that follow are for homemade stocks, and I urge you to use them whenever possible. With all of the high-quality products available at gourmet stores and via the Internet, it might seem quaint or old-fashioned to make your own stocks, but there's simply no substitute for the depth of flavor in a true, homemade stock, or for the luscious body imparted by the gelatin in the bones. Those qualities, especially when deployed in the service of a sauce, are among the most important cornerstones of classic French cooking, which means they're integral to much of what we do at Chanterelle. My experience is that these characteristics are lacking in even the best mass-produced stocks, no doubt because of the volume in which they're made. If it isn't already common practice in your kitchen, try making your own stocks. It's easy, and many of the recipes are economical, calling for little more than bones and a handful of vegetables and herbs. I also find that stock-making fills your home with a pleasing aroma, and that there's nothing like having an assortment of stocks in your freezer to entice you to cook.

Mushroom Stock

10 cups water or homemade Chicken Stock (page 292) or high-quality low-sodium chicken stock, or a mixture of the two

1 medium onion, unpeeled, cut into large chunks

3 medium carrots, unpeeled, cut into large chunks

2 garlic heads, in their skins, cut in half horizontally

2 cups mixed dried mushrooms, well ground in a food processor

1 to 2 cups mushroom trimmings, or 1 cup white mushrooms, cleaned and trimmed

MAKES ABOUT 4 CUPS

A combination of fresh and dried mushrooms gives this stock its complex flavor. If using dried, I suggest purchasing a mixed bag of mushrooms if you can because they are relatively inexpensive; you can also use a single variety, but don't use black trumpets or Chinese black mushrooms (dried shiitakes) exclusively because they will make the stock too dark and lend it a very distinct flavor. If using fresh mushrooms, the best time to make this stock is after cooking a dish that leaves you with mushroom trimmings (i.e., stems), because it's a way to use the entire vegetable.

Put the water, onion, carrots, garlic, ground mushrooms, and mushroom trimmings in a heavy-bottomed stockpot over high heat. Bring to a boil, then lower the heat so the liquid is simmering and cook for 1½ hours.

Strain the broth through a cheesecloth-lined strainer set over a large bowl. If not using right away, cool the stock. To do this, fill a very large bowl with ice, then set the bowl of stock in it, encouraging the hot liquid to cool quickly. The stock can be refrigerated in an airtight container for up to 3 days or frozen for up to 2 months.

Fish Stock

5 pounds bones from any white-fleshed, non-fatty, non-oily fish, such as halibut, sea bass, sole, and/or turbot

2 medium onions, peeled and cut into 1-inch chunks

3 medium carrots, peeled and cut into 1-inch chunks

2 garlic heads, in their skins, cut in half horizontally

32 cups (2 gallons) cold water

MAKES ABOUT 6 QUARTS

This is a good, all-purpose stock for fish recipes. Be sure to rinse the bones very well as indicated to ensure a clean-tasting finished product. The best way to obtain five pounds of bones is to call your fishmonger and ask him or her to set them aside for you to collect at the end of the day.

Put the bones in a pot and rinse very well under cold running water, letting the water run over them continuously and changing it 3 or 4 times until the water appears clear in the pot, with no blood or cloudy discoloration. Drain the bones and pat dry with paper towels.

Put the bones, onions, carrots, garlic, and water in a large heavy-bottomed stockpot over medium heat. Bring to a boil and skim the surface with a spoon to remove any scum that rises to the top. Reduce the heat so the liquid is simmering and cook for 45 minutes.

Strain the stock through a fine-mesh strainer set over a large bowl. If not using right away, cool the stock. To do this, fill a very large bowl with ice, then set the bowl of stock in it, encouraging the hot liquid to cool quickly. The stock can be refrigerated in an airtight container for up to 3 days or frozen for up to 2 months.

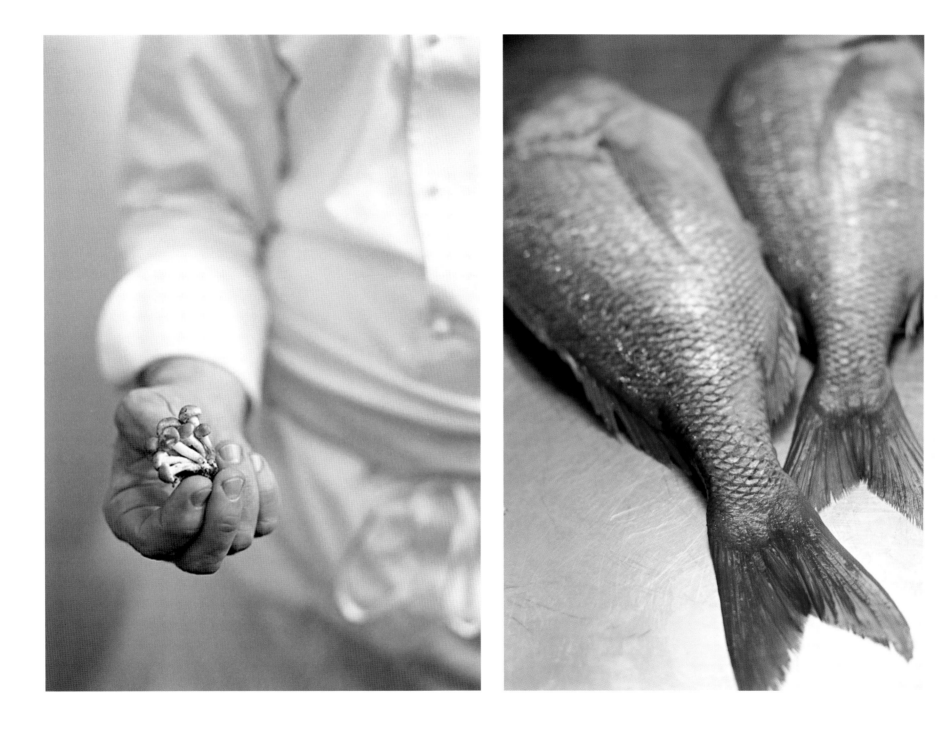

Lobster Stock

4 lobster bodies, each cut into
6 to 8 pieces

1 large carrot, unpeeled,
cut into 1-inch chunks

1 large Spanish onion, unpeeled,
cut into 1-inch chunks

1 garlic head, in its skin,
cut in half horizontally

1 tablespoon tomato paste

MAKES ABOUT 3 QUARTS

For sauces and soups featuring lobster, there's no substitute for the intense flavor of a true lobster stock. You can purchase lobster bodies frozen at most fish stores.

Put the lobster pieces, carrot, onion, garlic, and tomato paste in a large heavy-bottomed stockpot. Add enough cold water just to cover. Bring to a boil, then reduce the heat so the liquid is gently simmering and cook for 2 hours.

Strain the broth through a cheesecloth-lined strainer set over a large bowl. If not using right away, cool the stock. To do this, fill a very large bowl with ice, then set the bowl of stock in it, encouraging the hot liquid to cool quickly. The stock can be refrigerated in an airtight container for up to 3 days or frozen for up to 2 months.

Chicken Stock

5 pounds raw chicken carcasses, necks, backs, and trim (I usually include chicken wings, which add a lot of flavor and gelatin)

2 large carrots, unpeeled,
cut into 1-inch chunks

1 medium onion, unpeeled,
cut into 1-inch chunks

1 garlic head, in its skin,
cut in half horizontally

32 cups (2 gallons) cold water

MAKES ABOUT 6 QUARTS

This is probably the most called-upon stock in any restaurant kitchen. My version is fairly streamlined, with no peppercorns, herbs, or celery to distract from the essence of the chicken.

Put the chicken, carrots, onion, garlic, and water in a large heavy-bottomed stockpot over medium heat. Bring to a boil and skim the surface with a spoon to remove any scum that rises to the top. Reduce the heat so the liquid is simmering and cook, skimming the surface periodically to remove any scum, until the stock tastes unmistakably of chicken, about 4 hours. (If the water drops below the top of the solids during that time, add a few more cups.)

Use tongs or a slotted spoon to discard as many of the solids (especially the bones) as possible from the pot.

Carefully strain the stock through a cheesecloth-lined strainer set over a stainless steel bowl. If not using right away, cool the stock. To do this, fill a very large bowl with ice, then set the bowl of stock in it, encouraging the hot liquid to cool quickly. Skim off the fat that rises to the surface. The stock can be refrigerated in an airtight container for up to 3 days or frozen for up to 2 months.

Thickened Chicken Stock

4 cups (1 quart) Chicken Stock
(page 292)

2 tablespoons unsalted butter,
softened at room temperature

2 tablespoons all-purpose flour

MAKES ABOUT 4 CUPS

At Chanterelle, we use this stock, which we call "Thick Chick," to speed the production of certain pan sauces, eliminating the need to reduce them and giving them extra body and stability from the get-go.

Bring the stock to a boil in a medium heavy-bottomed saucepan.

In a small bowl, knead the butter and flour together to form a paste. Reduce the heat under the stock so the stock is simmering and whisk the butter mixture into the boiling stock. Cook for 10 minutes.

Strain the stock through a fine-mesh strainer set over a large bowl. If not using right away, cool the stock. To do this, fill a very large bowl with ice, then set the bowl of stock in it, encouraging the hot liquid to cool quickly. The stock can be refrigerated in an airtight container for up to 1 day, but should not be frozen.

Red-Cooking Broth

16 cups (1 gallon) Chicken Stock
(page 292), high-quality low-sodium
store-bought chicken stock, or water,
or a combination of stock and water

3 cups soy sauce, preferably
a dark soy such as Kimlan Aged Soy,
but Kikkoman® is fine as well

¼ cup dry sherry

1 pound Chinese rock sugar (light
brown sugar may be substituted)

2 bunches scallions (white and
green parts), ends trimmed and
cut into 3-inch lengths

2 cups whole star anise
(about 8 ounces)

12 dried shiitake mushrooms
(Chinese black mushrooms)

6 large pieces dried orange
or tangerine peel

One 4-inch piece fresh ginger,
unpeeled, rinsed and cut into
¼-inch-thick slices

Two 3-inch-long cinnamon sticks

MAKES ABOUT 4 QUARTS

This Chanterelle staple imparts a distinctly Chinese flavor to braised duck legs, oxtail, and other long-simmered dishes. One ingredient may be unfamiliar: Chinese rock sugar, which is similar to rock candy. It can be mail ordered or purchased in Asian markets, or you may substitute light brown sugar.

Put all of the ingredients in a large heavy-bottomed stock-pot and bring to a boil. Reduce the heat so the liquid is simmering and cook for 45 minutes.

If not using right away, cool the broth. To do this, fill a very large bowl with ice, then set the bowl of stock in it,

encouraging the hot liquid to cool quickly. The broth can be refrigerated in an airtight container for up to 3 days or frozen for up to 2 months.

Hock Stock

3 smoked ham hocks
(about 8 ounces each)

2 medium carrots, unpeeled,
cut into 1-inch chunks

1 large Spanish onion, unpeeled,
cut into 1-inch chunks

2 garlic heads, in their skins,
cut in half horizontally

16 cups (1 gallon) Chicken Stock
(page 292)

16 cups (1 gallon) cold water

MAKES 4 TO 5 QUARTS

Call on this stock to add a smoky note to recipes. For example, it would be a fine choice to bring the ham flavor front and center in split-pea soup.

Put the hocks, carrots, onion, and garlic in a large heavy-bottomed stockpot. Pour in the stock and water and bring to a boil. Reduce the heat so the liquid is simmering and cook, skimming the surface occasionally with a spoon to remove any scum that rises to the top, until the stock tastes nicely of ham and smoke, 3 to 4 hours.

Strain the stock through a fine-mesh strainer set over a large bowl. If not using right away, cool the stock. To do this, fill a very large bowl with ice, then set the bowl of stock in it, encouraging the hot liquid to cool quickly. The stock can be refrigerated in an airtight container for up to 3 days or frozen for up to 2 months.

Veal Stock

5 pounds veal bones (preferably with some meat left on them, and preferably a variety of types of bone, including some leg bones), all cut into 2- to 3-inch pieces

1 calf's foot (about 2½ pounds), cut into 2-inch chunks (have the butcher do this for you)

1 beef shin (about 2½ pounds), cut crosswise into 1-inch-thick pieces (have the butcher do this for you)

¼ cup canola or other neutral oil

2 medium carrots, unpeeled,
cut into 1-inch chunks

1 large Spanish onion, unpeeled,
cut into 1-inch chunks

1 garlic head, in its skin,
cut in half horizontally

32 cups (2 gallons) cold water

MAKES ABOUT 6 QUARTS

Most butchers will be happy to sell you bones for making this stock. Ask the butcher to cut them into small pieces; it really needs to be done by a professional for both safety and practical reasons. Preheat the oven to 400°F.

Put the veal bones, calf's foot, and beef shin in a large roasting pan and drizzle with the oil. Roast in the oven, stirring occasionally to ensure even browning, for 30 minutes. Add the carrots, onion, and garlic and continue to roast, stirring, until the bones and meat are well browned and the vegetables are also taking on color but are not as browned, about another hour.

Transfer the bones and vegetables to a large heavy-bottomed stockpot. Set the roasting pan over two burners on the stovetop. Turn the heat under both to medium. Pour in 4 cups of the water and cook, stirring to scrape up any crusty browned bits on the bottom of the pan. Pour the liquid into the stockpot and add the remaining 28 cups cold water to cover the bones and vegetables well. Bring to a boil, then reduce the heat so the liquid is simmering and cook, skimming the surface occasionally with a spoon to remove any scum that rises to the top, for at least 6 hours and up to 10 hours. (If the water drops below the top of the solids during that time, add a few more cups.)

Use tongs or a slotted spoon to discard as many solids (especially the bones) as possible from the pot. Very carefully strain the stock through a cheesecloth-lined strainer set over a stainless steel bowl. If not using immediately, cool the stock. To do this, fill a very large bowl with ice, then set the bowl of stock in it, encouraging the hot liquid to cool quickly. Skim off the fat that rises to the surface. The stock can be refrigerated in an airtight container for up to 3 days or frozen for up to 2 months.

Venison Stock

You will need to plan ahead to make this stock, which I use for making sauces to accompany venison, by procuring the bones from a butcher or saving them from your own cooking. You can also use venison osso buco (available from D'Artagnan, see Sources on page 298).

Preheat the oven to 400°F.

Put the bones in a large roasting pan and drizzle with the oil. Roast in the oven, stirring a few times to ensure even browning, for 25 minutes. Add the onions, carrots, and garlic and continue to roast, stirring, until the bones and meats are well browned and the vegetables are also taking on color but are not as browned, another 45 minutes to 1 hour.

Transfer the bones and vegetables to a large heavy-bottomed stockpot. Discard the fat from the roasting pan and set the pan over two burners on stovetop. Turn the heat under both to medium. Pour in 4 cups of the water and cook, stirring to scrape up the crusty browned bits from the bottom of the pan. Pour the liquid from the pan into the stockpot and add the remaining 28 cups cold water to cover the bones and vegetables well. Set the pot

over high heat and bring to a boil. Reduce the heat so the liquid is simmering and cook, uncovered, skimming the surface occasionally with a spoon to remove any scum that rises to the top, for at least 6 hours and up to 10 hours. (If the water drops below the top of the solids during that time, add a few more cups.)

Use tongs or a slotted spoon to discard as many solids (especially the bones) as possible from the pot. Very carefully strain the stock through a cheesecloth-lined strainer set over a stainless steel bowl. If not using immediately, cool the stock. To do this, fill a very large bowl with ice, then set the bowl of stock in it, encouraging the hot liquid to cool quickly. Skim off the fat that rises to the surface. The stock can be refrigerated in an airtight container for up to 3 days or frozen for up to 2 months.

5 pounds venison bones, preferably with some meat left on them, or venison osso buco

¼ cup canola or other neutral oil

2 medium Spanish onions, unpeeled, cut into large chunks

2 medium carrots, unpeeled, cut into large chunks

2 garlic heads, in their skins, cut in half horizontally

32 cups (2 gallons) cold water

MAKES ABOUT 6 QUARTS

Lemon-Saffron Aïoli

This vibrant condiment is delicious with cold poached fish, as a dip for artichokes, and over cold cooked vegetables. It's also wonderful served with fried shellfish, such as calamari.

Hydrate the saffron in the water in a small heatproof bowl for 5 to 10 minutes. Transfer to a blender and add the garlic and egg yolk. With the motor running, add the olive oil in a thin steam to form a thick, creamy emulsion. Add the lemon juice, mustard, and salt and blend.

Transfer the aïoli to a small bowl, using a rubber spatula to scrape as much as possible out of the blender. The aïoli will keep in an airtight container in the refrigerator for up to 2 days.

¼ teaspoon saffron threads

2 tablespoons hot water

1 medium garlic clove

1 large egg yolk

¾ cup extra-virgin olive oil

1 teaspoon freshly squeezed lemon juice

½ teaspoon Dijon mustard

½ teaspoon salt

MAKES ABOUT 1¼ CUPS

Preserved Lemons

15 lemons, plus more if needed

½ cup kosher salt

2 tablespoons black peppercorns

1 tablespoon coriander seeds

MAKES 5 PRESERVED LEMONS

Use these lemons to flavor Middle Eastern–themed dishes, such as the monkfish dish on page 153. Note that these must be allowed to develop in the refrigerator for at least 3 weeks.

Juice 10 of the lemons, then cut the remaining 5 into quarters, leaving them attached at one end—don't cut all the way through. Sprinkle the insides of the quartered lemons with a little salt.

In a clear plastic or glass container, sprinkle half the remaining salt and half the peppercorns and coriander. Place the quartered lemons on top. Add the remaining salt, peppercorns, and coriander. Pour the lemon juice over, which should be enough to cover the lemons; if not, squeeze enough additional lemons to cover them with juice. Place a plate or something else on top to weight the lemons down and keep them under the juice. Cover tightly and refrigerate for at least 3 weeks or up to 2 months before using.

Duck Stock

2 duck carcasses
(from 4- to 5-pound ducks),
each cut into quarters or sixths with
a heavy kitchen knife or shears

2 medium carrots, unpeeled,
cut into 1-inch chunks

2 medium Spanish onions,
unpeeled, cut into 1-inch chunks

1 garlic head, in its skin,
cut in half horizontally

32 cups (2 gallons) cold water

MAKES ABOUT 6 QUARTS

This rich stock is essential to creating the best flavor in duck-based soups and sauces.

Preheat the oven to 400°F.

Put the duck pieces in a large roasting pan and roast, stirring the liquids that accumulate and draining the fat on occasionally by carefully pouring or siphoning it out with a basting bulb.

After 1 hour, add the carrots, onions, and garlic and stir to coat them with the fat. Continue roasting until the duck and vegetables are lightly browned, draining the rendered fat along the way, about another hour.

Use a slotted spoon to transfer the duck and vegetables to a large heavy-bottomed stockpot. Set the roasting pan over two burners on the stovetop and turn the heat to medium on both. Add 4 cups of the water and cook, stirring to scrape up the crusty browned bits on the bottom of the pan. Pour the liquid from the pan into the stockpot and add the remaining 28 cups cold water to cover the ducks well. Set the pot over high heat and bring to a boil. Reduce the heat so the liquid is simmering and cook, skimming the surface occasionally with a spoon to remove any scum that rises to the top, for at least 4 hours. (If the water drops below the top of the solids during that time, add a few more cups.)

Use tongs or a slotted spoon to discard as many solids (especially the bones) as possible from the pot. Very carefully strain the stock through a cheesecloth-lined strainer set over a stainless steel bowl. If not using right away, cool the stock. To do this, fill a very large bowl with ice, then set the bowl of stock in it, encouraging the hot liquid to cool quickly. Skim off the fat that rises to the surface. The stock can be refrigerated in an airtight container for up to 3 days or frozen for up to 2 months.

Pasta Dough

Making your own pasta dough is easier than you might think. While you can certainly purchase fine, ready-made fresh pasta in stores today, it's worth doing it yourself at least once. There's nothing like homemade pasta, and it's essential for making homemade ravioli because store-bought varieties of pasta sheets are not as malleable.

1½ cups all-purpose flour, plus more for dusting the work surface

2 large eggs

1 teaspoon heavy cream

Cornmeal, for dusting

MAKES 12 OUNCES PASTA; ENOUGH FOR 4 STARTER OR SIDE PORTIONS

Lightly flour your work surface and mound the flour in the center. Make a well in the flour and break the eggs into it. Add the cream and, using a fork, whisk the eggs and cream together, incorporating the flour gradually while whisking.

Once the flour is fully incorporated, knead the dough together by hand. It will be stiff at first, but it will become smooth and bouncy after 5 to 10 minutes. If it still feels sticky after this time, add a little more flour and knead to incorporate it. If it feels dry and crumbly, incorporate a few drops of water at a time until you get the consistency you want.

Wrap the dough in plastic wrap and refrigerate for at least 1 hour or overnight.

To make fettuccine or other shapes, cut the dough into quarters. Working with one piece at a time, flatten it out and generously flour it to keep it from sticking as you work. Run it repeatedly through a pasta machine or a stand mixer fitted with the pasta attachment, gradually lowering the setting on the machine until you reach the thinnest setting. Change the attachment to the desired pasta shape (e.g., fettuccine), and roll the pasta through the machine. Lay the pasta strands out on a parchment-lined baking sheet and sprinkle with cornmeal to keep them from sticking together. Repeat with the remaining quarters of the dough. Your pasta is ready to cook.

Sources

Artisanal Premium Cheese
American and international cheeses.
(877) 797-1200
www.artisanalcheese.com

Asian Food Grocer
Fish sauce, oyster sauce, dried shiitake mushrooms,
soy sauce, mirin, hoisin, nori rolls, sesame oil, spring
roll wrappers, and other Asian ingredients.
(888) 482-2742
www.asianfoodgrocer.com

Browne Trading Company
Fish, shellfish, smoked fish, and caviar.
(800) 944-7848
www.browne-trading.com

The Chef's Garden
Micro-greens, micro-herbs, and specialty vegetables.
(800) 289-4644
www.chefs-garden.com

Chefs' Warehouse
Hard-to-find gourmet ingredients, including
olives, capers, oils, chocolates, and flours.
www.chefswarehouse.com

D'Artagnan
Duck and duck products, game birds, poultry,
smoked, cured, and specialty meats, truffles,
truffle oil, and veal demi-glace.
(800) 327-8246, ext. 0
www.dartagnan.com

Hudson Valley Foie Gras
American foie gras and prepared duck products.
(845) 292-2500
www.hudsonvalleyfoiegras.com

Jamison Farm
Lamb and lamb products.
(800) 237-5262
www.jamisonfarm.com

Kalustyan's
Spices, herbs, honeys, mushrooms, fish and seafood products, preserved lemons, salts, tamarind, white soy sauce, and hundreds of other specialty items.
(800) 352-3451
www.kalustyans.com

Niman Ranch
Beef, lamb, and pork.
(866) 808-0340
www.nimanranch.com

Nueske's
Artisanal bacon.
(800) 382-2266
www.nueskemeats.com

Salumeria Biellese
French and Italian charcuterie.
(212) 736-7376
www.salumeriabiellese.com

The Truffle Market
Fresh, frozen, and dried truffles and truffle products.
(866) 481-9221
www.trufflemarket.com

Williams-Sonoma
Kitchen equipment and tools, and specialty items.
(877) 812-6235
www.williams-sonoma.com

Equivalency Charts

	OVEN TEMPERATURES	
Gas Mark	°F	°C
½	250	120
1	275	140
2	300	150
3	325	165
4	350	180
5	375	190
6	400	200
7	425	220
8	450	230
9	475	240
10	500	260
Broil	550	290

LIQUID/DRY MEASURES	
U.S.	Metric
¼ teaspoon	1.25 milliliters
½ teaspoon	2.5 milliliters
1 teaspoon	5 milliliters
1 tablespoon (3 teaspoons)	15 milliliters
1 fluid ounce (2 tablespoons)	30 milliliters
¼ cup	60 milliliters
⅓ cup	80 milliliters
½ cup	120 milliliters
1 cup	240 milliliters
1 pint (2 cups)	480 milliliters
1 quart (4 cups; 32 ounces)	960 milliliters
1 gallon (4 quarts)	3.84 liters
1 ounce (by weight)	28 grams
1 pound	454 grams
2.2 pounds	1 kilogram

Acknowledgments

This book, like Chanterelle and most other endeavors, does not represent just one person's work, but many, and I would like to acknowledge the contributions of my colleagues:

My wife, Karen, who somehow both inspires and grounds me; Andrew Friedman, who found the perfect tone and helped me express my thoughts so clearly and elegantly; Maria Robledo, our gifted photographer, for her patience and artistry—thanks for another collaboration and another beautiful book; Susan Ginsburg, my literary agent, who moved us along, always had the perfect advice, and never lost confidence; Pam Hoenig, our editor, whose early belief and tireless efforts helped create a book which exceeds even our highest expectations and which we will treasure always; Carolyn Mandarano, who brought the project down the home stretch with great care and attention; Carol Singer, who lent her keen eye and boundless enthusiasm to all aspects of the art direction; the team at Mucca Design, for "getting it" and capturing the spirit of Chanterelle in their exquisite design; Melissa Possick and Pam Duevel at Taunton, and Chloe Mata at Baltz & Company, for getting the word out; Don Linn, publisher of Taunton, for his unwavering and very generous support. Kate Zuckerman and Michael Klug, pastry chefs present and past, for their great taste and talent, and contributions to the dessert chapter (without them, there wouldn't be one); The talented trio who helped test, write, and organize the recipes: Cathy Charnack, Lisa Leonard, and Alex Bisset; Amy Ehrenreich, for invaluable help that went far above and beyond the call of duty (or job description)—thanks for doing it all with a smile; Ivy Ronquillo, for her diligence in editing the recipes; Steve Jackson and Keith Harry, sous chefs at Chanterelle, for holding down the fort while I was in the basement poring over recipes and pages, maintaining our high standards at every turn; Roger Dagorn, George Stinson, and Adrian Murcia, three of the brightest stars in the Chanterelle constellation; the Chanterelle staff, front and back of the house, past and present, for coming to work every day and helping me realize my dream. Adam Gopnik, for his flattering and generous foreword—we're glad he and Martha found their way into the restaurant all those years ago; Bill Katz, who belongs in a category all his own; his guidance and aesthetic sense continue to infuse everything at Chanterelle, and we would not be what we are without him; The artists, so much a part of Chanterelle, for generously sharing their remarkable talent with us; Our investors, the unsung heroes of the Chanterelle story, for literally putting their money where their mouths were; All of the reviewers, reporters, and bloggers who have been so kind to us over the years; and Chanterelle's clients, for their loyalty over three decades, two neighborhoods, and the ever-changing New York dining scene.